QUALITATIVE RESEARCH METHODS FOR EVERYONE

An Essential Toolkit

Karen O'Reilly

P

First published in Great Britain in 2025 by

Policy Press, an imprint of
Bristol University Press
University of Bristol
1–9 Old Park Hill
Bristol
BS2 8BB
UK
+44 (0)117 374 6645
bup-info@bristol.ac.uk

Details of international sales and distribution partners are available at
policy.bristoluniversitypress.co.uk

British Library Cataloguing in Publication Data
A catalogue record for this book is available from the British Library

ISBN 978-1-4473-7214-1 hardcover
ISBN 978-1-4473-7215-8 paperback
ISBN 978-1-4473-7216-5 ePub
ISBN 978-1-4473-7217-2 ePDF

Cover design: Andrew Corbett
Cover image: Getty/imaginima

Contents

Contents

List of boxes and figures

Boxes

Figures

Acknowledgements

I find it daunting to write acknowledgements because I am sure I will leave out someone important. In short, everyone I have ever taught, worked with, undertaken research with, or told about this book (apologies) has been supportive, insightful and/or motivating in some way. Even those puzzled looks and questions about retirement (you know who you are) motivated me to do what I love.

I want to especially thank the Social Research Association (SRA) for everything they do for researchers within and outside academia and for giving me the opportunity to provide training for, and therefore to meet, so many conscientious, kind and committed individuals. I never knew, until I knew the SRA, there was this whole army of researchers working hard to understand social life for the benefit of those who live it. I hope they find this book useful.

Thank you, of course, to Policy Press and especially Paul Stevens and Isobel Green for encouraging me in the first place and all the way along. Thanks also to those who reviewed the book. I know you are busy people doing this for the academy, for qualitative research, and for me. I hope I have done justice to your support and encouragement.

There are hundreds of excellent qualitative methods books and articles out there, and I have not been able to do justice to the entire body of work in the field of qualitative research (my list of references is already close to ten per cent of the book), but I want nevertheless to acknowledge everyone who has contributed to the vast amount of knowledge in this area. This book stands on their shoulders.

Those individuals who have especially helped me intellectually will, I hope, find themselves cited here and therefore can easily see who they are. Where would any of us be without friends? Thanks and love to numerous friends, many of whom are also colleagues – a double whammy. Love and thanks to all my family for their love and support, but especially to Trevor and to Kelly because they show absolute faith in me, give me the confidence and strength to keep going through difficult times, and even forgive me when I am being utterly selfish and absorbed.

1

Designing qualitative research

What this chapter is about

Welcome to your qualitative research journey. This chapter (along with the next two) provides you with the tools you need to get started, helping you develop a rigorous, clear, coherent, and convincing qualitative research proposal. The book provides a toolkit for qualitative research: a collection of expert skills, knowledge, procedures, tools, or information. The first tools in this chapter are built on the fundamental principles of qualitative research, five questions to help you develop clear and achievable aims and objectives, and how philosophy might help as underlabourer. The latter part of the chapter introduces the distinction between methodology and methods, and shows how practical choices of method relate to the goals of qualitative research.

> **FOR YOUR TOOLKIT**
> We do qualitative research because we want to understand people's experiences, feelings, emotions, meanings, and expressions. We are also interested in how these shape their decision-making practices, because we hope that somewhere along the line having a better understanding of people's practices will lead to making the world, or a tiny part of it, a better place.

The fundamental principles of qualitative research

Qualitative research is designed to understand and interpret people's feelings and emotions, as these are shaped by experiences, and as they shape actions. Qualitative research findings take the shape of insights and understandings, presented as themes, patterns and processes that respect the complexity and diversity of human lived life. Qualitative research proceeds in a flexible and responsive manner so that we can learn as we go from our participants and from our own experiences. Qualitative research relies on diverse methods that involve listening, hearing, watching, and thinking, co-creating, and reflecting. Qualitative research is iterative-inductive and engages ethical and reflexive practice.

FOR YOUR TOOLKIT

Interpretive, in its basic meaning is 'to interpret' or 'to make sense'. We aim to make sense of other people's worlds, first for ourselves and then for others. This is an ongoing act of interpretation.

Qualitative researchers are interested in the feelings, experiences, perceptions, norms, habits, and choices of individuals and groups. These are our data, which are detailed, rich and complex in quality. We are also interested in how these shape decision-making practices, because we hope that somewhere along the line having a better understanding of people's practices (our insights into what shapes their world and their responses to it) will lead to making the world, or a tiny part of it, a better place. Let's examine in detail this quote from Irene Vasilachis de Gialdino (2009: 8): 'Qualitative methods entail and manifest the assumptions of the interpretive paradigm, the grounds of which lie in the need to grasp the meaning of social action in the context of the life-world and from the actors' perspective.'

The 'interpretive paradigm' is discussed in more detail a little later; in short it means *making sense*. To understand other people's experiences and feelings, and the meanings behind them, we work hard to help them to clarify and express them, then to make sense of them for ourselves in the context of our own lives and experiences, and finally to interpret or make sense of them for others so that our readers can make sense of them in the context of their own experiences.

The word 'action' in the quote from de Gialdino recognises that a qualitative stance or sensibility sees humans as agents who have the ability (though they may not always use it) of thinking things through and making choices rather than simply reacting to external stimuli. We cannot predict or identify cause and effect in any simplistic or direct way; instead, we try to understand the meanings and understandings behind people's choices, and perhaps work towards understanding how they might act in future, given certain conditions. Finally, the concept of 'lifeworld' is invoking the state of affairs within which any world is experienced, the shared context, behaviours, expectations, experiences, or the universe of what is self-evident or given for any specific agent. I return to this later.

FOR YOUR TOOLKIT

Qualitative research findings take the shape of insights and understandings, presented as themes, patterns, and processes that respect the complexity and diversity of human lived life.

Qualitative research is committed to retaining the diversity and complexity of the social world and therefore does not attempt to reduce it to causal explanations or neatly defined categories of response (see Braun and Clarke 2022: 7). Qualitative results or findings take the shape of interpretations, presented as insights, themes, patterns, and processes, illustrated and explained with rich descriptions and examples. Qualitative research retains a respect for the uniqueness of individual cases, to discover insights from any one person at any one time, as well as search for comparative themes and patterns that can help us understand what people do and what they might do, so that we can perhaps develop policies or interventions that lead to better outcomes.

> **FOR YOUR TOOLKIT**
> Qualitative research proceeds in a flexible and responsive manner so that we can learn as we go from our participants and from our own experiences.

To achieve these meaningful interpretations we use flexible, non-standardised methods that we adapt for our participants and for ourselves as we learn and understand more. Our research design is always less important than our ability to respond to participants' responses (Ravitch and Carl 2020).

Qualitative research relies on diverse methods. To interpret people's lives, we may need more than our participants can tell us or show us, to read between the lines, to hear what has *not* been said, to observe what was done rather than (just) what was said. We will also want to make sense of our interpretations in the context of wider structures and constraints, power and resources, what was possible and what was not.

> **FOR YOUR TOOLKIT**
> Qualitative research is iterative-inductive: constantly iterating between being inductive (open-minded, bottom-up, learning from the field) and deductive (testing out existing and new theories and concepts to see if they help clarify understandings), with an inductive approach retaining the upper hand.

Qualitative research employs a mainly 'inductive' rather than 'deductive' analytical process. We identify and develop emergent (or co-constructed) insights rather than rely (only) on a priori concepts. I call this iterative-inductive (see O'Reilly 2012a). A *deductive* approach to research is one where a hypothesis is derived from existing theory and the empirical world is explored, and the data collected, to test its truth or falsity. A simplistically *inductive* approach is one where the researcher begins with as open a mind and as few preconceptions as possible, allowing theory to emerge from the data. An *iterative-inductive* approach recognises that researchers have preconceived ideas and theories about how the world works – they will read the literature and study the field a little, they will have had experiences. But they should hold these ideas lightly and test out (in as open-minded a way as possible) where and when they might be helpful in clarifying emerging insights, oscillating between theory and practice (Cubellis et al 2021). They should be open to being wrong and tune in to things that surprise them and challenge their preconceptions, and open to discarding, changing, and developing new theories and concepts. As Virginia Braun and Victoria Clarke (2022: 8) insist: 'Themes do not emerge from data but are actively produced by the researcher through their systematic engagement with, and all they bring to, the dataset.'

While pure objectivity (in terms of not imposing our own feelings and thoughts) might be an *apparently* admirable goal it is in fact neither achievable nor fully desirable. Instead, we need to engage in ethical and reflexive practice that uses our experiences and insights intelligently and carefully to learn from others (see Chapter 3). Relating with someone as if they are an object and you are a detached and unemotional data collection tool is never likely to attain any kind of truth, still less understanding. Using verbs rather than nouns, being ethical and being reflexive invokes an ongoing consideration of the relationship between the researcher and those researched. Reflexive practice is a version of reflexivity that is collaborative, responsible, iterative, engaged, agile, and creative; it is adaptive to surroundings, communities, experiences, and perceptions.

Five difficult questions

Some years ago, Jennifer Mason (1996) suggested that addressing five difficult questions at the outset of a qualitative research project will aid the design of clear aims and objectives. She has updated these as the years have passed (Mason 2018) but I have adapted her original formula as it has served me well for teaching purposes. The questions should not be treated as separate steps but as overlapping and intertwining. I like to think of them as points on a star that help reveal the heart of the star – the heart of your project. The five questions (adapted from Mason 1996 and 2018) ask:

- What is your ontological approach?
- What is your epistemological approach?
- What is the broad topic area?
- What is the key intellectual puzzle?
- What/who is the research for?

The ontological approach

Your ontological approach is your understanding of the realm of entities your research project recognises (Benton and Craib 2023). Note that while Mason (2018) refers to your ontological perspective, I prefer to think of an approach and how it relates to a given project. This requires you to think a little systematically about what things your project is interested in: for example, people, groups, social actors, minds, psyches, rationality, emotions, understandings, beliefs, the self, individuals, texts, stories, narratives, experiences, languages, processes, institutions, underlying mechanisms, nature, genes, rules, norms, morality, interactions, social constructions, social structures, practices and outcomes, the material world, the social world. Note that this is not an exhaustive list; Mason (2018: 5) has a more extensive list that is still not complete. Ontology relates directly to any broad frameworks or research fields you are working within. I work within a practice theory framework and so my ontology includes, among other things, structures, agency, and processes (Box 1.3). Penny Curtis and colleagues (Birch et al 2007) work within a framework that includes children as social actors (Box 1.1).

FOR YOUR TOOLKIT

Your ontological approach is your understanding of the realm of entities your research project recognises. Epistemology asks how the things you are interested in can be known or understood.

The epistemological approach

Your epistemological approach is your understanding of what might represent knowledge or evidence, as opposed to belief or prejudice, of things: how things can be known (Benton and Craib 2023). Here Mason (2018) uses the term 'epistemological position', whereas I want you to think about your approach to a specific project. Epistemology draws from various philosophical traditions and so a deeper understanding of philosophy (as discussed later in this chapter) can be helpful. It is important to relate it overtly to methodology: ask yourself how the things you are interested in can be learned about; what would count as evidence or knowledge, for example, of children's actions, choices, social structures? Here are some suggestions for what might represent knowledge or understanding:

- What participants tell you (descriptive phenomenology)
- What they do not tell you (critical realism)
- What participants write or do (critical theory, practice theory, hermeneutics)
- What you deduce (critical theory)
- What participants say they are thinking (interpretive phenomenology)
- What they say they are feeling (descriptive phenomenology)
- Facts that you uncover (positivism)
- The norms that you identify (practice theory)

I would not recommend trying to spell out in any great detail your ontological or your epistemological approach, except for a specialist reader. You do not even need to mention them in a proposal, though there is no harm doing so if you feel confident enough. However, understanding and clarifying for yourself at least some of the things you want to understand, and how, will help you develop a good proposal and will ensure your methodological approach is coherent.

The broad topic area

Qualitative research tends to use topic areas and puzzles to enable research questions to be phrased in open and exploratory ways. A project written as a question can be too narrow. The broad topic area for Sonali Shah and Nia Jones (2023) in their study 'RIghts and CHoices (RICH) for women with cerebral palsy' (see Box 8.1) was 'a qualitative study to understand what works in the provision of their maternity care'. As Mason (2018: 10) argues, the choice of topic will usually 'express something of the researcher's ontological or epistemological position'. Ontologically, the RICH study design suggests maternity care is something diverse that can be known about. Epistemologically, the researchers could aim to know more about this via discourses, institutional rules and regulations, actions, or feelings, what people say or what they do not say, what the researchers intuit, the contradictions or consistencies. As it is, the research question – what shapes the experiences and choices in relation to pregnancy, childbirth and the postnatal period for women with cerebral palsy in the UK? – clarifies it is experiences and choices, and the conditions or experiences that shape these, that will be the focus and will inform the methodology and methods.

The intellectual puzzle

The intellectual puzzle forms the backbone of research, and as Mason (2018) says, should be open to revision. Being iterative-inductive, qualitative researchers begin with topic areas and intellectual puzzles to explore and be guided by theory, not fixed or rigid hypotheses to test. This aids objectivity in the way I understand it: we aim to learn from and with our participants, not to impose our views of the world on them through our predetermined research questions. Intellectual puzzles are informed and shaped by wider literature (Chapter 2).

Research puzzles in qualitative research can have an exploratory, explanatory, evaluative, or generative focus, or more usually a combination. *Exploratory (or definitional) research puzzles* attempt to explore, discover, and portray in detail the form and nature of a phenomenon; the range of meanings, beliefs, experiences; the structure of groups or settings. They ask what it is like to be in a certain situation. *Explanatory research puzzles* aim to explain the reasons behind identified patterns and associations. They ask why people believe or behave as they do. *Evaluative research puzzles* wish to appraise or evaluate a phenomenon. They ask what it is like to deliver or be at the receiving end of something. *Generative research puzzles* work towards aiding the development of initiatives, strategies, policies, theories. They ask what can be done to improve a situation. This distinction is discussed in more detail by Jane Ritchie and Rachel Ormston (2014), using the concepts of contextual, explanatory, evaluative and generative research functions. In my experience, the most likely approach is to work your way through all of these in turn as each informs the next, and the extent to which you use each type relates to your goals towards pure basic research or applied research.

FOR YOUR TOOLKIT

Being iterative-inductive, qualitative researchers begin with broad topic areas and intellectual puzzles to explore, not fixed or rigid hypotheses to test. Objectivity here means we aim to learn from and with our participants, not to impose our views of the world on them through our predetermined research questions.

Who is it for?

Mason (1996) suggests we simultaneously consider what and who the research is for. The literature review (Chapter 2) locates our work in the context of relevant academic knowledge, substantive knowledge and policy debates, and thus begins to address potential audiences. You should also think about the extent to which you are content to reveal rich insights that contribute to academic debate, and to the development of the intellectual imagination, or hope to overtly make policy recommendations. Perhaps you intend to develop interventions, or work towards transformative action or design (Morosanu 2016; Pink et al 2022), as discussed in Chapters 2 and 7. Addressing the five difficult questions of the five-point star is useful in developing coherent aims and objectives.

FOR YOUR TOOLKIT

Look through research funders' databases for proposals, or ask colleagues, and get successful or useful models to help guide your design.

Aims and objectives

It is useful to distinguish aims, or vision, as expansive and enticing statements setting out what the research intends to achieve, its broad or general ambitions; and objectives, or goals, that clarify how the aims are to be accomplished, itemising specific steps or tasks. Aims can be ambitious; objectives should address the more immediate project outcomes and be focused, precisely described and feasible.

FOR YOUR TOOLKIT

Aims (or vision) set out what the research intends to achieve, its broad or general ambitions. Objectives (or goals) itemise the steps to take or specific tasks that clarify how the aims are to be accomplished.

Other items such as relevance, cost, contribution and so on can then be tackled in relation to aims and objectives (vision and goals). And of course, this all overlaps with methodology and sampling, but before I move on to that (in Chapter 2) I use Penny Curtis and colleagues' Space to Care study to illustrate how addressing the five difficult questions of the five-point star is useful in developing a coherent vision and goals (Box 1.1).

The *broad topic area* is children, care and space (Box 1.1). The aims and objectives clearly, succinctly, and coherently establish and constitute the *intellectual puzzle*. The stated aim of the study suggests that, *ontologically*, Curtis is interested in understanding the experiences and perceptions of children, as social actors. She also includes, ontologically, the spatial characteristics of different hospitals. *Epistemologically*, spatial characteristics need to be known in a way that can be documented (perhaps through observation), and experiences and perceptions need to be understood in a way that takes account of the spaces within which children are located. So, when I look further, I am hoping (and indeed am satisfied) that the plan is to use interviews (listening), participant observation (hearing and watching in context), and the collection of other evidence through observation and existing documentation, in diverse settings. *Who the study is for* is laid out in the second two objectives: to deduce what strategies may help in planning of hospital spaces.

Box 1.1. Illustrating aims and objectives: Space to Care

Space to Care: Children's Perceptions of Spatial Aspects of Hospitals aimed to explore how children, as social actors, perceive and experience the internal, spatial characteristics of different hospital environments. Four objectives were identified: to document the physical and social characteristics of the spaces provided for children within a range of different hospital settings; to explore children's own experience and use of these different internal spaces and the meanings they attribute to them; to develop strategies that enable children's needs to be considered alongside those of adults in the planning and utilisation of internal spaces in hospital; to develop a set of child-centred research tools that will contribute to theoretical and methodological developments within childhood studies (Curtis et al 2007; and see Birch et al 2007).

The remainder of this chapter is dedicated to the philosophy of social science because of its fundamental role in informing rigorous qualitative research. I aim to give context and detail for those of you who need it but to keep it as simple and straightforward as possible for those of you who really need to just get on with the job of designing and undertaking good-quality qualitative research.

The philosophy toolkit for qualitative research

The toolkit logic asks you to put philosophical approaches in a virtual toolkit and make them available as possibilities to consider. Philosophy should provide the role of underlabourer: it is there to help us make sense of the choices we are making and the assumptions implicit in them (O'Reilly 2012a; Benton and Craib 2023). The categories and concepts developed (inductively) by philosophers to help interpret social research should not become straitjackets that constrain us or coats that we put on to identify which club we belong to. Instead, a qualitative research project is best when somewhat informed by different philosophies that in turn will shape the approach to ontology and epistemology. There are often elements of different philosophical approaches in any one piece of work. My advice is to spend a bit of time understanding the language of the philosophy of the social sciences and then to move on and get on with the job of doing your research: avoid disappearing down the philosophy rabbit hole. To that end, I introduce a few key terms with reference to some of the key (or my favourite) literature. *All qualitative research is informed by the interpretivist paradigm*, but let's start at the beginning, with positivism.

FOR YOUR TOOLKIT

Philosophy should provide the role of underlabourer, helping us to make sense of the choices we make and their implicit assumptions, not dictating decisions.

Positivism

Early social scientists hoped to develop a science of society that could be as rigorous and positive as the natural sciences appeared to be. They thus designed approaches that were as close to the empiricist model of natural science as possible: they attempted to approach social science with no preconceptions (with the mind as a blank sheet), to test for cause and effect in social life, to control for external factors in experiments, to search for broadly applicable laws of society, and to be objective by denying the role of researchers' and participants' understandings, interpretations and meanings of the questions being asked.

In practice, a positivist or objectivist approach leads to the design of fixed research hypotheses based on the researchers' prior knowledge and to rigidly designed questionnaires, or interview schedules, with predetermined answers from which the 'respondent' must select. Researchers maintain a detached demeanour that leaves participants feeling ignored or misunderstood and thus unlikely to share their thoughts. A positivist (or objectivist) approach fails in its own purpose because at every step of the way it imposes the researcher's view of the world (Westmarland 2001). Qualitative research now is a more ethically moral approach, more empathetic, caring, and understanding than positivist approaches.

A strict adherence to positivism (and to objectivity) is now considered naive given the broad consensus on the many critiques I will go on to outline. In short, humans think and then act based on their feelings and experiences; they do not simply react to external stimuli. There is no direct access to feelings, experiences and meanings; these are not easily shared or discussed, they are complex and sometimes even taboo. We now attempt to discover them using focus groups, interviews, conversations and so on. Questionnaires and fixed interview schedules are too crude, too shaped by our own views of the world. Further, it is impossible to approach human agents and social life with no preconceptions at all, but we try to reduce these through interaction, conversation and interpretation, not through imposing rigid schedules in a false attempt to be objective. Finally, we aim to understand the patterns of meaning behind lived experiences. This is an act of interpretation, or sense making.

One thing we can take forward from positivism is Auguste Comte's desire to develop an approach to understanding social life that is *positive* in informing better futures (Benton and Craib 2023). As discussed, qualitative research is designed to understand and interpret people's meanings, feelings, and emotions as these are shaped by experiences, and they shape actions. Findings take the shape of insights and understandings, presented as themes, patterns, processes or stories, that respect the complexity and diversity of human lived life. These help us understand what people do and what they might do, so that we have the confidence to develop policies or interventions that lead to better outcomes. Qualitative research can identify the needs of diverse and seldom heard people and help overcome unconscious bias, in research and in policy, by giving participants a voice. Qualitative research is more likely to be truthful or of value because it understands complexity and context, and practice. Qualitative research is therefore positive because it gives us hope (Chapter 2). The various forms of interpretivism provide much more nuance for *understanding* social life in this positive way.

> **FOR YOUR TOOLKIT**
>
> A positivist or objectivist approach fails in its own purpose because at every step of the way it imposes the researcher's view of the world.

Interpretivisms

First, and with emphasis, *all qualitative research is informed by the interpretivist paradigm*. Interpretivism is an umbrella term that encapsulates many of the philosophies of social science discussed later that endeavour to understand and make sense of social life from the perspective of the human agent, within the context of their societies and cultures, histories, and meanings. Interpretivisms were developed as a response to positivism and are often seen as opposing it with the arguments that, on the one hand, the empiricist view of science has been challenged even within natural science; on the other hand, empiricism does not make sense as a model for understanding human agents. For interpretivists, it is essential to see humans as *actors* in the social world rather than as simply *re-acting* as objects in the natural world (humans are not like Pavlov's dogs).

FOR YOUR TOOLKIT

All qualitative research is at least loosely informed by the interpretivist paradigm as a positive, sense-making endeavour.

Interpretivists agree it is impossible to approach human agents and social life with no preconceptions at all. We have research questions, we review literature, we understand something of the lives we are interested in, and we live our own lives. The best we can do is work with the tools we have to achieve the best research possible. Rather than pretend we have no feelings or thoughts ourselves, as with objectivist approaches, we need to consider their role in our research. Of course, we should try not to be biased or prejudiced but we can work with and challenge our insights through reflexive practice (Chapter 3).

As an aside, objectivist grounded theorists who argue we should leave reviewing any literature until after the research has been completed are influenced by positivism in trying to have a blank mind and discover independent facts (Taghipour 2014).

Interpretivists understand humans are not predictable in the same way natural phenomena can be: humans make choices, think, reflect, imagine, and then make decisions. They cannot always tell you how these decisions were made or on what basis; these are shaped by their norms and socialisation, and constrained by rules and conditions. Nevertheless, there are patterns and likely or possible outcomes that follow complex pathways (see Pink et al 2022); and we can try to understand why certain types of people follow certain patterns and what compels and constrains them. Such insights can inform policy interventions or actions, but as Ted Benton and Ian Craib (2023: 46) have argued: 'Any particular policy intervention is likely to be modified in its effects by complex interactions between social processes, and unless there is some means of taking these into account, reform strategies are liable to generate unintended and possibly unwanted consequences.'

Finally, while we would not want as social researchers to uncritically make value judgements, nevertheless if we make no judgements at all, and we do not permit those of others, how on earth can we hope to work towards making the world a better place? For this we need to move beyond positivist approaches to critical ones. 'When they encounter cultures in which systematic torture, female circumcision, endemic racism or capital punishment is accepted as morally proper, most social scientists are liable to find their capacity to suspend judgement sorely tested' (Benton and Craib 2023: 7).

FOR YOUR TOOLKIT

It is impossible to isolate causes and effects of human behaviour (as in positivism). Nevertheless, there are patterns and likely or possible outcomes that follow complex pathways; and we can try to understand why certain types of people follow certain patterns and what compels and constrains them.

Phenomenology

During the 1960s and 1970s it became popular to describe qualitative research as phenomenological, meaning in its simplest application, obtaining the actors' point of view, tapping into their lived experiences, feelings, and meanings, how they relate to the world.

> The discipline of phenomenology may be defined initially as the study of structures of experience, or consciousness. Literally, phenomenology is the study of 'phenomena': appearances of things, or things as they appear in our experience, or the ways we experience things, thus the meanings things have in our experience. Phenomenology studies conscious experience as experienced from the subjective or first person point of view. (Smith 2018)

FOR YOUR TOOLKIT

Phenomenology simply means obtaining the actors' point of view, tapping into their lived experiences, feelings, and meanings – how they relate to the world.

There is no direct access to feelings, experiences and meanings; they are shared with researchers via focus groups, interviews, conversations and so on, in the form of our participants' *interpretations*. Hence phenomenology is an interpretivist approach.

Given the range of diverse approaches to phenomenology that have emerged over time and the lack of clarity about the origin of the term, Heath Williams (2021) advises us not to get hung up on the term's source or etymology. Loosely, a *phenomenon* is anything that can be experienced and *logos* means to study. Just as we no longer feel we must do science as Newton conceived of it, or sociology as Durkheim did, Williams suggests we freely adapt any notion of traditional phenomenology, making it work for ourselves and our research. Nevertheless, two authors have been particularly influential in developing the term: Husserl and his student Heidegger.

FOR YOUR TOOLKIT

A descriptive phenomenology is focused on describing lived and embodied experiences as natural phenomena with no need for interpretation. An interpretive phenomenology attempts to understand the idiosyncratic and mutual *patterns* of meaning behind lived experiences.

Annelie Sundler and colleagues (2019) distinguish 'descriptive' and 'interpretive' phenomenology in their work on the lived experiences of patients, families and professionals in the fields of nursing and midwifery. Descriptive phenomenology, informed by the work of Husserl and Merleau–Ponty (Dowling 2007; Williams 2021), is focused on *describing* lived and embodied experiences as natural phenomena with no need for interpretation. As I discuss in Chapter 9, a descriptive phenomenological account can be useful and insightful, as a starting point, in focusing on what people tell us about how they feel or on *their* perspectives and understandings (see Statham 2019). But we are usually looking for something more, some sort of explanation or answers to the why question. Williams (2021: 369) notes:

> [T]here are disadvantages to approaches which rely too heavily on the description of simple experience. Firstly, singular descriptions are open to charges that what is described is merely an idiosyncratic feature of the describer's mental or conscious life. Until researchers begin to generalize to shared or structural features of experience, it is hard to know whether we are dealing with something general and therefore important, or something eccentric.

In the end, for our work to be useful, we need to explicitly interpret our findings. This is where Heidegger can help. Heidegger, through the concept of *Dasein* (see Giddens 1984), locates presence and daily life within wider structural conditions and thus gives us the logic with which to understand how we might go beyond simply what people tell us to interpret or make sense of *lived* experience in the context of the human need to adapt to those around us. This is why some interpretivists argue that human behaviour needs to be understood in the context of a particular society or culture (as in ethnography), or that social structures (norms, rules, laws, finances) are always present in experience, meanings and emotions (as in practice theory, Box 1.3).

FOR YOUR TOOLKIT

Interpreting does not mean making it up and is not purely subjective. It involves rendering experiences meaningful in the context of what it is possible to understand given one's own experiences.

This approach to interpreting in context is often summarised as a hermeneutic or structured phenomenology (for example, Teskereci and Boz 2019). 'The process of understanding is paradoxical, involving 'the hermeneutic circle': we cannot know the part without understanding the whole of which it is a part, and at the same time we cannot understand the whole without understanding the parts that make it up' (Benton and Craib 2023: 103).

Hermeneutics comes from the Greek word 'to interpret' or 'to clarify' and it conceptualises an attempt to understand groups within cultures but also across cultures. The analytical process in interpretive psychological analysis (Wertz et al 2011; Statham 2019) is often described in terms of a double hermeneutic or dual interpretation process because, first, the participants make meaning of their world, and second, the researcher tries to decode that meaning making (Pietkiewicz and Smith 2014: 8). Benton and Craib (2023: 102–5) spend a lot more time exploring this philosophical approach than I can provide here, but it makes intuitive sense and I use the logic (often without using the term or using the term structured phenomenology) throughout this book (Box 1.2).

Box 1.2: Structured phenomenology in action: one world is not enough

In 'One world is not enough: the structured phenomenology of lifestyle migrants in East Asia', Rob Stones and colleagues (2019) explain how British migrants in Hong Kong and Thailand, and Hong Kong Chinese migrants in China, lived and understood their lives and how these experiences and meanings were themselves shaped by wider conditions and experiences. The article's Heideggerian phenomenology allowed us to home in on the specifics of everyday moments of involvement, practice, and interaction. We could focus inductively on what 'shows up', what is 'cared about' from moment to moment in the mundane horizons of lifestyle migrants. The approach thus directed us to the moods and internal textures of everyday *ways of being*. For example, we noted the celebration of a Westernised lifestyle and a break from monotony on the part of the Chinese migrants; and the celebration of an escape from Westernised living on the part of the British migrants. But the approach was also 'powerfully enhanced by close attention to how these inner lives are deeply interwoven with relevant structural contexts' including an acknowledgement that any of them could be described as relatively privileged but structurally marginalised (Stones et al 2019: 44). See O'Reilly and Scott (2023b) for a further example of the use of a structured phenomenology.

Relativism, realism and critical approaches

For some scholars the argument that all feelings and experiences emanate from within a particular context and perspective led to an extreme form of relativism. This is the doctrine that if knowledge, truth, and morality always exist in relation to culture, society, or historical context, they can never be absolute and thus all claims to knowledge have equal validity. It can be interesting on a descriptive level to see where different constituents of a community are coming from, and how their perspectives contradict or complement each other – descriptively comparing world views, of patients and doctors for example. But we usually require more analysis, and if we want to go further and argue that one of those views is wrong, we come unstuck and need to use a critical approach.

A critical approach might begin with the ontological argument that not only are there phenomena in the shape of experiences and feelings from a given perspective, there are also *real* phenomena, that exist independently of anyone's view of them.

> *As an aside,* people (scholars, researchers, philosophers, all of us) use the word realism in many different ways. Some equate it with objectivism and deny the role of interpretation (O'Reilly 2012a).

A critical realist philosophy of social science is grounded in critical theory and posits the existence of *real* phenomena that may not be directly observable via any of our research methods (see Fell et al 2022): that human beings' conceptualisations and interpretations (the phenomenological) exist alongside, and in interaction with, wider patterns and processes of which an individual may not be aware. Critical realism is a vast subfield of the philosophy of social science, and I cannot do it justice here (see Benton and Craib 2023). However, it offers tools for those who want to get on with the job of doing social research. You begin by exploring the phenomenology of what Rob Stones (2005) calls the agent in focus (the participant). Having interpreted your findings and looked for patterns and differences, you might look further and ask: What are the mechanisms that lead to what outcomes under what conditions? What is happening here? This approach to realism has informed much of the work in co-production, participatory methods, and activism, that I turn to in Chapter 7.

Most researchers now acknowledge the real existence but infinite complexity of the social world, and concede that this social world can only be known through the focused collection and generation of evidence alongside an analytical interpretation. They also accept that all knowledge is limited, open to being proved false, and requires constant reflexive elaboration (O'Reilly 2012a; Benson and O'Reilly 2020b). Traditions and prejudices, prejudgements, and old ways of viewing the world need bringing to the light in an iterative-inductive oscillation, because without confronting our prejudices (our prior views) we cannot see whether they need adapting in light of history.

> The basic assumption is the same: the social sciences are concerned with understanding meaningful human action, but the approaches discussed in this chapter all emphasise the significance of the wider culture, whether we call it a language game, a form of life, a tradition or a community. The individual and the meaning of individual action is framed by the wider culture in the same way perhaps as the sentences that I speak as an individual are framed by the rules of the language in which I speak. But they all leave us with an interesting question: To what extent are we prisoners of our own tradition,

our culture? And can we see outside it or beyond it? How can we question it? (Benton and Craib 2023: 105)

And so, I turn finally to practice theory, which views social life, cultures and meanings, patterns and processes, as the outcome of the ongoing, historically shaped, interaction between structure and agency in the practice of daily life.

> **FOR YOUR TOOLKIT**
> A structured phenomenology, as in practice theory, interprets the subjective experiences of participants (their phenomenology) as always anchored within, and infused by, past and present structural contexts.

Practice theory

My own work is informed by practice theory with the help of strong structuration theory (Stones 2005; Hughes et al 2022). People create social lives through their actions but not under conditions they themselves have always chosen. Social life plays out through structures and actions; actions are shaped by how individuals think and feel, and social structures are, in turn, over time, the outcomes of social interactions. In this emergent tradition, projects explore the conditions of existence (the laws, norms, rules, culture) as well as the feelings, experiences, emotions of individuals, in groups and societies, as they interact over time (Box 1.3, and see O'Reilly 2012b). Philosophically, this represents a somewhat eclectic use of (some of) the approaches in this chapter, that understands their limitations and strengths, and works towards a meta-theoretical framework for social science. Again, as Benton and Craib suggest, maybe the approaches are not always as incompatible as has been argued:

> Durkheim's use of statistics, and his positing of social facts (his positivism) and society as being over and above the individual (his holism) takes us only part of the way – they tell us that we might expect more suicides in Protestant communities, but not all Protestants commit suicide. There is still an explanatory space to be filled by individualist and interpretive processes. This argument points to the fact that the social world might be composed of different types of being, in this case, *social structures, social processes* and *individuals,* and that they are different from each other. (Benton and Craib 2023: 88, emphasis added)

Further, these ontologically different types of being interact with each other and shift and alter as social life is lived on a daily basis, in practice, over time (Stones et al 2019). I return to this, illustrating its application, when I address the analysis and interpretation of qualitative research in subsequent chapters.

Box 1.3: Practice theory in action: Brexit and the British abroad

The Brexit and British People Abroad project (Benson 2020; O'Reilly 2020a) was designed around a practice theory approach to understanding migration (O'Reilly 2012b). Practice theory (for example, Schatzki 2005; Stones 2005; Shove et al 2012) views social life as the outcome of the ongoing interaction of social structures (institutions, laws, policies, norms) with the activities (or actions) of human agents in the practical living out of their daily lives. This is a model for understanding social life that recognises that why and how people do what they do is at once historical, institutional and individual. Adopting such an approach to understanding Brexit, its effects and outcomes, takes seriously time, space and process. It sees Brexit as an ongoing process that influences the everyday practices of individuals and communities, in this case, those of the British living in Europe, while also giving rise to new formations as policies change and practices emerge in response. Such new formations are often creative and at times unexpected, arising out of the interplay of cultural contexts and mediated frames of reference. In turn, these new formations shape and inform the activities of (perhaps other) human agents, though with the recognition of the differential levels of power and influence of individual agents to initiate change in line with their own desires (Benson and O'Reilly 2020b).

Other approaches

There are numerous philosophical understandings of social science that I have not been able to discuss. I advise you to learn a little and move on and then return to philosophy as and when you need help understanding what you hope to achieve or when you read something that inspires you. The philosophy of social science is a vast field to which scholars have committed entire careers. New concepts and approaches are being developed for diverse situations and to address new ways of seeing the world. Sometimes complex terminology is employed by authors assuming a high level of former knowledge of philosophy, for example when Maria Törnqvist and Tora Holmberg (2021) adapt Merleau-Ponty's work on embodied phenomenology as a means for understanding the role of vision in dance. At other times language is used in a new way, such as when Lorenzo Pedrini and colleagues (2021) elaborate in extensive detail a methodology that draws from Mauss and Bourdieu to understand embodied and encultured aspects of the antifascist boxing body *boxe popolare*. Focusing on embodiment for them adds an 'emergent phenomenological dimension' that helps understand how 'political belief is as much embodied as it is intellectual' (Pedrini et al 2021: 311). Others are employing neologisms such as queer phenomenology (Ahmed 2006) and critical phenomenology (Chandler 2019). Do not worry about the labels; instead, view these as exciting examples of how to think through, conceptualise and vocalise what matters to us as researchers.

How to use the philosophy toolkit

I recommend you decide for yourself what philosophical positions or debates help you understand what you want to do and what you think is important. There is so much inconsistency around the various terms and their uses that you cannot find the one true path. Rather, find a way to think about your own approach and explain it to your reader, with references to literature you have found useful, including this book (and see Box 1.4). Using your own words demonstrates you have understood the philosophy and makes it more understandable for readers (excluding philosophy experts or purists, of course). As Williams (2021) suggests, provide a short definition of a concept from an established expert followed by an explanation of how you understand and apply it.

Box 1.4: How you might describe your philosophical approach

My work fits within the interpretivist paradigm, especially a structured phenomenology, by which I mean loosely that I see human agents as actors in the social world, and my role is to try my best to render their lives meaningful in the context of their societies, histories, and cultures. I understand this is an interpretive act in as much as I am always understanding others as a social subject myself; moreover, my work is for others who are themselves human agents located in their own milieus. I am informed by positivism in as much as I want to attempt not to be biased or prejudiced, while also recognising my own positioning will inform my reflexive practice. My work draws from phenomenology in aiming to explore the experiences and meanings of the lives of my participants while recognising that they cannot always express in words what they think and feel. I may at times take a critical realist stance that identifies patterns and systems of which the participants are not immediately or directly conscious.

Let's now move on to thinking about how to select methods that are relevant in terms of a given philosophical approach and set of aims and objectives.

Methodologies and methods

It is important to distinguish methodology and method: methodology is the understanding (ology) of how the research will be approached, the logic (informed by the philosophical debates and considerations discussed earlier) behind the decisions made as to what actual methods to use, and how and when, as well as other decisions about sampling and selections, ethical issues, and so on. Methods are the means through which data are collected or generated, the practical steps employed to achieve your aims. For example, for its practice theory approach, the Brexit and British People Abroad study (Box 1.3) used expert interviews, in-depth case studies involving participant observation and narrative interviews, a citizens' panel, and interpretive analysis of texts, documents and discourses (Benson and O'Reilly 2020a; O'Reilly 2017b, 2018a).

> ## FOR YOUR TOOLKIT
> *Methodology* is the understanding (ology) of how the research will be approached, the logic behind decisions about what methods to use. The *methods* are the means through which data are collected or generated.

As an aside, constructivist approaches to qualitative research – a range of approaches that treat what are commonly thought of as independent, real objects as social or cultural 'constructs' (Benton and Craib 2023: 278) – will often avoid using words such as data, collection, or gathering and will instead talk about creating understandings with participants or data generating. They argue that 'data' sound like little chunks of objective facts, and that trying to collect or gather them denies the role of the researcher. I use the terms 'data', 'collection' or 'gathering' in this book but please take it as given that I mean insights and understandings that are somewhat co-created, not free-floating facts that are gathered, independently, directly, and entirely objectively.

The methods toolkit

I introduce here some of the many methods and tools available to researchers to consider how they relate to the above considerations. This is not meant as an exhaustive list but to open your mind to what is possible and to think carefully about how to get the best information for your purposes in the most appropriate and sensitive ways. The section also provides an introduction to subsequent chapters. The toolkit logic asks you to put these methods in a virtual toolkit and make them available as possibilities to consider. In my toolkit I have put *interviews, focus groups, ethnography,* and *creative methods.* This pretty much covers everything, as we shall see.

Interviews

The most widely used method in qualitative social research is semi-structured interviewing. I introduce different types of interview for your toolkit in Chapter 4, including life history, oral history, narrative, spontaneous interviews and conversations. Qualitative interviews are always semi-structured, with an emphasis on open questions; they can include the opportunity for participants to be asked a few specific and standardised questions, such as 'How many times did you visit the clinic last week?' But mainly the goal is to enable them to discuss the topics that you raise, in the way they want to interpret them, as well as some they may wish to raise themselves. A discussion guide allows you to focus, to stay on track and to guide the conversation but you will use this flexibly to enable induction and iteration.

In Chapter 4, I distinguish focused, conversational and discovery approaches to interviewing. Focused approaches are more often used in applied and policy research, in evaluations, and assessment-type interviews, where there is less scope for conversation and discovery. Conversational approaches ask for the person's own story or narrative with minimum interruption from the interviewer and are more exploratory. Discovery approaches are more iterative, working with participants to discover insights together. It is crucial to think carefully about what sorts of interview are available to you as you design your research, and especially how they relate to your research aims and objectives. What sorts of insights will interview data reveal?

Interviews: what sorts of insights?

Interviews are an opportunity for participants to think through and express how they understand things, what they mean to them, what they have experienced. They help you begin to understand their lives, but only as much as they are prepared to tell you or can express. Interviews yield insights into *how* people express themselves, to whom, and how they interpret things. Interviews can also tap into aspects you might not have thought of before.

Interviews do not necessarily reveal what a person actually did or would do. You should not say 'from our interviews we found that five would vote Tory and five would vote Labour' but 'half of those we spoke to *said* they would vote Tory' and so on. It is what they *said* that is interesting and is all you can be sure of. If phenomenology, in its simplest application, means obtaining the actors' points of view, tapping into their lived experiences, feelings, and meanings, how they relate to the world, then interviews are one way of accessing the phenomenological.

Interviews additionally enable some discussion of context to enable a nuanced understanding of what people might do in given circumstances, and to inform a hermeneutic approach. Vignettes and scenarios can help contextualise, as can the use of photographs and other creative techniques. These help people think a bit more about aspects of their lives about which they might be ambivalent, things people feel it hard to talk or even to think about.

Interviews do not have to be one-off opportunities to extract information from a single individual. They can take the shape of lots of little conversations, with individuals and with groups, even using social media. In Chapter 6, I discuss how to build relationships with participants to help address concerns around how people felt at a given time or juncture, and to give them time to think and reflect, to contradict themselves or to share ambiguity around an issue. In Chapter 7, I talk about how creative methods help people to share through creating or doing rather than talking. Interviewing will be affected by how participants see you (and maybe you can alter that); it may require a sharing of views. Also, interviews can be democratic in giving people a voice. I return to these notions in Chapters 3 and 4.

> **FOR YOUR TOOLKIT**
> Put guided conversations, semi-structured interviews, focus groups, and group conversations in all their diversity into your methods toolkit and consider their role in achieving your research aims and objectives.

Focus groups and group conversations

Focus groups and group interviews are covered in detail in Chapter 5, with lots of advice on how to conduct successful ones. Here I introduce the main approaches you can add to your toolkit. You are probably already familiar with the political and market research model. These typically involve four to 12 participants who have been purposefully selected because of their relationship to what you want to know. In this approach the participants are often strangers, to each other and to the researcher. A moderator runs the focus group and guides the conversation in ways predetermined (to an extent) by the researchers. These may be conducted in a series, may take place in institutional settings, and participants may be paid or compensated for their time and costs.

Focus groups are a useful technique but guided group conversations can employ other diverse styles and approaches. In ethnographic work, for example, we might talk to two or more people at any time in spontaneous ways. You can plan an informal guided conversation, or even slip in some of your questions into a spontaneous group discussion (see O'Reilly 2012a). In these cases, participants may already be part of a naturally occurring group or may know each other. Focus groups with vulnerable adults or children, or on sensitive topics, can take place in familiar settings and can be collaborative, ethical, and based on trust and rapport. But what sorts of insights do they yield?

Groups: what sorts of insights?

Groups are creative and dynamic and are a good way of generating phenomenological insights into how people feel, think, talk about something, as well as ideas you hadn't considered. People bounce ideas off each other but also affect each other, making them feel they can/not or should/not express a position. Nuance and ambivalence can be lost as groups work towards consensus or to avoid confrontation. But groups can be useful for observing interaction and power dynamics. They can yield insights into normative assumptions; they can lead to consensus or yield deep rifts. They can be useful for examining sensitive topics where people share experiences and feel more able to talk openly. They reflect, and therefore your interpretation must recognise, the socially produced nature of knowledge and ideas.

Ethnography and participant observation

Ethnographic methods and the methodology of ethnography are covered in Chapter 6. My goal here is to introduce ethnographic methods for your toolkit. Despite the foundational myth that ethnography should be arduous, long and lonely, there have been numerous advances, amendments and adaptations of the approach that respond to changes in the real world, as well as to our developing understandings of ethnography's place in social science research. Given these many adaptations (and their adjectives), in Chapter 6 I present ten enduring key principles for ethnography.

Participant observation is the main method of ethnography, and it involves taking part – maybe as a member of a community, maybe merely as an observer who joins in – while noting and recording theoretically informed observations (see O'Reilly 2012a). Ethnographers also talk to people in diverse circumstances. They use opportunistic, short interviews and many other forms of data collection, including creative and participatory ones, and document or structural analysis. Ethnography (or a bit of ethnography) is increasingly being used in applied settings to help build an evidence base for actions, policies and interventions, especially in settings such as health, medicine, policing, social work and education.

Ethnography: what sorts of insights?

The insights and understandings yielded using ethnographic methods include the difference between what people do and what they say they do (Shah 2017; Cubellis et al 2021) and the opportunity to talk to people as they do things. Interviews and conversations in ethnography are always context relevant. Ethnography also enables you to tap into the complexity of people's lives and decision making, as well as their experiences, meanings, and understandings. Devoting time to build rapport and trust, doing things with people, and sharing in their lives, gives you the time to explore ambiguity and ambivalence and gives them time to express alternative views and perspectives. Talking with participants at different times means you are less affected by mood and moment than in a one-off interview. If you are left with puzzles or doubts about what you have heard or seen, you can go back and ask for more clarity. You can take the time to tap slowly and carefully into things people find difficult to express (perhaps through the creative approaches in Chapter 7). Over time you come to understand some of how people's beliefs and understandings are shaped by communities, and can examine how norms are practised and shaped, as sought by a Heideggerian (structured) phenomenology and by practice theory.

> **FOR YOUR TOOLKIT**
>
> Put ethnographic methods, and creative and participatory methods, into your methods toolkit and consider their role in achieving your research aims and objectives.

Creative methods

The term 'creative methods' has been used for diverse approaches being developed ever since people started doing qualitative, especially ethnographic, research. Yet still in some circles the hegemony of a specific (positivist) view of science and of certain approaches that have come to be accepted as valid, such as semi-structured interviews, has often served to exclude or deny creativity and imagination. With a specific focus on doing things differently, Chapter 7 explores some of the many ways conventional approaches to data collection have been adapted, developed, altered, reimagined, and recreated. Again, my goal is to inspire you to think outside the box, to open your minds and your imaginations, to learn from others, and to be brave enough to be creative and imaginative about what you could do as part of your research.

Five approaches to being creative are introduced in Chapter 7: creating, doing, mediating, combining, and collaborating. Collaborating is a way of thinking creatively about methods that includes the participants in the creativity as well as in other stages of the research. This is my opportunity to introduce co-participation, participatory action research and decolonising methods. What sorts of insights and understandings do these methods yield?

Being creative: what sorts of insights?

Qualitative research is essentially creative, flexible and responsive: putting a spotlight on being creative merely encourages us to embrace that creativity. Being creative with methods can support: descriptive phenomenology by helping people express themselves; an interpretive phenomenology by working with participants identifying patterns; and structured phenomenology by locating understandings in the lifeworld. Creative approaches can be transformative in transforming yourself, the participants and the wider world. Collaborating can involve working on interventions together that are useful and meaningful. Being creative is a means of ensuring excluded voices have been heard. Creative and imaginative approaches help you to locate things in context, to observe the passing of time and processes as they unravel.

When being creative, think carefully about your aims and objectives. It is useful to distinguish data as writing, found data, and creative production. 'Data as writing' refers to (often visual) data that you produce, perhaps collaboratively, to support your case when writing up or disseminating findings. While not exactly data collection it might overlap in practice as you make photographs or even restage events to illustrate insights. 'Found data' are data that existed prior to the research, and are analysed interpretively, or using discourse analysis or semiotics. 'Creative production' is where data are produced collaboratively to create meanings or insights, or are used as prompts to encourage discussion about meanings and feelings.

Previously existing or found data

I would like to end with a few thoughts about the analysis of previously existing and external data, documents, and texts (found data). Here I am thinking about the secondary analysis of pre-written diaries, of visual displays that preceded your entry to the research arena, the analysis of open-ended survey questions, the secondary analysis of previously collected qualitative data, of websites, policies and rules, and other data that were not created or generated for your research. Jennifer Mason (2018) contrasts researcher-generated data and data that are 'out there'. Such 'found data' cannot be treated iteratively and inductively in the ways I describe in this book because they predate or are external to your research.

The most likely way you would analyse previously existing or external data is through interpretive analysis, by making sense of their role in the lives, experiences and actions of the participants in the study (O'Reilly 2012a). Projects often begin their sense making by looking at previously existing data, for example organisational websites, rules and policies (Hughes et al 2022), regulations (Benson and O'Reilly 2018), or even the built environment (Birch et al 2007). This might provide background and contextual information (see Chapter 8). As the project proceeds, they might go on to analyse (using structured phenomenology) how these contextual elements shape the agency of the participants, and are shaped by them (Box 1.2). Paul Willis and Mats Trondman's (2021) holistic view of ethnographic analysis contends that as well as understanding people's actions, thoughts and feelings we must also pay attention to the role of structures (institutions, patterns, and norms) and cultural products or artefacts and their use. The latter can include analysis of online forums and group cultures. Michaela Benson and I (Benson and O'Reilly 2018) include analysis of 'expat' forums, for example, in understanding the way of life of British people in Malaysia. Others might use narrative, semiotic or discourse analysis, to analyse documents and texts (Chapter 8), but these are traditions with their own cultural norms. When using previously existing data you need to think especially carefully about their role in the project; they will be mentioned again as the book proceeds.

Final thoughts

We have covered the logic of qualitative research, the philosophy underlabourer role, how to develop clear and precise aims and objectives, and selecting appropriate methods. You are now well on your way to being able to design rigorous and good-quality qualitative research. The next chapter provides intellectual and practical tools for conducting interpretive sampling, reviewing the literature, designing tools for participants, and for assessing the quality of qualitative research.

Speaking of design

(Thanks to Daniel Kahneman (2012) for this idea as a substitute for conclusions.)

'I know what I'm interested in and why but I'm going to have to be pretty flexible and responsive if I want to learn from participants how the world works for them.'

'Philosophy is great for helping me think things through: I am not a blank sheet on which facts can be written, I know I can't isolate cause and effect with human agents, but I hope I can identify some patterns and likely or possible outcomes that follow complex pathways.'

'There are so many possibilities when it comes to methods, each offering their own type of insights. I'd like to be imaginative with my own research but I must remember my research goals.'

'I mustn't forget to think about things people can't or won't talk about such as social and other structures, conditions and constraints.'

Taking things further

Benton and Craib's (2023) *Philosophy of Social Science* is a journey through **philosophical thought** and its relationship to social science. There is also a shorter introduction to **philosophy** in *Ethnographic Methods* (O'Reilly 2012a). For more on Husserl, Heidegger and **phenomenological** approaches, see Dowling (2007) and Williams (2021). See Sam Ladner (2014) for a thorough **critique of positivist** (and factist) perspectives in the context of private sector ethnographies. For those who want to go further with respect to **practice and structuration** theory, I recommend O'Reilly (2012b), and Hughes et al (2022). Jennifer Mason's (2018) book, *Qualitative Researching*, includes a host of good advice, and I recommend it for her six difficult questions and discussion of **research questions**. The edited volume by Pope and Mays (2020) includes contributions from highly respected qualitative researchers in **healthcare**.

Listen to the related episode for this chapter on Qualitative Research Methods for Everyone podcast:

2

Developing the design

What this chapter is about

In this chapter we move on from the first stages of planning a research project to making coherent and interpretive sampling selections, the role of the literature review in iterative-inductive research, planning other materials that you might use, conducting a pilot study, and assessing the quality of qualitative research. The goal here, together with Chapters 1 and 3, is to comprehensively address any particulars you may need to consider in order to have research approved by an ethics or funding committee, or other gatekeeper, and to get you ready to start with confidence.

Interpretive sampling

In the following comprehensive discussion, I introduce a new set of concepts developed specifically for this book to clarify procedures in qualitative sampling and selections. First, I introduce the concept of *interpretive sampling*, that respects the interpretive and iterative-inductive nature of qualitative research introduced in the previous chapter. I then delineate *initial, ongoing and final samples* and their role in the iterative-inductive process. I use the concept of *sample fitness* to define how to assess and demonstrate the value of initial, ongoing and final selections. I finish the section with an extensive example of how selections might be made and assessed using these new concepts.

> *As an aside*, I use the words 'sampling' and 'selections', almost interchangeably, because this is language people are familiar with. But it is important to recognise the problematic nature of the language of sampling and how it can be interpreted. The notion is taken directly from natural science, where a blood or urine sample (for example) is expected to contain what is in the whole. In social science research (quantitative or qualitative) the way in which a sample or selection represents others (if at all) needs to be thought through and clarified.

Qualitative research falls within the *interpretivist* paradigm, meaning it is designed 'to interpret' or 'to make sense' and to render meaningful. It is essential, therefore, to eventually include in the research whoever and whatever will enable you to make sense of the phenomenon and all the dimensions of it that you are interested in rendering meaningful. An interpretive sample must also link overtly and clearly back to what was described in the design of the research.

> **FOR YOUR TOOLKIT**
>
> Qualitative research falls within the *interpretivist* paradigm, meaning it is designed 'to interpret' or 'to make sense' and to render meaningful. It is essential, therefore, that your interpretive sampling includes whoever and whatever will enable you to make sense of the phenomenon and all its relevant dimensions as you come to understand these.

An interpretive sample will be iterative-inductive (see Chapter 1), constantly iterating between being inductive (open-minded, bottom-up, learning from the field) and deductive (testing out existing and new theories and concepts to see if they help clarify understandings), with an inductive approach retaining the upper hand. In qualitative research we usually aim to represent *types* of people or behaviours, or a *range* or diversity of experiences or perceptions, as these relate to the problem we are addressing and in the context of certain conditions. However, there is a good chance that we do not know at the outset what typologies will be meaningful, how diverse the responses will be or what conditions are relevant. We must start somewhere, with an *initial sample*, but this may not remain adequate. Further, in qualitative research, because we are including hard-to-reach groups, or researching sensitive or complex issues, access can be challenging and we need to tread gently. For these reasons, interpretive samples will need to be drawn and redrawn as the research progresses.

> **FOR YOUR TOOLKIT**
>
> Interpretive samples will need to be drawn and redrawn as the research progresses, as initial, ongoing and final samples.

The initial sample

The *initial sample* is designed purposefully. This is a technique widely used in qualitative research for the identification and selection of information-rich cases related to the phenomena of interest (Palinkas et al 2015). Statistically, random samples cannot usually be relied on to yield enough complexity and richness and are likely to exclude some minority, valuable and insightful instances. The main objective of a purposeful sample is to intentionally include groups, individuals, or other characteristics that can logically or thematically be assumed to be representative of the population. The sample at this stage is representative of the wider population conceptually, not numerically. Purposeful samples select for relevant diversity in relation to the research problem (such as those who experience a certain range of experiences, or take certain types of medication), as well as more generic (but still relevant) variables such as social class, ethnic group, age, and so on. Initial samples may be heterogeneous or homogeneous with respect to different variables, depending on the focus of the research (for example we may wish to select a homogenous group of people with a specified disability but from a heterogeneous diversity of backgrounds).

> *As an aside,* I make no apology for using the concept of variable though it is more commonly known in quantitative research. I am using it to mean characteristics according to which the population or context varies.

It is worth noting that not only is designing an *initial sample* a sensible and logical way to proceed but those giving funds, permission or access for your work will need an idea how you intend to start. In funding applications, initial sample design is your opportunity to demonstrate (and ensure you have) confidence in your knowledge of the population and circumstances. Explain how you can access the relevant groups and contexts, discuss what issues may arise and how you might overcome them. And remember, selections can include individuals or groups (for example, children of certain ages, people with specific disabilities), organisations (such as political institutions, charities), settings (locations, places), events (routine and special, such as religious festivals, staff meetings), time frames or periods (such as day, evening, after work), and previously existing data (such as web pages, adverts, displays, news).

There are other sampling techniques that you can draw on when designing your initial sample, such as convenience samples and case studies. Snowball samples will be discussed later.

FOR YOUR TOOLKIT
The initial sample is designed purposefully. Purposeful samples select for *potentially relevant diversity* in relation to the research problem as well as more generic relevant variables.

Convenience samples

Convenience or ad hoc samples are not really samples, but a means of access. People, groups or contexts should not be included in a study purely because it was convenient or because they were added ad hoc. However, there may be reasons that one has to use existing contacts or known groups (for example, in the case of hard-to-reach or 'invisible' groups), and there are times we might even include someone because they offered themselves or just turned up and seemed interesting. All selections should have a justifiable rationale and should always be made on the basis of their relevance for the study, and you should carefully assess the relationship of those included to the wider population or in terms of their relevance for the study (revisit this later when thinking about the final sample). So, feel free to include a discussion in your initial sample design about how some people/groups/contexts are conveniently available and what, or how, they will contribute to the study, in terms of the insights these will offer. This is a positive thing, but to call this a convenience sample suggests selections have been lazy or not fully thought through.

Case studies

Care must be taken in any research design using the language of case studies because of its diverse array of meanings. Clarify exactly how you are using the term, what aspects make yours a case of what, and what aspects are different or exceptional. Arya Priya (2021) provides a useful overview of the current state of the debate; however, I still find Robert Stake's the most useful interpretation of the term (also see O'Reilly 2009: 23). Stake (2003) distinguishes an instrumental case study and an intrinsic case.

In an instrumental case study, the study is designed to focus on a specific case of something that is more widely known. Individuals, groups, settings, organisations, and so on, can provide cases, where in the final writing or communicating of research the findings are used to indicate more broadly relevant social processes. It is difficult to avoid the (often implicit) assumption that the selected case will perfectly represent a case of something that also exists more widely or elsewhere, while in truth there is never a perfectly representative case of anything in social life, since humans are always somewhat unpredictable and actions are always context dependent. Nevertheless, we can attempt to loosely locate some of the things (variables) we are interested in: specific areas, groups, places, or times, and these can constitute cases. Most researchers do research some place, with some group, as a way of understanding issues of wider concern, without always using the language of a case study. Lydia Hayes (2017), for example, was interested in how, broadly speaking, the work of homecare (in clients' homes and residential/nursing homes) is perceived, interpreted and influenced in the context of wider legal and political frameworks. Sarah Wall (2015) concludes her findings for self-employed nurses in Canada, not just the ones in her study. I return to representativeness later in this chapter.

Sometimes two or more cases are studied comparatively in a comparative case study. Here, some aspects will be comparable and held constant (perhaps similar types of industry), while others vary for comparison (perhaps different types of labour migrant). Think of a Venn diagram, where some aspects of interest vary from one case to another while some aspects overlap or are similar. It should be aspects crucial to the central theme that are constant.

> *As an aside,* I have often heard people working in applied rather than academic settings using the notion of a case study to mean choosing someone to represent their argument. This is in fact an illustrative case, in writing or dissemination, not a study (see Chapter 9).

In an intrinsic case study, situations, groups, institutions, people, or even behaviours are studied because they are intrinsically interesting – the review of a specific policy or intervention or one particular instantiation, for example (see Stake 2003). This might be because they are different or cutting edge, or could even be because the researcher has exclusive or privileged access. Here, again, the language of 'case' can be off-putting because it implies we are talking about a case (an instance) of something wider.

> **FOR YOUR TOOLKIT**
> An instrumental case is selected instrumentally as somewhere to locate the study. An intrinsic case is studied for its intrinsic interest. An *illustrative case* is used to illustrate, and is related to writing not design.

Whatever techniques you use to locate participants, always clarify who and what are included in your initial sample and why with respect to your initial aims and objectives.

The ongoing sample

Interpretive sampling continues as the research proceeds, through ongoing assessment of the relevance of data for your eventual findings and, where possible, making adjustments to who and what are included (Malterud et al 2016). This iterative-inductive process involves (1) selecting an initial set of people, groups, contexts and so on; (2) beginning to collect, or generate, and analyse data (learning from the participants and the field); (3) annotating, coding, sensitising, memoing; and (4) drawing further ongoing samples to refine understandings and better understand the complexity and variability of the topic. Ongoing sampling also moves from open and broad to more discriminating and strategic as you learn more.

> **FOR YOUR TOOLKIT**
> Ongoing sampling involves returning to (more or the same) people, to examine emergent ideas, new topics, developing insights, and reviewing what, where and who are included as *known relevant diversity*.

The selection of *ongoing samples* could include snowballing, but as with convenience sampling discussed earlier, 'snowballing' is a technique for making selections, not a type of sample. Snowballing is where a few initial selections are made, then the sample grows through networking or linking to known contacts. It is a useful way of reaching people but it is crucial to think critically about who is included and what you are learning from these inclusions and exclusions.

Ongoing sampling involves returning to people, or including others, to examine emergent ideas, new topics, developing insights, and reviewing what and who is included as analysis proceeds. In the design of a project or proposal, I explain to readers why ongoing sampling will be crucial and how that will be practically achieved, perhaps through convenience or snowball sampling. A reviewer of a research design will have more confidence in your ability to achieve your goals if you have thought carefully about how people, groups, topics, and contexts might be included where they will inform the developing insights. Of course, the extent of ongoing sampling that can be achieved will be limited by access, time and resources, and this should also be noted where relevant.

The final sample

Eventually, you will conclude the study and will be able to describe your final sample: the people, groups, contexts, and other variables that you ended up including. Describe how the final sample relates to any dissemination or outputs as it provides the scope and limits of your study. It is important that the sample you end up with gives you confidence to be able to say what you want to say (see Chapter 9). Conversely, you can only make claims to understand something you have fully researched, and this includes who has or has not been included, as well as what topics, the extent of the interviews, the nature of the research, and so on. This takes us on to the topic of sample fitness.

> **FOR YOUR TOOLKIT**
> The final sample is the people, groups, contexts, and other variables and topics that you finally included, which will reflect *required relevant diversity* for specific outputs.

Sample fitness and the thorny issue of sample size

The question 'what size should my sample be?' arises over and over again, as Sarah Baker and Rosalind Edwards (2012) acknowledge and as I have found myself through decades of teaching and supervising. Worse, there is a tendency to skim over the question in the research methods literature, or to address it with statements such as 'numbers are not relevant for qualitative research' or 'we are looking for depth not breadth'. This is not helpful, especially when confronted with people with a more quantitative or positivist mindset who tend to denigrate qualitative research as subjective or anecdotal. As interpretive sampling should fit with interpretivist logic, then the question should be *does the sample fit?*

Initial sample fitness should address fitness for the design stage of a project, ongoing sample fitness should be addressed in relation to the iterative-inductive design of the research, and final sample fitness should be assessed in terms of the claims made in final reports and other dissemination.

Initial sample fitness

Initial sample fitness asks: Does the initial sample fit with the aims and objectives of the project? This is partly about size, as Kirsti Malterud, Volkert Dirk Siersma, and Ann Dorrit Guassora (2016: 1754) contend: 'an approximation of sample size is necessary for planning, while the adequacy of the final sample size must be continuously evaluated during the research process'. To provide costings and to plan the timeline, you need to estimate how many interviews or focus groups you might do, how much time you might spend doing participant observation or using creative techniques, with whom and how many people. But the number or size of the initial sample is far less relevant in terms of fitness than whether you have included the breadth of people (and other variables) to at least begin to address the aims and objectives.

> **FOR YOUR TOOLKIT**
> Initial sample fitness asks whether the proposed samples or selections fit with all of the project's important design issues. Does it address potentially relevant diversity?

Initial sample fitness asks: Does the initial sample fit the desired depth and breadth of the proposed project? Is it designed to be exploratory with few variables or broader in nature with a diverse set of variables? Rich, in-depth research that will use historical, narrative, or longitudinal interviews or intense periods of participant observation will yield a phenomenal amount of data to explore and write up into many types of output. Here, using a large sample would require possibly years of writing up. On the other hand, research that is making broad claims that you hope someone might act on in terms of policy development, for different groups of people under different situations, will require a more diverse and heterogeneous sample. The diversity of these latter studies inheres in the quality of the sample rather than in the quality of responses. A more targeted and tightly defined study will have a smaller and more tightly defined sample.

Initial sample fitness asks: Does the sample fit the proposed methodology and methods? Remember that methodology is the logic behind methods selection and methods are the techniques used. Different disciplines and research fields have their own expectations. In oral history and in narrative research, because of the depth and richness of the data yielded, it is usual to have small numbers of participants but a richness of topics. Ethnographic research usually involves a considerable amount of time in settings, yielding complex and rich data. In applied research, the tendency is to have more targeted sampling, directed at specific types of people and to address more focused questions.

Initial sample fitness asks: Does the sample fit the role of qualitative research in the overall project? This is related to the richness of data expected, and whether or not the qualitative aspect is central to the project or supplementary to other kinds of (perhaps quantitative) data. Relatedly, will the qualitative research be required to produce a chapter, an article, a small report, or an entire thesis or book?

Initial sample fitness asks: Does your sample fit with the location of your research in wider literature? Have you identified gaps and addressed those in your sample design? The role of theory and prior research will inform how you identify relevant variables for the initial sample.

Initial sample fitness asks: Does your sample fit with other important practical and ethical project design issues? (see Baker and Edwards 2012). The sample will be constrained in terms of what time, money and other resources are available, what access you can expect to achieve, how lightly you must tread ethically, what you are expecting to write/produce for whom in what time scale. You will also need to satisfy the demands of reviewers, funders, your discipline, and colleagues. Your sample needs to fit with external constraints and expectations.

To conclude, initial sample fitness considers how rich and exploratory the research aims to be, the variables identified early on, the diversity of the topic and population, the expected breadth or depth, expected external and practical limitations, as well as where the research is likely to be published and who will assess the work.

Ongoing sample fitness

Ongoing sample fitness asks how your continued selections and choices fit with the interpretivist logic of learning as you go and developing grounded insights. Even where qualitative researchers are more applied or focused (for example in policy research), or those who are overtly testing a theory, I would nevertheless hope they would amend their selections or focus (if only in terms of what they ask of whom and how) as they learn more and their own assumptions are challenged. Alternatively, if little is known on the topic already or if the researcher suddenly finds dimensions that had been previously overlooked, then they may need more time or more participants. In other words, we want to reach out broadly initially and become more targeted later, as our understandings develop iteratively. Amending your sample can, of course, include adding more dimensions to the topic, more questions to ask the same people, or different people to be asked similar things, perhaps related to different contexts.

As with the initial sample, your ongoing sample also involves adjusting who and what, and how much time, is included for practical and ethical reasons. As Malterud et al (2016) note, sensitive topics and complex issues require a sensitive approach and may involve returning to participants, being creative with methods, or finding different participants in order to fully understand the problem.

FOR YOUR TOOLKIT

Ongoing sample fitness asks how your continued selections and choices fit with the interpretivist logic of learning as you go and developing grounded insights. Does it address known relevant diversity?

Final sample fitness

Final sample fitness asks: Does my final sample fit my conclusions? Given what I now wish to argue (in whatever article, report, or paper), do I have a good sample with which to talk about this confidently? Does my sample or selection fit my claims? This is similar to what Clive Seale (2018: 172–3) calls sample adequacy: 'Have I got enough here to say something new and original and to back up my claims with a decent amount of evidence?' Or to put it another way: 'The results presented in the final publication will demonstrate whether the actual sample held adequate information power to develop new knowledge, referring to the aim of the study at hand' (Malterud et al 2016: 1759).

Final sample fitness requires you to address to what extent you now aim to be representative. Are you sharing individual diverse insights or developing themes, typologies, or processes that represent broader phenomena (see Chapter 9)? The answer depends on what you are writing, be it a report, an article, a book, a PhD, and whether these are comprehensive results, a few key findings, developmental results, or selective findings (White et al 2014). Crucially, this is about having enough people and richness to be able to speak with confidence in relation to your goals. If what you are saying is very complex and rich then you will need a rich sample (of people or themes) to illustrate that complexity. If there is a lot of diversity in the population in relation to your argument, then you have two options: either you need to make sure you have enough information to be able to talk with confidence about that diversity, or you need to acknowledge that there is some diversity, some different types of people or situation, that you were unable to cover in sufficient depth.

The fitness of the final sample also depends on whether you are doing research for one particular output or you are researching something out of interest that may be written up over a long period. During my first ethnographic project, in Spain, I met and spoke with over 250 people. I have been able to write from this research for many years, including a book and several articles. Over the years, I have met some of these people again and again; now I write more longitudinal or reflective analyses that focus on process and change, thus my selections (of topics and people) have been ongoing as have my analyses (see O'Reilly 2017a).

> **FOR YOUR TOOLKIT**
> Final sample fitness assesses the quality of the sample for the claims you are making. Does it have the richness and complexity of material to argue with confidence? Does it address required relevant diversity?

I have introduced, for the first time anywhere, the conceptualisation of sampling as *interpretive sampling*, using the concepts of initial, ongoing and final samples, that are assessed using the notion of sample fitness. I now illustrate this with an extensive example from my work with Michaela Benson.

Interpretive sampling in action: Brexit and the British abroad

The Brexit and British People Abroad project 'Freedom of Movement, Citizenship and Brexit in the lives of British Citizens living in the EU–27' was funded from 2017 to 2019 by the Economic and Social Research Council's Brexit priority scheme and was part of the UK in a Changing Europe's suite of activities. The project, led by Michaela Benson with myself as co-investigator, had an overall *aim* to examine the impact of Brexit for the estimated 1.2 million British citizens living in the EU-27 whose rights to live and work in the EU were renegotiated as part of the Brexit Withdrawal Agreement between the UK government and the EU Commission. There are more details in Box 2.1.

Box 2.1: For illustration: Brexit and the British abroad

The project's *objectives* were outlined as follows: to examine what Brexit, as it unfolds, entails for Britons resident, part- or full-time, in several national and local contexts in Europe, populations who have benefited from the freedom of movement and related entitlements; to question how Brexit shapes what it means to be an expatriated Briton living in Europe and how this relates to the values they place on their British and European citizenship; and to explore how such populations become part of Brexit.

The proposed methodology, methods, and review of the literature were outlined in full in the case for support. In short, we proposed to supplement decades of past research with British populations in France and Spain with new empirical data combining: approximately 20 expert interviews with national decision makers, local stakeholders, migration intermediaries, civil society organisations and support services; in-depth case studies with expatriates in France and Spain (the EU member states hosting the highest numbers of expatriated Britons), supplemented with a citizens' panel composed of Britons resident in Ireland, Germany, the Netherlands, Greece and Cyprus (countries that are home to the largest populations of Britons after France and Spain); and interpretive analysis of texts, documents, discourse, media and policy debates, and decision making (Benson 2020; Benson and O'Reilly 2020a; O'Reilly 2020b).

Brexit and the British abroad: the initial sample and its fitness

Our *initial sample* was designed to fit the relevant diversity of the population, given our aims and objectives. The expert interviews included officials across EU countries and organisations to capture how institutional actors with responsibilities for British populations understand, communicate, manage and mediate the effects of the Brexit negotiations. They formed a small and specific part of the overall project and interviews were relatively focused and specific in terms of topic. Given the project was initially designed to last just a few months, this seemed to fit well with our overall design and practical limitations such as time and funds, as well as expectations that such interviewees were unlikely to be able to afford to give us much time.

For the in-depth case studies (by which we simply meant locations to focus on) we estimated 50 interviews with Britons living in France and 50 in Spain, exploring their aspirations and goals, but also an understanding of how these change, given the wider, structural context. These were designed to be in-depth, narrative-style interviews with a longitudinal perspective. We selected France and Spain as field sites because they represent a large majority of British people living in the EU, and we have both done extensive research in these destinations in the past and could provide detailed longitudinal context (O'Reilly 2000; Benson 2011). For practical reasons, we were confident we could locate a diverse sample in sufficient time. We decided to supplement interviews in the study sites with participant observation at key events (O'Reilly 2012a) to give us direct access to some of the contexts and communities that shape activities of migrants. This was important for our practice theory framework.

The citizens' panel, inspired by the Mass Observation Project, was to comprise 100 British residents living in Ireland, Germany, Greece, the Netherlands and Cyprus, with the aim to keep a finger on the pulse of how the populations of these destinations were witnessing and responding to changing rules and regulations, and the changing nature of Brexit negotiations in a range of geographical settings and cultural contexts.

As with the expert interviews, the purpose here was to tap into a wide diversity, without expecting great depth of interview. We planned to return to respondents several times so this had a longitudinal element. We also hoped the countries we selected would represent different types of EU democracy, economy and geography.

Brexit and the British abroad: the ongoing sample and its fitness

Our reflexive and iterative sampling is discussed at length in our article arguing for reflexive practice (Benson and O'Reilly 2020b). There were various ways in which we felt it necessary to amend our sample as we went along, for practical reasons such as time, access and geography, but also to reflect our developing, grounded interpretations. We were lucky enough to obtain volunteers from every European country, and so our citizens' panel was extended to include 200 people, who contributed varying amounts via emails, online interviews, social media, and other media. As we said:

> As we learned more about the relevant diversity of the population, and questioned our own positioning, we worked to navigate our sample, seeking ways of engaging British People of Colour, leave voters, younger working people, people with disabilities and UK nationals living in Ireland ... We also shifted the geographies of the research to reflect the knowledge that British citizens who have

taken advantage of Freedom of Movement are a success story of European citizenship, integrated into local and European labour markets and dispersed throughout the EU27; research in France was extended to include Toulouse, and in Spain to include Granada. In this way, navigating inclusion in the research was directly related to our desire to communicate the diversity of this population, their life circumstances and migration, and the uneven outcomes of Brexit as we came to understand all these. (Benson and O'Reilly 2020b: 187)

We also supplemented our emerging insights through the use of two online surveys (Benson et al 2018; Benton et al 2018), as well as making efforts to include younger participants (Danby and O'Reilly 2018). Note that reflecting on your own ongoing sample fitness is also an opportunity to acknowledge what you learn about the population but are unable to pursue, or cases you cannot include.

Brexit and the British abroad: the final sample and its fitness

An assessment of final sample fitness asks: Was it fit for purpose? I address this with respect to two different outputs from the project: Benson and Lewis (2019) and Benson and O'Reilly (2020a). 'Brexit, British people of colour in the EU-27 and everyday racism in Britain and Europe', written by Michaela Benson and Chantelle Lewis (2019: 2211), begins:

This paper focuses on how British People of Colour living in the EU-27 make sense of Brexit. As we reveal through original empirical research, their views on Brexit are shaped by personal experiences of everyday, structural, and institutional racism. Importantly, such experiences were a feature of their lives before and after Brexit, in Britain but also in their places of home and work in other European countries. This research provides empirical grounding that supports an understanding of Brexit as unexceptional, as business as usual not only in Britain but also in other European nations. Further, it contextualises the experiences of these British People of Colour in longer European histories of racism and racialization and the routine racial exclusion at the core of collective imaginings of who is British and who is European.

This article in a peer-reviewed journal is approximately 8,000 words long and was only possible because the final sample was extensive enough for us to be confident about our claims. One of the earliest findings in the project was that Brexit was generating (for the British in Europe) some often unpleasant forms of othering. As time passed, however, it became clear that for people of colour this othering was not experienced as particularly exceptional. Indeed, for them, Brexit proved merely to amplify already existing and longer standing experiences of structural and institutional discrimination and everyday racism. We realised we would need to adapt our strategies to improve recruitment of British people of colour to the project. Our colleague, Chantelle Lewis, who was working with us on the project thus took primary responsibility for recruitment, drawing on personal contacts and mutual acquaintances over a period of a year starting in 2017, to recruit an extra 30 participants for in-depth interviews. The participants ranged in age from 24 to 50 and lived in eight different EU countries.

We assess this final sample as fit for purpose. It does not attempt to statistically represent all people of colour of all types, geographies, ages, and backgrounds; instead, it analyses a quality of feeling that people of colour shared in common; it highlights, especially through the use of theory (see Chapter 9), issues that were meaningful to those involved and that others can relate to or find illuminating. The sample also enables us to throw a new light on perspectives about EU relations 'in stark contrast to accounts that pitch Britain, and indeed other locations in and around Europe, as *newly* racist and xenophobic' (Benson and Lewis 2019: 2224, emphasis added).

The article 'British citizens in Europe left navigating the (Brexit) swamp' (Benson and O'Reilly 2020a) is a short piece for a wide audience on a website hosted by UK in a Changing Europe. At just over 1,000 words, there is little space for any in-depth discussion, but the claims we make are based on the entire project. Because of the extent and breadth of the final sample, we have the confidence to talk of emotions being rife across the entire population of British citizens in Europe. Our ongoing documentary analysis facilitated a rich and complex understanding of which ongoing negotiations were affecting our participants and our interviews articulated these as lived experience. We were able to link the article to other reports we had produced (for example, Danby and O'Reilly 2018), as well as to other useful informative websites. We could argue with confidence that governments across the EU and the UK were slow to offer support, that legal agreements were limited or inadequate, that Britons developed their own support groups but that this reflected deep-seated anxieties and frustrations, and that gender, age, disability, race and class, alongside personal circumstances, are all factors which shape the extent to which people can overcome some of the challenges Brexit presents to them. The diversity of our final sample, the longitudinal nature of our research, and its breadth, depth and quality, as well as the methods employed, mean our final sample was fit for this purpose.

Reviewing the literature

Chapter 1 addressed the logic of qualitative research, the philosophy underlabourer role, how to develop clear and precise aims and objectives, and how to select appropriate methods. Chapter 2 has so far thought through the logic of making coherent and interpretive sampling selections. It is time to consider the role of the literature review in iterative-inductive research, planning other materials that you might use, conducting a pilot study, and finally, how to assess qualitative research.

The role of the literature review in qualitative work is to locate your work in existing studies; to familiarise yourself with what else has been done and how; to sensitise your work to potential theories, results, and concepts; to identify gaps in knowledge; and to form sensitising concepts, foreshadowed problems, or guiding theoretical problems (discussed later), *not* to form fixed hypotheses. It should open your mind, not foreclose it.

FOR YOUR TOOLKIT

The role of the literature review is to locate, familiarise, sensitise, and identify gaps, not to form fixed hypotheses. It should open your mind, not foreclose it.

Scientific work should be cumulative, and you cannot begin to contribute to existing substantive, theoretical or policy knowledge until you have some idea what that consists of. A *substantive review* asks what is already known about the topic, substantively. You might examine work that has used quantitative, qualitative and mixed methods, but you are likely to spend more time on the qualitative research, especially when it comes to identifying gaps or inadequacies. A *policy review* asks how this topic is shaped by policy. It is specifically important for those who want to consider how policies constrain or enable participants' choices and for those who wish to contribute in some way towards policy as part of the research. A *theoretical review* asks how this area has been understood, theoretically and conceptually. What tools have been developed to aid understanding in the area? Alice Goffman (2014), for her ethnographic study of policing and surveillance practices as experienced by predominantly Black young people in Philadelphia (see Chapter 3), reviewed the literature on criminal law in the US, the policies known as the 'war on crime and drugs', as well as the theoretical literature on crime, punishment, mass incarceration, and inequality.

In qualitative research, any prior knowledge and/or theory should be used with scepticism, and researchers have devised ways of conceptualising how to use pre-existing theory and concepts in an iterative-inductive way (O'Reilly 2012a). Constructivist grounded theorist Kathy Charmaz (2014) draws on the concept of 'sensitising concepts', which sensitise you to certain ways of thinking that might eventually prove useful, but that must earn their way into one's analysis. Anthropologist Bronislaw Malinowski used the concept of 'foreshadowed problems' as a way to conceptualise the problematic nature of preconceived ideas. Preconceived ideas, he said, 'are pernicious in any scientific work, but foreshadowed problems are the main endowment of a scientific thinker' (Malinowski 1922: 9). In my book on ethnographic methods I use the notion of guiding (theoretical) problems (O'Reilly 2012a; and see O'Reilly 2009); inspired by (perhaps lay) theoretical ideas about the world, these are not rigid or fixed but can be adapted or discarded as research progresses.

> **FOR YOUR TOOLKIT**
> Guiding theoretical problems are theoretically informed ideas about the world that shape intellectual puzzles and can be adapted or discarded as research progresses.

In an iterative-inductive approach, that moves back and forth between what you think you know and what you learn in a constant oscillation, you will need to review literature at the outset of a project, as orientation, as you go along, to aid sense making, and at the end, to ensure there was nothing crucial published that you had overlooked and to strengthen and give form to your final arguments.

Framing the work theoretically

Theoretical frameworks, or what Virginia Braun and Victoria Clarke (2022: 189) call Big Theory, tend to be conceptual, broad-brush, or macro frameworks that apply to general phenomena. These may be discipline specific or relate to a field of research. They will thus shape the research design. They may be epistemological, as in practice theory (O'Reilly 2012b). They might be critical, starting from the position that inequalities exist, such as when we used theoretical perspectives on the concepts of neoliberalism and postcolonialism in our research on lifestyle migration in Malaysia and Panama (Benson and O'Reilly 2018). They may be more substantive, such as the sociology of childhood (Morrow 2001; Birch et al 2007), which views children as active social agents. They may be used to conceptualise broad social changes, as with researchers in the field of international labour migration and globalisation (O'Reilly and Rye 2021). Crucially, some will not fit with a qualitative sensibility because they are already too rigid and do not permit the oscillation between theoretical frames and lived practice that shapes good qualitative research (see Cubellis et al 2021). Theories of change, for example, should be used carefully and permit opportunities to learn from participants in a creative and flexible manner. If a design is too rigid it will not allow for serendipity (see Chapter 6): exploratory research should not be subjugated to its initial design or to frameworks (see Pink et al 2022).

> **FOR YOUR TOOLKIT**
> Theoretical frameworks tend to be conceptual, broad-brush, or macro frameworks that apply to general phenomena. They shape the research design, and as such can be too rigid to permit the oscillation between theoretical frames and lived practice that shapes good qualitative research.

Designing tools for participants

I will talk much more about the various tools and techniques that might be used with participants as I work through subsequent chapters. However, you might need to prepare some materials to illustrate plans to ethics committees, funding committees, or other gatekeepers. These usually include participant information sheets, consent forms, interview or discussion guides, and some consideration of the role of visual and creative methods and how they will be employed.

Participant information sheets and consent forms

Participant information sheets and consent forms are crucial to obtain informed consent. You may need slightly different versions for different types of participant, such as for children, parents, patients, and clinicians. Their design and use will affect how research proceeds; they will often be the first thing that participants see and the first that they know of you and your work; they will shape opinions and interactions. A participant information sheet should include, in an accessible format: your aims and objectives and broad topic area; the anticipated extent and nature of participation; any inclusion or exclusion criteria (who the participants are expected to be, in terms of demographics). They should raise any risks or dangers that participants might confront, and the benefits you hope might be forthcoming. They should clarify privacy and confidentiality details, should include contact details and affiliations, and can include references to literature and other useful information. They should be attractive and enticing as well as informative and clear. Many examples are available via a fairly routine internet search. Familiarise yourself with different models and choose one that works best for you. I also recommend that you ask colleagues for theirs and share yours so that, within your own team at least, you develop best practice and a bank of good examples.

When a participant information sheet is well designed, the consent form can simply ask the participant to acknowledge they have seen the information sheet and understood it. It can itemise the various different components, such as interview styles, observation, participation, visual data, creative methods, dissemination, and storage of data. In the next chapter, I talk about when and how best to use participant information sheets and consent forms, and in subsequent chapters, I talk more about their design and implementation as part of the practice of doing qualitative research.

FOR YOUR TOOLKIT

Participant information sheets, consent forms, and other materials will need to be prepared in the design of a project but should be used flexibly and ethically in practice. Share models with colleagues and develop a bank of good examples.

Discussion guides

Design your discussion guides in advance as these steer the interview/focus group for you and give gatekeepers (and participants, if you decide to share them in advance) a sense of scope. But remember, and advise all participants and gatekeepers, that the guide will be used loosely and flexibly, allowing the participant to guide the interview in directions they wish to go, at least to some extent. Qualitative interviews have the advantage of being interactive and allowing for unexpected topics to emerge (Busetto et al 2020), so we must design our discussion guides in such a way that we are in a position to take up newly emergent topics.

Discussion guides should not be too lengthy, so consider a hierarchy of questions where sub-topics are stacked underneath main headings. And think carefully about layout. Simple, visually pleasing designs are easier for you to consult in the moment. Discussion guides guide discussions; they are not topic guides. Although they will include potential topics, you can also add introductory statements, flow statements, probes, prompts, any information participants need to know, and plan some ending statements. I return to the topic of discussion guides in more detail in Chapters 4 and 5.

Other materials to prepare

If you hope to be creative or participatory with methods (Chapter 7), to use visual or other data as part of a research interaction, or to mediate research, you will need to clarify in advance the extent and nature of participation. Possibilities include: photos the participants have taken/displayed previously; images you have brought with you; photos you ask participants to take in advance of an interview (with the topic in mind); objects in the home; other images and documents. You might ask participants to draw maps, or even play with Lego. Funders, commissioners and ethics committees may need/want to know some of this in advance, and you may find it useful to plan some of this ahead of entry into the field, especially if you or the participants need to prepare materials. Of course, in the flexible, ethical, responsive approach to design that I argue for, this is not always possible. Sometimes the best you can do is to estimate possibilities in advance and then return to participants and funders, ethics committees and other gatekeepers to update them where necessary. If qualitative research is ongoing, iterative and inductive, then so must our relationships be.

> **FOR YOUR TOOLKIT**
> If qualitative research is ongoing, iterative and inductive, then so must be our relationships with participants, gatekeepers and funders.

Conducting a pilot study

Qualitative researchers rarely undertake pilot studies because it is difficult to *explore* things with people more than once. However, you can try out your discussion guide with a few people who will not be included in the sample, or get advice from experts and key participants, or from colleagues and friends who have expertise in the field. You could even try some role-play as you test out your interview techniques. You can, of course, also work with participants in the design of your discussion guide, using what you learn here as part of your overall learning process. Collaboration exists on a continuum, from working together at different stages to full-blown participatory action research, and including participants in your writing and dissemination (see Chapter 7). This, like much of the above, raises the issues to address at the design stage of a project, which must also be managed and negotiated in practice as the research proceeds.

FOR YOUR TOOLKIT

Many aspects of qualitative research – aims and objectives, methodology and methods, sampling and selections, preparing materials, ethical issues and reflexive practice – are designed at the outset but navigated in practice as the research proceeds.

Evaluating qualitative research

Qualitative research should be evaluated by criteria related to its aims, strengths and possibilities, established at the design stage of the project: does it achieve what it set out to achieve? Qualitative research is designed to understand and interpret people's meanings, feelings and emotions, as these are shaped by experiences, and as they shape actions. Findings take the shape of insights and understandings, presented as themes, patterns, processes or stories, that respect the complexity and diversity of human lived life. These help us understand what people do and what they might do, so that we have the confidence to develop policies or interventions that lead to better outcomes. Qualitative research can identify the needs of diverse and seldom heard people and help overcome unconscious bias, in research and in policy, by giving participants a voice. Qualitative research is more likely to be truthful or of value because it understands complexity, context, and practice. Qualitative research achieves representativeness through being broadly meaningful, by developing themes and typologies, and evoking shared meanings, enabling transference, or by using theory and concepts. Qualitative research can give us hope.

Is the research valid?

In *quantitative* research the concept of validity is used to ensure the instruments used (survey questions) are good indicators of concepts. It asks whether the study 'measures' or captures what it was intended to. Does qualitative research address what it intended to? Is it valid? The UK Alzheimer's society has a good summary of why qualitative research works well (is valid) for research with people living with Alzheimer's. They argue that qualitative research is especially useful for 'identifying the needs of people with different characteristics' and in 'overcoming unconscious bias by giving people affected by dementia the opportunity to bring things to attention that would not otherwise be asked about or noticed'(Alzheimer's UK 2024: np). Good qualitative research ensures participants have been listened to, and has given them the opportunity to consider, expand, change their minds, and elaborate. Good qualitative research provides richness, complexity, depth, and diversity. It challenges our and others' preconceptions. Good qualitative researchers will clarify their interpretations, and show where they have been critical or interpretive, or analytical. Good qualitative research will include analysis of the wider context, such as opportunities, rules, norms, culture, and conditions.

FOR YOUR TOOLKIT

Good qualitative research ensures participants have been listened to, and has given them the opportunity to consider, expand, change their minds, and elaborate. It challenges our and others' preconceptions.

Is the research transparent, rigorous, and reflexive?

In *quantitative* research the concept of reliability asks if the research has any interviewer effect, or if it is objective and detached from the researcher. If the research were to be done again by someone else, would they have the same findings? In *qualitative* research we agree it is impossible to approach human agents and social life with no preconceptions at all. We have research questions, we do a literature review, we understand something of the lives about which we are interested, and we are living our own lives. The best way to be reliable is to work with the tools we have to achieve the best research possible. Rather than pretend we have no feelings or thoughts ourselves, we address their role in our research. Of course, we try not to be biased or prejudiced, but we work with and challenge our insights through reflexive practice (Chapter 3). Our work is reliable if it is transparent (clear and open), rigorous (careful, considered and thorough), and reflexive (an adaptive practice of continually considering the relationship between the researcher and those researched).

FOR YOUR TOOLKIT

Qualitative research is reliable when it is transparent, rigorous and reflexive.

Is the research useful or applicable?

Some of us want our research to intervene in some way using the insights from our qualitative research. Maybe we value the evidence it provides on which we can base practice, or we value the way it can address the theory–practice gap and impact service delivery because of its attention to the meaningful everyday practice of agents (Cubellis et al 2021). The surprises and contextual detail that qualitative research reveals can inform product innovation (Ladner 2014: 17). In the tradition of emancipatory social science, Maria Mies (1983: 124, cited in Westmarland 2001: 4) suggests that the truth (or value) of a theory depends on 'its potential to orient the processes of praxis towards progressive emancipation and humanisation'. That is to say: might it be useful? Might it work? Or perhaps, more overtly and concretely, we can value the research for the way it can inform a realist evaluation:

> Realist approaches ask not just 'what works?', but also 'for whom, in what circumstances and why?'. They place emphasis on understanding the mechanisms by which outcomes of interventions (such as policies) come about and, crucially, how this depends on contextual factors. This can inform action based on existing learning from a wide range of sectors and disciplines – action that is tailored to be effective in specific contexts, and can respond to the potential for unjust outcomes. (Fell et al 2022: 916)

To assess usefulness or applicability, then, we might ask whether the research gives us the confidence to design or imply interventions. Is there enough relevant contextual detail for others to do the same? Has it had or does it offer some utility within the original context? Does it bring the public voice (their meanings and insights) to policy making?

FOR YOUR TOOLKIT
Good qualitative research gives us the confidence to design or imply interventions that are likely to work in practice.

Is the research representative?

Statistical generalisation is disingenuous without a statistically representative sample; it also reveals a poor grasp of the nature of both quantitative and qualitative research. Qualitative research achieves representativeness through being broadly meaningful, developing themes and typologies, evoking shared meanings, enabling transference, or by using theory and concepts.

If insights are *broadly meaningful*, they can be meaningfully acted on. Suppose we did some research trying to understand why some people avoid going to the dentist and one person said they don't go because they don't like the noise of the drill, and they wish the dentist would play rock music to drown out the noise. Before dentists decided to play rock music, they might reasonably ask whether this was a majority or minority response. What they really want to know is to what extent this is a *broadly meaningful* response. A survey might test for the *extent* of such a superficial answer; a qualitative project pursues the *nature* of the response, for this respondent and for others. We ask people how they feel about noise and music, and this will probably tap into other things about the dentists' environment that we had not thought about, some nuanced understandings about sights and sounds, which are both meaningful and useful. Because our insights are developed through iterative–inductive interpretation (and ongoing sampling) we add richness and nuance to our insights. The fact that some people like rock music might be a minority response; the fact that some people fear the noise of the drill and would prefer to listen to other sounds is likely to be a meaningful majority response that dentists can have the confidence to act on. Rich and complex data are good evidence of and material for complex insights and understandings that are useful.

FOR YOUR TOOLKIT

Qualitative research achieves representativeness through being broadly meaningful, developing general themes and typologies, evoking shared meanings, enabling transference, or by using widely applicable theory and concepts.

We also aim to be somewhat representative through the *themes and typologies* we develop as part of our interpretive understandings (see Chapter 9). When talking about patterns and processes we imply that these are generally applicable to certain types of people and situation (Box 2.2). It would be useful if we clarified this more often and specified any situations or conditions that we are aware of where our insights might not apply. This links to the logic of sample fitness (discussed earlier), and the argument that samples and selections should fit with the interpretive nature of qualitative research and with the claims you are making.

Box 2.2: Evoking a type: North Americans in Ecuador

Matthew Hayes (2018), in *Gringolandia*, which is about geo-arbitrage (moving to somewhere economically cheaper to purchase a better quality of life), illustrates representative types of people using evocative descriptions. For example, he describes Colin and his wife as in many respects 'representatives of an important subset of North American migrants in Ecuador … like many participants, Colin and his wife were motivated to look for a lower-cost place to live to afford the retirement they wanted, and for them that meant living abroad … Colin learned about Ecuador on the internet' (Hayes 2018: 35). In this brief account we learn of some types of common decision-making processes of North Americans in Ecuador and some of the shared meanings behind them. Representativeness is thus both evoked and categorised.

There are those who argue that qualitative research needs only to be *evocative*, evoking feelings that on a general level readers can relate to, share, or empathise with. This is especially the case for those working in the postmodern tradition (see O'Reilly 2009), but also in the field of evocative ethnography (O'Reilly 2012a). Caroline Ellis (Ellis et al 2011) for example, hopes people will recognise the feelings and emotions she shares, and that they will be broadly meaningful to readers and listeners. Hayes (2018: 215) also says he 'aimed to gather socially significant narratives rather than representative ones' – stories and accounts that mean something to readers as well as to the participants (Box 2.2). Matei Candea (2018: 85) says that ethnographies often show rather than tell, because 'description captures quick changes from moment to moment, replicating the unpredictable qualities of social interactions'. This can be evocative.

Some address the *transferability* of findings to similar settings (cf. O'Reilly 2009; Kvale and Brinkmann 2015; Leung 2015). Transferability as a concept enables us to make generalising more tangible, but it calls for the researcher to either (1) do the work for the reader, by explicitly suggesting other contexts where the research might be relevant, and how and why, or (2) giving enough explicit and relevant detail about the specific case and context so that readers are able to do some transferring to similar settings for themselves. We can be intentionally modest about such claims. Using the concept of *moderatum* generalisations, Geoff Payne and Malcolm Williams (2005) apply the following logic: these views/experiences exist, we are not saying how frequently they will be found, and we acknowledge that parts of the 'map' may be missing, but we can act on this as far as we know. The term 'intentionally modest generalisations' might be a useful one to employ for all the instances in this section (see O'Reilly 2009).

Qualitative researchers also use *theoretical* or *conceptual generalising*. Of course, this is common in grounded theory where the explicit purpose is to develop a theory from the ground up that addresses the specific problem, issue or concern at hand (Charmaz 2014). But when we think about it more carefully, any theory or concept is used to help us understand or to conceptualise a broader phenomenon. Theory can be defined as an account of how the world works, and concepts are ideas to help us think about how the world works.

Does the research give us hope?

I am confident that we all value the characteristics of qualitative research because we hope its insights might eventually make the world a better place; we all wish to be transformative (see Chapter 7). However, our aspirations in that direction might not take the form of applied social science, of actually designing interventions or directing policy. Instead, we might simply and loosely care about the world. We might be content with insights that challenge existing knowledge, or make us think in a different way. This is true for research that falls into the category of pure or basic research. We might ask whether the study *contributed* to wider knowledge or understanding. We would hope it was linked to, and located within, wider literature and to findings from other research. We could evaluate how far knowledge and understanding have been extended by the research, and in what ways. We can assess the extent to which it complements other forms of data revealing gaps, new knowledge, new insights. Or as Sarah Pink and her team put it, understanding configurations in progress reveals *possibilities*:

> [O]ur ethnographic engagements with people, technologies, other species, and other things, as their relationships play out, and as they learn about one another, have played an important role in our learning about the complex configurations through which technologies emerge when they are part of the world in progress. In such a world, there might not be the design solutions, but rather, arrays of possibilities. (Pink et al 2022: 16)

Or we can ask if the research at least gives us hope, with thanks to Les Back (2021: 4):

> Our work may be of value precisely because it documents remarkable things that are not remarked upon and in so doing creates an archive of emergent alternatives, directions or possibilities. I think in a way this has been a latent or tacit commitment in all the work I have done without really comprehending it. As scholars the attentiveness we pay to the world is part of hope's work.

FOR YOUR TOOLKIT

We all wish to be transformative, but our aspirations might not take the form of applied social science, or of designing interventions or policy. Instead, we might simply and loosely care about the world. Qualitative research can give us hope.

Final thoughts

Chapter 1 took you well on your way to being able to design rigorous and good-quality qualitative research. Chapter 2 has taken you forward to consider sampling and other design issues, and to assess qualitative research. The next chapters start to examine specific methods, starting with interviews.

Speaking of developing the design

'I have settled on a few people to include that I think would be helpful. I might have to include others and ask different questions as I learn more. I will work towards having a good sample given what I decide to write.'

'I've got a good sense of how this topic has been studied and conceptualised in the past but I've got an open mind about what theories might help me understand what I learn as I go.'

'The ethics committee asked for lots of detail, a participant information sheet and even a copy of my discussion guide. It's been useful to design them, but I've made it clear they will be used flexibly.'

'It is important to me that my research gives people a voice. I'm aiming for it to speak to people, so they can identify themselves or others in it. And it would be great if it could at least give readers hope that things could be different.'

Taking things further

There are numerous good textbooks already available that will support you in **reviewing the literature** for a project, but I recommend reading about the role of wider literature in qualitative research, in Emerson et al (2011), Charmaz (2014), and Braun and Clarke (2022). Many research councils, funding bodies, universities, research organisations and professional organisations now offer (online) guidance on **preparing materials** for participants and gaining informed consent: for examples see the National Institute of Health Research, UK Research and Innovation, and the Social Research Association. There is more on **assessing the quality** of qualitative research in Braun and Clarke (2022), and O'Reilly (2009). Grounded theorists use **theoretical sampling** in a similar way to what I have described as ongoing sampling but with more focus on overtly developing a theory from the ground up (see Charmaz 2014: 129–212).

Listen to the related episode for this chapter on
Qualitative Research Methods for Everyone podcast:

3

Being ethical and reflexive

What this chapter is about

This chapter addresses being ethical and reflexive as ongoing practices that should shape and inform your work in an enduring process from inception, through design and implementation, all the way through the various interactions that constitute research, to conclusions, dissemination and beyond. Ethical issues are multi-dimensional and layered, ongoing, and require engagement and reflexivity. Be ethical by adhering to the moral principles that guide you through your organisation, discipline or funding body, as well as your own personal moral guide. But also, be kind – to yourself and to others through being considerate, thoughtful and generous in spirit.

Being ethical is too vast a matter to cover here in comprehensive detail. Rather than tackle it from a broad, philosophical perspective, my approach is to address those issues most likely to confront qualitative researchers in the practice of their research. Nevertheless, I would recommend you become more widely informed and to have various perspectives to guide you. To that end I take a close look at the content of some published ethical guidelines, and suggest further reading, later in this chapter.

Specifically, the chapter covers: informed consent; the participant information sheet; the consent form; gaining and ensuring consent; understanding public and private spaces; respecting confidentiality and anonymity; being trustworthy and building rapport; assessing risk and avoiding harm; dealing with thorny issues; and gaining ethical clearance. In line with my argument for being ethical as a continuous practice, ethical issues will continue to be considered as the book proceeds.

The second part of the chapter turns to discussing reflexive practice, a term elaborated by Michaela Benson and Karen O'Reilly (2020b) that emphasises its scientific underpinnings in broader sociological theory, locates it within an interpretivist methodological framework (that is dynamic, agile, and flexible), and draws on the concepts of positionality and positioning to argue for reflexivity as a collaborative, iterative, and creative practice. Remember that qualitative research proceeds in a flexible and responsive manner so that we can learn as we go from our participants and from our own experiences. Qualitative research relies on diverse methods that involve listening, hearing, watching, thinking, co-creating, and reflecting. Qualitative research is iterative-inductive and reflexive. These are its special features and its strengths and form the basis of how it should be evaluated.

> **FOR YOUR TOOLKIT**
> Being ethical and reflexive are ongoing practices that shape and inform
> our work in an enduring process from inception, through design and
> implementation, to conclusions, dissemination and beyond.

Being ethical

As a general rule, we should do our best to protect the rights of anyone involved
in the research process while accepting that at times this can prove an extremely
difficult balancing act, necessitating on-the-spot calculations and choices. Formal
guidelines and codes can sensitise us to issues that may arise, and can clarify any
cases or situations where consensus has been reached (for example, that covert
research should not be undertaken without very good reason; Calvey 2021).
However, like Martyn Hammersley (2009), I am also nervous that overly rigid
rules can stunt the development of innovative, exciting and important research.
No potential project, if worthy enough to pursue, should be abandoned
with the excuse that the ethical issues seemed too difficult to resolve. Ethical
considerations should not usually be a reason *not* to conduct research but should
require us to be constantly rigorous, reflexive and critical (and careful and kind).
Let's start by thinking about how to get people to participate. We would hope
their agreement, their consent, is based on their full understanding of what they
are agreeing to. This is known as gaining informed consent.

Informed consent

Gaining informed consent is crucial for qualitative (and any) research. Participants
can only agree to take part in a project once they have been fully informed,
and understand, what the research is about, what is going to happen during
the research, and what will happen to the material afterwards. We can inform
people through a participant information sheet that we give them beforehand,
but we should also take every opportunity to answer questions and clarify things
as we go along. Different people need to be informed in different ways and
at different times, and we must remember that people vary in terms of their
levels of understanding, even of the word 'research' and what that means. Our
information needs to be accessible, user-friendly, and timely, and a participant
information sheet can help with that.

The participant information sheet

Participant information sheets are short leaflets or pamphlets or a few paragraphs
that explain about the research in more detail. They can be clear, concise
and colourful with photographs or images where relevant. They are great for
participants and you to refer back to, or for participants to proudly show their
family and friends what they are contributing to. They are also a good place

for you to put quite a lot of information succinctly but comprehensively. If the participant information sheet holds a good amount of information, the consent form can be much shorter, and therefore less intimidating. There are lots of examples available through a good internet search, but I would recommend building a depository of examples of good practice to share within your institution. I have also discussed the design of participant information sheets in Chapter 2.

The consent form

A consent form should be much briefer than the participant information sheet. It usually acts as a checklist and reminder of the items discussed or summarised; the assumption is that the participant has been fully informed and they are happy to consent to move forward. Using a consent form is an opportunity for clarification and confirmation. There is a danger that a consent form can be treated as a tick-box exercise, giving the researcher confidence to move ahead with the project having got the ethics 'out of the way'. Filling in the forms together provides a useful time to fully clarify any issues and agreements, but this is not enough on its own. Consent needs to be reclarified and renegotiated any time difficulties or concerns arise. Being ethical is not only a formal procedure (requiring forms); it is a process.

> **FOR YOUR TOOLKIT**
> Consent to take part in research should be fully informed and reclarified and renegotiated as issues arise. It is more ethical that people feel comfortable and informed and happy to ask more of us, than to ensure we have covered our backs (or satisfied an ethics committee) by getting a form filled in.

Gaining and ensuring consent

Gaining consent is an ongoing, negotiated and sometimes tricky process. We want people to feel relaxed and comfortable and able to open up to us, and if we ask them to sign a form before they start this can stifle all subsequent disclosure. I often hear *If I asked my participants to sign a consent form before they started, I'm afraid that they would then be very careful what they tell me because it all feels so formal.*

One possibility is to tell them about the research and ask them to sign a form afterwards. Indeed, signing a form is not even always necessary. We can get verbal consent and record it as we record the interview, focus group or whatever. During participant observation, we often rely on informal consent that is gained as we go along.

Asking people to sign forms can trigger strong emotions or fear linked to prior experiences of bureaucracy, red tape, or rules and regulations. Sometimes too much formality can be frightening for participants. Another common response

I receive is along the lines of *I work with refugees, there is no way I can ask them to sign consent forms.* In that case, the fact that participants understand the research and know what they are taking part in and what will happen to the data is far more important than whether or not they have signed an official form. It is more ethical that people feel comfortable, than to ensure we have covered our backs (or satisfied an ethics committee) by getting a form filled in.

Specific issues arise with participatory research and with co-production techniques, where conflicts over ownership of data and its production and dissemination might justifiably arise (see Chapter 7). I recommend honest and open team discussions at the beginning of the research as well as at every new stage: consent is a matter of constant negotiation and clarification. Intervening and informing interventions is shaped by one's ethical principles, as Sarah Pink's *Design Ethnography* team recognise. Their goal is to work with participants of all levels, to ethically understand ongoing change as much as finished products, to share their work as always emergent, like life:

> [D]esign ethnography also needs to tread carefully by acknowledging the tension between the theoretical and ethnographic commitments that lead us to understand futures, and the practical and institutional motives that our research partners and research participants may have for engaging with futures quite differently. Our ambition is not to resistantly come up against other people's futures, but rather to complicate them in such ways that foreground ethics and responsibility. (Pink et al 2022: 18)

In any research, conflicts of interest can arise. Being ethical is a living practice with each issue needing attention on its own terms. Some must deal with competing power relations; sometimes participants' needs and rights contradict professional, institutional and regulatory body guidelines and preferences; and sometimes these conflict with your own preferences and moral stance. No one ever said ethical practice was easy.

Understanding public and private spaces

It can be a challenge to determine to what extent a space can be considered publicly shared or private. The Association of Social Anthropologists of the UK recommends understanding local definitions of what is public or private and taking all practicable steps to ensure you are at least introduced to people where possible. I have been asked questions like:

> I've been told to ensure consent in public and private spaces, but during participant observation in some settings, like a meeting, I can be very clear about consent with everyone there; in other settings, like a hospital outpatients department, there's no way I can make it

clear to everyone that I am doing research. How on earth do I deal with this?

This takes us back to informed consent. As a rule, wherever possible people should be informed but without making them feel uncomfortable or threatened. If you are making observations and broad notes, then it is not essential to get everybody's formal consent but where possible and/or relevant remind people what you are doing while you are there. Observation of broad patterns of behaviour in public spaces is acceptable where those observed would expect to be observed by strangers, but you must still be trustworthy and respect confidentiality.

This implies that research can sometimes be covert (and there is an argument that covert research can be less intrusive than overt research and can cause less harm). Covert research does happen in online research sometimes (Marzano 2021), but I am not sure it causes less harm. In covert research, participants have not given informed consent and therefore cannot be given the right to withdraw. Covert research is like lurking in online research; it can be that you are exploiting your power as a researcher or writer by researching or writing about things others would not have expected you to. People can accidentally disclose private information even in supposedly public spaces. To eavesdrop is generally unethical. Also, we must always think about how to treat the material (and the human beings) we are 'collecting'. Qualitative researchers using iterative-inductive and interpretive approaches (see Chapter 1) would find it difficult to simply analyse what was said or done without also engaging with participants.

On the other hand, covert research does continue to have its place in qualitative research, especially in public spaces where gaining consent would be impossible. It can be justified as long as the research can still be argued to be important, such as where powerful and exploitative people might be the ones opposing the research undertaking, or where declaring your presence might actually be dangerous, or where taking sides is a contentious or slippery issue (Calvey 2021). The distinction between being covert and overt in practice can anyway be a little muddy, so certainly avoid being obtrusive or invasive.

Incidentally, doing secondary analysis of pre-existing data (of archived qualitative research or of any online data) looks like covert research with little justification and it has the potential to reveal people's identities if researchers are not familiar with the field or context. Data may be publicly available (and for decades), but those who took part did not usually anticipate someone might be reading and analysing their words in the future. Once again, be kind, considerate and careful. As a bottom line, gain informed consent, be overt wherever possible and, where this is difficult, be sure that any decision to be even somewhat covert is made carefully and with good justification.

Respecting confidentiality and anonymity

Qualitative research usually promises anonymity and confidentiality, but it is not essential to assume everyone in a project should be anonymised. In some projects that is impossible (for well-known figures); in others, participants may well be happy to be known. In a journal article examining some of the long-term impacts of British migration to Spain's coastal regions, I took the opportunity to celebrate the work of two special migrants: Joan Hunt, who co-founded Cudeca, a cancer care organisation, and Charles Betty, who was the co-founder of Age Care Association, which gives advice and help to older British migrants in Malaga (O'Reilly 2017a). To respect my earlier promises of anonymity, I went back to them and asked if they would agree to me mentioning their names in relation to their public profiles (I continued to respect confidentiality by not sharing any private conversations or confidences). Joan and Charles were shown the article before publication to give them the opportunity to confirm they were happy with how they had been represented. Relatedly, one of the dissemination activities of a comparative study of British and Asian lifestyle migrants was an interpretive photography exhibition, held at Hong Kong University, in 2015 (Stones et al 2019). Although the researchers had promised anonymity with respect to data collection and dissemination, they wanted to use photos and quotes for the exhibition, so again it was necessary to go back to the relevant participants and ask their permission. They were asked to check their quotes and photos, to change anything if they wanted to, and were even invited to the exhibition. Interestingly, one couple did change a quote from their interview but in true interpretive style this led to an interesting conversation about who they had counted as friends as opposed to colleagues.

Respecting anonymity also calls for anonymising in writing, but what words do we use to speak of others? I use the language of participants rather than subjects or informants. Some use the word 'interlocutors' but that sounds a bit pretentious to me. In *Design Ethnography* Sarah Pink and colleagues explain how the term 'participant' indicates the flexible, negotiated nature of participation in a project, for multiple stakeholders, and other sentient and non-sentient beings. It is worth quoting them at length here as what they say applies broadly to my arguments in this book, especially with regard to ethical principles of collaboration:

> At the core of design ethnographic practice is the notion of the *participant*. This involves accounting for people in our investigations and interventions in ways that go beyond the various terminologies used to define them across design and ethnographic disciplines. In research characterised as human–centred, people are often siloed into categories of user, consumer or citizen. In anthropological ethnography people are, with good intentions, referred to as informants, interlocutors and through other terms that frame their participation and collaboration in research. These terminologies determine the kinds of voices and stakes people can have in processes of research and design … In this book, we generally write of research participants, but when we switch registers to define participants in more specific ways, we engage other terms. For example, where Debora writes of co-researchers in Chapter 6, or where Melissa writes of charity shop colleagues as everyday designers in Chapters 4 and 7. We also regard participants as experts from whom we learn within projects.
>
> We have chosen the notion of the participant because it provides a more open alternative; rather than determining the role of a person who becomes involved in the research, it enables that person to define their participation, the extent to which they wish to participate, if they wish to be named or shown or if they would prefer to remain anonymous and where they wish to draw certain lines and boundaries. This does not mean that participation is completely open for definition, since it is important to explain to participants what our terms need to be as well. (Pink et al 2022: 30)

In terms of style, for communicating, please avoid using numbers or letters. Even when there is a table with more information elsewhere in the document, it is frustrating if you must keep flicking back to another page. Pseudonyms are more common in academic work (see Spencer and Pahl 2006; Benson and O'Reilly 2018; Hayes 2018), where quotes are part of a more discursive textual commentary. Summaries are more common in policy and applied work, such as 'Male, aged 31–40' (White et al 2014: 393). But we use both pseudonyms and summaries in our article about harvest work and time (O'Reilly and Scott 2023b), because we want to both personalise quotes and indicate their relationship to the project, for example, Charlie, employer/manager, PFB project; Annabel, Bulgarian migrant, Glarus 2. As a word of warning, pseudonyms can raise issues about anonymity because they can indicate a type of person, or age, or ethnicity. I usually ask participants to choose their own pseudonyms, while still being careful that this will not inadvertently identify them. Finally, we must also take care to not reveal the identities of others through association or through the naming of places or other identifying features. Be warned that people might be known by their role in a community or by a certain way of expressing themselves.

> **FOR YOUR TOOLKIT**
> Writers often use free indirect speech (quoting a style of phrase rather than exact words), or blended stories (where accounts or stories are blended together to capture an essence rather than an identifiable person) to ensure anonymity, or when recording was not possible.

Techniques that are sometimes used to anonymise quotes or stories are free indirect speech and blended stories. In free indirect speech, the participant is quoted using their style of speaking but without using a direct quote that might be easily identifiable. Journalists use the technique liberally to recall something they heard but cannot precisely remember. It is the meaning that is deemed important to the writer and reader rather than the exact words. Blended stories (see Jones 2004) are accounts or stories blended together to capture an essence rather than an identifiable person. This is done to ensure anonymity, or when recording was not possible, or when evoking a type of event or emotion rather than a specific one.

Confidentiality is more complex than anonymity in as much as it involves being trustworthy, knowing when something has been shared in confidence and must be told carefully so as not to identify the author, or maybe not even shared at all. This is related to issues of trust and rapport.

Being trustworthy and building rapport

In qualitative research, we try to build a feeling of confidence about our trustworthiness and rapport (a feeling that we understand each other) because we want participants to share their insights and understandings as they reflect on them. At times they will share thoughts they have never shared before, or perhaps not even considered, sometimes sensitive issues or complex matters. They are not going to do this if they don't trust us or they feel we do not empathise. Working to establish rapport can feel a bit exploitative, as if we are making friends in order to extract information (or fake friendships; Oakley 2016). But hopefully you not only want to *build* trust and rapport, but you actually want to *be* worthy of that trust by actually *sharing* rapport with someone. Being trustworthy means that we try not to exploit them, that we respect their confidences and their diverse opinions. Building rapport means that we work hard to understand them, rather than pretending to understand them so that we can get good data. In this way, building trust and rapport are truly ethical ways of doing research, but they can be demanding. Consider giving participants your time beyond the boundaries of the project by simply being helpful or caring, by listening when it is not immediately relevant, by doing things that might not obviously help you pursue your own goals. This is good ethical research practice.

FOR YOUR TOOLKIT

Qualitative researchers aim to build trust and rapport with participants because we want them to open up to us, to share their insights and understandings, but also because we want to *be worthy of their trust* and *to empathise*.

Incidentally, being worthy of trust also involves safely guarding materials and recordings (photos, videos, transcripts, all data). If you have doubts about the security of your storage system, ask for advice. Trust also raises issues about the extent to which we should absolutely trust the words of our participants, as illustrated in the work of and debates around *On the Run*, by Alice Goffman (2014; see also Box 3.1). Sometimes qualitative researchers are interested in people's experiences and how they portray and share those, over and above facts, as it is the former that shape and inform actions: 'If a person perceives a situation as real, it is real in its consequences' (paraphrased from Thomas and Thomas 1928). Nonetheless, this does *not* mean facts are irrelevant, and we should not portray what we have heard as if it is fact, but rather as what we have heard.

Box 3.1: An ethical debate: Goffman's *On the Run*

Alice Goffman's (2014) *On the Run* is a rich, detailed, powerfully written study of the hidden practices of policing and surveillance as experienced by young people living in one relatively poor Black neighbourhood in Philadelphia. It is based on over six years of immersive ethnography with a deprived community, starting when Goffman was only 19 years old. *On the Run* depicts its research participants, the '6th street' boys, as continually subject to police surveillance and arrest. It portrays in graphic detail the ways in which the criminal justice system comes to play a central role in their lives (as well as those of their families) from a young age, and the relentless pressures, struggles, criminality, and dipping and dodging to try to avoid arrest as experienced by her participants.

On the Run received widespread praise and acclamation as soon as it was published. Later, it was subject to a torrent of criticism for a number of reasons. Goffman is accused of trusting her participants too much, accepting rumours as facts, and a lack of reflexivity, for potentially getting involved in crime herself, and for destroying her field notes. The main protagonist of the critique was Steven Lubet (2015a, 2015b and 2017). Crucially, Lubet is a lawyer and journalist and, in *Ethnography: Why Evidence Matters* (2017), he calls for fact checking of ethnographies. Some reviewers of the book agree with him; many do not, and his intervention appears to have shaped an ongoing debate about what ethnography should be. In a review of Lubet's book, Tim Hallett (2019) is quite scathing. He argues that Lubet does not understand ethnography as ethnographers do, that the bits and pieces of ethnography he has chosen to critique mostly end up being good, and says Lubet cherry-picks evidence in his attempt to 'push ethnography up against the evidentiary standards of law' (Hallett 2019: 256). Goffman's book raises a host of interesting issues related to ethics and reflexivity.

On occasion, we really do not like the things our participants tell us and can find their opinions challenging. This calls for us to engage in reflexive practice, as I discuss later. Working to gain trust and rapport can cause anxiety that we are being overly intrusive. I was once asked:

> One thing I feel anxious about is that when I ask people about my topic, I am going to affect them. I'm asking about things they haven't thought about before when I'm interviewing people with dementia and I'm going to make them upset. How do I deal with this?

It is difficult not to intrude into people's lives, no matter how we do research. In some ways I think this question is linked to the (positivist, objectivist) notion that we should be able to collect clean, unadulterated data. In qualitative research, we acknowledge that even where we think we have achieved such objectivity, we have not generated useful data (see Chapter 1). Taking this question from an ethical perspective takes us to the question of harm.

Assessing risk and avoiding harm

It is crucial to think through, in advance of a research project, what harm might be caused by intervening in people's lives. This is known as anticipating harm, and you will probably be asked to think about it when asking for ethical clearance for a project. First, think about the participants in the study and how the research might affect them at any stage from data collection to dissemination. Discuss how potential harm will be circumvented; how issues will be addressed as they arise. Also think about gatekeepers and other people who might give you access; think about interpreters or other intermediaries. Consider any researchers and research assistants. All of these need protecting, but also have the potential to cause harm, even if vicariously. We are responsible for anyone who engages in the research with us.

Remember also to think about any potential risks to yourself. One outcome of the risk assessment procedure we followed for research with British lifestyle migrants in Malaysia and Thailand (Stones et al 2019) was to ensure that when we were interviewing people alone in remote areas, someone would always know where we were going and when and we would have a contact on speed dial in case of any difficulties. We also included, in our schedule, time after the interview to share experiences with the team, to debrief. Following a full and thorough risk assessment procedure for all the research participants including yourselves is a useful practical and ethical exercise.

FOR YOUR TOOLKIT

We have responsibility as researchers to our participants (first), to ourselves, our team, any assistants or helpers, to our funders, to other colleagues, as well as even (at times) to our family and friends.

We must also avoid causing harm as we proceed. Not every outcome of our research or of our interactions with the social world can be anticipated, so we can never say we will cause no harm. But we should do our best to avoid it where we can. As with all ethical issues, specific examples are endless, and each situation needs addressing on its own terms. A good research design will reflect on all potential issues and address in detail how they might be dealt with should they arise. As a key principle: anticipate and avoid harm wherever possible.

FOR YOUR TOOLKIT

Anticipate and avoid harm wherever possible by following a full and thorough risk assessment procedure for all research participants including yourselves.

Dealing with thorny issues

Qualitative researchers, because of the sensitive and immersive nature of their work, can find themselves confronted with difficult or thorny issues (Box 3.1). Working with vulnerable adults, or children, and/or on sensitive topics can require constant vigilance with respect to one's moral and legal position. We must always consider the safety of our participants and avoid putting them in any danger, as well as the safety of the researchers and anyone helping us (gatekeepers, key informants, translators, transcribers and so on). I have known an interview transcriber become upset because she was reading a powerful, painful and emotive story. She needed support, just as we all might. As a general rule, you should not try to act as a therapist with research participants, even if you are trained as one. But you can prepare guidance as to where someone might turn for further information, advice and support. You can share contact details for people to seek medical care or counselling. It is important that we understand the law as far as we can and that we separate what is legally necessary from what is ethically important. Above all, seek advice, help and guidance yourself: you are not an expert on every eventuality in life – no one is. Do not try to deal with everything alone – lots of people before you have done research and there is a lot of expertise out there. Get advice, talk with other people, share insights and understandings, share successful research proposals, use or form a community of support.

> ### FOR YOUR TOOLKIT
> Do not confront all this alone. Learn about the legal/ institutional rules that you are governed by, as well as addressing moral concerns, get advice and support, and discuss ethics and reflexivity with colleagues.

Gaining ethical approval

In some institutions and for some funding bodies you will be asked at the design and planning stage of the research to explain in detail what ethical issues you have considered and how you hope to address them. In some cases, you will also be asked to do a full application for approval or clearance by an ethics committee (for example, with the National Institute of Health Research). While this can seem burdensome it also facilitates a coherent and rigorous approach to research. I recommend becoming familiar with a few institutional ethical guidelines or codes because these help us to think about what is or might be important to us and to our participants. It is also important to conceptually separate ethical clearance, which is about obtaining administrative clearance for your project, and being ethical (or ethical practice), which is something I hope we all want to engage in. When employing the flexible, responsive and creative methods I have described throughout this book, be careful to understand to what extent you are covered by the ethical approval of your institution or funding body as you proceed (Rashid et al 2019).

> ### FOR YOUR TOOLKIT
> Institutions and groups of colleagues should share ethical clearance applications and discussions about ethical practice to build a bank of examples of good practice.

Key issues raised by codes of ethics

There are many codes of ethics (or guidelines or statements) and all are useful in their own way – and, incidentally, are usually the result of a phenomenal amount of effort and consideration on the part of their authors. You should certainly be familiar with those produced by your own institution and funding bodies but read more widely than you need to. You can learn a lot about qualitative research more broadly by reading about ethics in education, for example, or gain fascinating insights about interviewing by reading about ethics in anthropology. Ethical guidelines should guide your qualitative journey.

Guidelines or codes I have found useful include those produced by the Social Research Association, the British Educational Research Association, the Association of Social Anthropologists of the UK, the European Commission (research ethics in ethnography/anthropology), and the American Anthropological Association.

Several of these codes start with a good definition of qualitative and/or ethnographic methodology, and if all qualitative research is (as I have described) flexible, responsive, agile, and creative, then we can all learn from guidelines that are more specifically designed for those using participatory and ethnographic methods. Many of the guidelines include fabulous (sometimes live or regularly updated) examples and illustrative cases, and some link to further reading in the field of morality, ethics and philosophy. Other key issues raised include quality, responsibility, informed consent, confidentiality and anonymity, power and conflicts of interest, and some now cover digital media and creative approaches. On quality, there is a consensus that it is ethical to conduct careful, rigorous and good quality research, to maintain standards of integrity, to protect our materials, to make results accessible, and to think about who benefits from our work. On responsibility, we are reminded of our responsibility to participants, as well as to sponsors, clients, stakeholders, our research community, and even to students who use our work in the future. We are encouraged to think of both long- and short-term impacts. They make it clear that consent should be ongoing and consensual, and that participants should know they can withdraw from all or part of the research at any time. On this, as a tip, you will need to make it clear that there will be a time when participants can no longer withdraw, for example once the work is published or disseminated. Some organisational guidelines include model consent forms or checklists and advice for creative methods, for working with young people, children, and individuals with cognitive impairment and anyone else who might lack or have limited capacity to give informed consent. All guidelines emphasise the ongoing nature of ethical considerations, the imperative for sustained discussion and consideration and of weighing competing obligations.

I now turn to the topic of being reflexive, which overlaps with being ethical and is also a stance and a practice that shapes research as a live issue. I also return to consider ethical and reflexive practice throughout the subsequent chapters, as they interweave with every aspect of research.

FOR YOUR TOOLKIT

Establish a good working relationship with your ethics committee or team, or establish your own if your organisation does not have one, and become familiar with a range of ethical guidelines, using them to guide your qualitative research journey in an ongoing way.

Being reflexive

Reflexivity became a bit of a buzzword during the latter part of the 20th century. In social science more generally it referred to insights already gained through philosophical approaches such as interpretivism, phenomenology and hermeneutics, which taught us we cannot isolate simple causes and effects in human life because humans are not predictable. However, the specific contribution the concept of reflexivity made was to draw our attention to the fact that all human beings are reflexive. That is to say, every single one of us makes decisions about the actions we take through reflexive action: through looking, considering, thinking, imagining, and planning in interaction with those around us. Reflexivity in practice in all our lives is adaptive to our surroundings, our communities, our experiences, and our perceptions. Human beings are not automatons; we are not reducible to algorithms. Key theorists included Giddens, Bourdieu and Archer (see O'Reilly 2012b) whose strength was in drawing attention to the limits of knowledge associated with the social scientist's membership and position in the intellectual field (especially, see Bourdieu 2003).

FOR YOUR TOOLKIT

Reflexivity affects all of us, researchers and otherwise. Every single one of us makes decisions about the actions we take through reflexive action, through looking, considering, thinking, imagining, and planning.

Around the same time, feminist writers and ethnographers were challenging the nature of authority in research data, drawing attention to the complex and myriad power contexts of relationships that are constantly being negotiated in interactions (see Skeggs 2001; Gunaratnam 2003). When translated into social research methods, this understanding of human life involves recognising that quantitative and qualitative researchers also are reflexive human beings, located within communities, relationships and histories that, in turn, are populated by other human beings who are also constantly being reflexive. This leads us to 'analysis of the interactional politics of research' (Oakley 2016: 197), including addressing gender, class, ethnicity, and other 'positionalities' that shape these power relations (Benson and O'Reilly 2020b).

The notion of a *live* sociology has been put forward by Les Back and Nirmal Puwar (2012; see also Back 2007, 2012) in their invitation to social researchers to be more agile and creative in responding to rapid social and political change at a wider level, as well as to the daily ongoing contingencies of research itself. They want to inspire 'creative, public and novel modes of doing imaginative and critical sociological research' (Back and Puwar 2012: 1), calling on us to embrace new platforms and technologies, both in data generation and in dissemination. This approach they hope will disturb linear and static understandings of the research process leading to what we are calling a more agile, contingent, and collaborative *reflexive practice* (Benson and O'Reilly 2020b: 181).

To put it simply, we will always affect each other in our interactions, in our constant negotiation of the (social) world's contingencies as they confront us and as we decide how we might act. This has more impact on qualitative than on quantitative methods, but the latter is not free from subjectivity. A quantitative survey will be designed by a person with their own biases and assumptions, questions will be interpreted by the respondent, and the findings interpreted by the researcher. But in qualitative research, interaction is continuous, or live (Box 3.1); indeed, this is its quality and strength. When interviewing participants, for example, they will try to second-guess what we are trying to find out, will bear in mind what they think we want to achieve as well as be shaped by what they themselves are hoping to get from the interaction. As an interview proceeds, we both reassess the situation and our insights based on how we behave and understand each other (see Chapter 4).

A positivist approach would try to clean out or deny personalities, thoughts and biases, attempting to take readings like a thermometer. Positivists develop techniques for gathering data such as surveys, designed around hypotheses, or interviews with fixed schedules and standardised questions. These techniques, rather than leading to understanding and insights will simply *lead* participants to respond in ways that are even more shaped by the relationship. Their respondents (as they are understood to be in such approaches) will answer quickly to try to get them out of the door, or they will tell them one side of the story based on what they've assumed the researcher already knows, or they will misunderstand and give superficial answers, and the researcher will be in no position to explain, or work towards an understanding. They will thus simply reproduce the misunderstandings they began with. There is no interaction without reflexivity.

FOR YOUR TOOLKIT

There is no interaction without reflexivity. Positivist approaches that attempt to be objective through standardisation, inflexibility, or fixed hypotheses, merely reproduce the misunderstandings that both researchers and participants brought to the interaction.

Another way that people try to reconcile interpretivist and positivist approaches is to simply write, at the end of a project, a reflection about what sorts of issues may have shaped the interview or focus group or other qualitative research interaction. This is reflective, not *reflexive*.

Interpretivists (indeed, most social researchers) now concede that to try to clean themselves out of an interaction is impossible and furthermore would not achieve what we are trying to achieve: an interpretive understanding of the experiences, meaning making and choices of participants. In qualitative research, we want to learn from the interaction, we want to be open-minded, to adapt our insights as we learn more and so we must find ways to think about the role of reflexivity as a positive aspect. We work to understanding and working within its role in the interaction, rather than simply working on how to ameliorate its effects. This argument has been made in many excellent theses; I really do not need to repeat it here (see for example Dean 2017; May and Perry 2017; Lumsden 2019).

FOR YOUR TOOLKIT

Reflexive practice is a version of reflexivity that is collaborative, responsible, iterative, engaged, agile, and creative (Benson and O'Reilly 2020b).

In my paper with Michaela Benson (Benson and O'Reilly 2020b), we argue that social researchers should engage in *reflexive practice* that is collaborative, responsible, iterative, engaged, agile, and creative. By 'collaborative' we mean involving people as participants in research (rather than as subjects, informants or respondents) enabling us to work together towards meaningful interpretations. By 'responsible' we mean it is incumbent on us to work towards meaningful and useful interpretations in an ethical way. With the terms iterative, engaged, agile and creative we are invoking the iterative-inductive, flexible, negotiated nature of live research discussed in Chapter 1. Reflexive practice involves continually considering the relationship between the researcher and those researched. We propose three strategies for engaging in reflexive practice: reflexive positioning, reflexive navigating, and reflexive interpreting. The strategies are not distinct from each other, they are ways of thinking about reflexive practice.

Reflexive positioning

Reflexive positioning requires us to include knowledge and awareness of ourselves as researchers and as human agents within our ongoing interpretation of the practices of social life. The concept of positionality suggests your relationship to the people you are working with is a fixed position. This can be useful in terms of thinking about gender, ethnic group, social class, and other attributes you and they bring to the interaction in the first instance. But the concept of reflexive positioning suggests that not only are we conscious of these attributes or positions, but that we continually reflect on how such attributes shape the interaction during the interview, focus group, ethnography or whatever, as well as during the interpretation (Benson and O'Reilly 2020b). Positioning is a process informed and shaped by statuses. Bourdieu's concept of participant objectivation is a useful way to think about this further. Put simply, the concept asks that we not only understand the worldview of the participants but also the wider conditions under which knowledge is produced, and include an 'exploration of this academic unconscious' (Bourdieu 2003: 285, in O'Reilly 2012c). In our paper (Benson and O'Reilly 2020b), we give some examples to illustrate how this reflexive positioning works in practice, with reference to our personal and academic backgrounds and our engagements with participants and the research.

> **FOR YOUR TOOLKIT**
> Reflexive positioning calls for us to be reflexive about our positionality as it shapes interaction with participants, and with the research itself, in an ongoing process (Benson and O'Reilly 2020b).

Reflexive navigating

Reflexive navigating acknowledges the dynamic, flexible and agile aspects of reflexive practice. It involves working reflexively – through constant and conscious changes, developments, and responses – as our research shapeshifts in real time (Benson and O'Reilly 2020b). Methodologically, it means embracing creative techniques and new technologies; ethically, it means responding to needs and demands as required. In terms of developing insights, it involves thinking about how positionalities are shaping these. In our Brexit and British People Abroad project, for example, our desire to be inclusive in terms of the diversity of British people abroad involved amending our selections through ongoing sampling (Benson and Lewis 2019; and see Chapter 2).

Reflexive navigating is also personal and emotional. Mary Holmes (2010: 140) defines reflexivity as:

> an emotional, embodied and cognitive process in which social actors have feelings about and try to understand and alter their lives in relation to their social and natural environment and to others. Emotions are understood not in terms of some that may retard reflection and some that may enhance it; rather reflexivity is thought to be more than reflection and to include bodies, practices and emotions.

This intervention alerts us to be aware of our own emotions, to tune into them in order to achieve empathy and understanding, and to be kind and generous. Reflexivity as a practice is social, negotiated, adaptive, requiring self-reflection from researchers towards their location in everyday relational struggles.

> **FOR YOUR TOOLKIT**
> Reflexive navigating is dynamic, flexible and agile and requires us to navigate our research through constant and conscious (and reflexive) changes, developments, and responses (Benson and O'Reilly 2020b).

Reflexive interpreting

Reflexive interpreting acknowledges the reflexivity and positionality of the human individuals and groups with whom we undertake research, and therefore views social life itself as a (constantly shifting) reflexive process of negotiating and accommodating (Benson and O'Reilly 2020b). It involves an awareness of our role in the interpretation of the data and that our interpretations of the social world are made through and informed by our engagement with it. But more than that, it recognises that we in turn are shaping the social world that we are part of, while the social world and the individuals within it are also adapting to and negotiating changes and developments. In our Brexit and British People Abroad research, for example, we needed to tune into the ebbs and flows of changing emotions – replete with contradictions and continuities – that were undoubtedly a reflection of Brexit as a deeply unsettling and constantly changing process (Benson and O'Reilly 2020b). We also witnessed the rise of new forms of mobilisation among British people abroad with campaign groups becoming more established and influential. Our participants were being reflexive and active with regard to their own lives, and responding to (what they saw as) the failures of the UK government to take care of their best interests. Reflexive practice entails considering social life as a reflexive process and drawing interpretations that recognise this.

FOR YOUR TOOLKIT

Reflexive interpreting requires us to intellectually tune in to the ebbs and flows of daily social life for all human individuals engaged in it, to eschew static and superficial interpretations and representations (Benson and O'Reilly 2020b).

Reflective journaling

Keeping a reflective journal throughout (and perhaps before and after) a research project is an exceedingly useful activity. I use the term *reflective* rather than reflexive here because I refer to the act of reflecting on (looking back after the fact) things that have happened or been said that you might wish to record and think about. Reflective journaling is a great aid to reflexive practice. There are many ways it can be done, but simply, it means keeping a diary of your thoughts, opinions, concerns and doubts, and anything else you wish to reflect on that may have shaped your research in some way, which you may need to act on in the future, all while using this diary to inform your reflexive practice.

FOR YOUR TOOLKIT

Reflective journaling, or keeping a personal diary, is a great aid to reflexive practice.

Kyu Ha Choi (2020) has written a useful blog on the topic of reflective journaling, especially noting its subjective nature and the fact that writing itself can encourage us to think and to process thoughts. He also notes how the data can become research data in their own right, in a version of auto-ethnography. More than that, a reflective journal is a means of explicitly mapping the research role, making the entire process more visible. I have found a diary also dovetails with analysis as a place to record any practical tasks I need to do, the considerations I need to make (see Chapter 8). Keeping a personal diary (O'Reilly 2012a) as part of research practice has caused me to rethink some things I took for granted, helped me to challenge language I was using, enabled me to redirect my analytical perspectives, and generally facilitated the flexible, iterative-inductive approach to analysis I advocate in this book. However, a personal diary or a self-reflective journal only aids reflexivity if you make it part of your reflexive practice of positioning, navigating and interpreting within a framework that views social life itself as a (constantly shifting) reflexive process of negotiating and accommodating (Benson and O'Reilly 2020b).

Final thoughts

Being ethical and being reflexive are ongoing practices that shape and inform your work in an enduring process from inception, through design and implementation, to dissemination and beyond. Be ethical by adhering to the moral principles that guide you formally as well as following your own personal moral guide. Reflexive practice is a version of reflexivity that is collaborative, responsible, iterative, engaged, agile, and creative.

Speaking of ethics and reflexivity

'I've designed participant information sheets and consent forms but I'm going to talk to people as well and explain things as I go.'

'Reading some of the ethical guidelines has really opened my eyes. I didn't even know what covert meant before.'

'You hear about building trust and rapport with participants. Surely the best thing is to *be* friendly, reliable, and trustworthy.'

'I'm not a thermometer, I'm a human being with feelings and emotions of my own, but I can work with that, and it might make our interaction more ethical and kind.'

Taking things further

To read more about **reflexivity in practice**, see: Benson and O'Reilly (2020b), Dean (2017), May and Perry (2017), Lumsden (2019). Braun and Clarke (2022: 15–22) include a lengthy consideration of reflexivity as process. For more on **multi-positionality, positionality in flux**, and **positionality as a toolkit**, see Dodworth (2021) and Reyes (2020). Goffman's (2014) *On the Run* and the debates around it provide a great case study for discussing **complex ethical issues** and the nature of ethnography and qualitative research more broadly. Read it alongside Lewis-Kraus (2016), Lubet (2015a, 2015b, 2017), Hallett (2019), as well as the further references cited in Hallett's review. For a useful chapter on **creative research methods and ethics**, see Kara (2020: 61–76). For a fascinating discussion about **covert research** and how it has been stigmatised, see Marzano (2021), and see Iphofen and O'Mathúna (2021) for more on covert research. Nicole Brown (2021) has a great book and companion website on **research journaling**.

Listen to the related episode for this chapter on
Qualitative Research Methods for Everyone podcast:

4

Interviewing

What this chapter is about

This chapter provides the tools to conduct sensitive, rich, meaningful, and insightful interpretivist qualitative interviews. I start by revisiting (from Chapter 1) the logic of the interpretivist paradigm especially with regard to how this informs and shapes qualitative interviewing. Many approaches to interviewing have been developed that work towards shaping and navigating conversations for diverse types of people and context: the individual life story, narratives and storytelling interviews, group interviews, and interviews within ethnography. I appraise these to give you a grounding in interviewing techniques, but go further with your own reading. I then spend the rest of the chapter focusing on the most commonly used approach – the individual, semi-structured interview – and on designing a good discussion guide, arranging and navigating the interview. I end by addressing some of the challenging issues I have been confronted with over the years.

> **FOR YOUR TOOLKIT**
>
> Interpretivist qualitative interviews are conversational-style exchanges of communication where one person in the exchange has a specific purpose and the other person's role is to freely participate, engage, assist, and respond. The most common approach is the individual, in-depth, semi-structured interview.

The logic of interpretivist qualitative interviewing

A qualitative interview is not a survey interview, a casual conversation, a job interview, or a police interrogation. It is a conversational-style exchange, where one person in the exchange has a specific purpose and the other person's role is to engage, assist, and respond comfortably and voluntarily. Qualitative interviews are usually informed by the interpretivist rather than the positivist paradigm.

In a positivist or survey-style interview, researchers first deduce (using what they think they know about the world) what questions to ask and the potential answers to expect (see Chapter 1). Questions are then asked and responses recorded in exactly the same way and in the same order for every respondent. This standardisation is an attempt to be objective, to clean out, or control for, the effects of the interviewer, because the positivist approach emulates a specific understanding of natural science that, as in experiments, controls for external conditions in order to isolate and predict cause and effect. The approach aspires for the interviewer to be a neutral data collection tool, who will obtain the same answers from the 'subjects' no matter what mood either is in: perhaps it would be better if a robot did the interview. Questions are predominantly closed, with a list of options for the 'subject' to choose from. This is for ease of processing but also to rule out too much variance; the researcher is looking for patterns and generalisations rather than nuance. Data collection in this model is a static and linear process, in which responses are not analysed until after data collection is completed. There is no opportunity for clarification, exploration, or discovery. Ironically, in its determination not to be biased, this approach writes its biases into the design (Westmarland 2001).

FOR YOUR TOOLKIT

Positivist approaches to interviewing write their biases into their design and have no tools for learning new insights from participants. They can be exploitative, unethical, and yield off-the-cuff, untruthful or poorly considered responses.

I am bemused by the extent to which this approach still has power and influence. We see it when researchers, students, or teachers try to be detached, to not lead their respondents, to not talk about themselves too much, to hide their emotions, to stick to their topic guide no matter what happens, and to ask questions the same way no matter the response. If you have been taught to do interviews like this, it is time to think again. I give you the tools to challenge this logic and to do useful interpretivist interviews that might be messy and loosely structured but at least enable you to listen and hear, think and learn.

There have been numerous critiques of the positivist influence on interviewing. Ann Oakley's (1981, 2016) longitudinal interview research with women who were becoming mothers for the first time is one of the most memorable. Oakley was taught to keep her emotions to herself, to be detached, to listen but not talk too much, which was especially challenging when her participants asked her questions about herself, or expressed fear and anxiety about pain, or shared their concerns about medication. Reflecting on how she was supposed to respond when one woman asked her which hole the baby would come out of, Oakley (2016: 197) said 'the conventional methodological advice would have been that I should not answer her question because this would bias the data'. Oakley argued that this detached, unemotional model of science is masculinist, denying the value of a more feminine approach to understanding that could benefit from sharing and caring. Further, trying to maintain distance from a supposedly passive research subject (discussed in Gubrium and Holstein 2012) is unethical and exploitative, she contended, giving nothing back, not even a bit of empathy, making participants feel uncomfortable. Finally, she said, this approach does not even achieve a full or honest account because participants will simply provide answers they think will satisfy interviewers to get them out of the door as quickly as possible. The harder we try to be objective and detached, the more we risk introducing biases, shaping the interview, and closing down conversation. This is true of both survey research and in qualitative interviews if they are not done in a sensitive way, informed by interpretivism.

Later, Nicole Westmarland (2001), invoking Oakley's argument about the masculinist nature of a positivist approach, showed how the association of male with form and female with formlessness goes back to ancient Greece, and although the feminism of the 1960s and 1970s went some way to challenging the dichotomy it nevertheless retains a hold in the imagination and informs the many calls we see for *reliable* research to be objective, detached, and unemotional. Social science knowledge, Westmarland contends, is *situational*: people will naturally say different things at different times depending on the situation. Instead of working hard to get standardised answers according to our predetermined design it is better to work with our participants to obtain insights that are useful in helping us understand the complexity of a phenomenon and to think carefully about the situation and how it shapes the interview for better or worse (as in reflexive practice, Chapter 3).

FOR YOUR TOOLKIT

Because social science knowledge is situational, we need to analyse the situation within which research was conducted to achieve meaningful and useful insights.

Later still, Lauren Cubellis, Christine Schmid and Sebastian von Peter (2021), using ethnographic methods in health research, argued that to address the common divergence between theory and practice in social research, methods must be adaptable and sensitive to on-the-ground lived processes. This is as relevant for good qualitative interviews as much as for ethnography: interviews can be conducted ethically, flexibly (even longitudinally), sensitively and thus interpretively. Interviews can be used to listen and to hear, and we can adapt by using a flexible discussion guide rather than a predetermined and rigid topic guide or questionnaire that would only serve to impose our prejudgements.

As outlined in Chapter 1, qualitative research is usually informed by a version of interpretivism, loosely translated as understanding others and making sense of their lives in light of our research problem. Interpretivists view the social world as working through the actions of people who make sense of the world around them based on what they already know and what they have experienced; they think, consider, weigh up options, imagine possible outcomes, and finally take actions that are shaped by norms, rules and possibilities. As William Thomas and Dorothy Thomas (1928) famously suggested: 'If a person perceives a situation as real, it is real in its consequences.' Thomas and Thomas use the example of a prisoner who violently attacks other prisoners because he believes they are calling abuse at him. It was the perception of abuse that led to the action, and so it is perceptions we need to understand. In Chapter 2, I used the example of going to the dentist: if I believe it is going to hurt, I may well avoid going, and if I go it may well hurt because I am so tense. My belief has an effect, despite any factual evidence to the contrary.

FOR YOUR TOOLKIT

Qualitative interviewing is interpretivist interviewing: it involves interpreting what the world means to people, rendering it meaningful to ourselves, and then to others.

If interviewers want to understand behaviour then they need to understand beliefs, shaped by experiences, imaginations and desires, perceptions, and norms. We need to understand our participants' understandings of the logic behind their decisions, what options are available to them, what they feel they can or should (not) do. These may be things they cannot easily talk about, things they may never even have realised themselves, things it takes some work for them to think through and express. This means the subject matter is different from that imagined in a positivist approach: the subject matter is meanings, experiences, feelings, thoughts, imaginations, choices and so on. We probably only have a vague idea what these are in advance so we can only loosely design a discussion guide with potential topics.

> *As an aside,* we may also be interested in what participants can and cannot do (physically, normatively, materially, or with respect to power and resources) no matter how they feel about it. We might also be interested in what they do without thinking about it, or in what they cannot talk about. In all these cases qualitative interviewing might not be adequate. We might need to also use participation, observation, impromptu conversations, or creative approaches. So, please read other chapters in this book to open your mind to possibilities that might be more relevant for your research than you had realised.

A qualitative interview is more like a conversation (see Rubin and Rubin 2011) than a survey interview; it involves a sharing of views (see Kvale and Brinkmann 2015) but one where the researcher has a specific goal. What I refer to as *interpretivist interviewing* is responsive: researchers listen and then respond as 'conversational partners' (Rubin and Rubin 2011). While we begin with a discussion guide, we also use unscripted responses that are employed in the moment. Our questioning and guiding will be flexible as we listen, hear, and respond, in our attempt to come to a shared understanding of a situation.

This is an ethical approach that emphasises building a relationship of trust that is not confrontational or interrogative, but acknowledges the emotions of both participants and considers how these shape the interview (Rubin and Rubin 2011). We empower our conversational partners in the ways questions are asked, by not being afraid to give something of ourselves while also monitoring through reflexive practice (Chapter 3) our own reactions so as not to judge or foreclose. This also involves searching for context, complexity and richness along the way, through discussion, clarification, and enquiry. With such a fluid approach, we may not be as in control as we like to think we should be, but control is both unethical and biased.

To conclude, qualitative research is interested in how people feel, what they think, how they react, what experiences they have had. This will include things they cannot easily express, things they have mixed feelings about, or have not thought about before, how they imagine something, future plans, what they do or did in practice rather than what they 'should' do. Our research will include people who are difficult to access, sensitive topics, and complex issues. So, how can we best design our interviews to do this well?

Qualitative interview styles for your toolkit

Following the toolkit approach of the book, I introduce a selection of interview styles so that you can put them and others in your toolkit. Of course, there are other styles to learn about; this is not an exhaustive list but an attempt to open your mind to possibilities. I then elaborate the more generic notion of an individual, semi-structured, qualitative interview.

> **FOR YOUR TOOLKIT**
> Interviews are usually conducted with individuals who have taken time out of their normal lives to share a focused conversation: they are thus out of context. Other approaches offer ways to put the context back in.

Individual life histories and oral histories

Life histories have a long tradition in social science. They focus on (emergent) themes in the context of a person's life, informed by a phenomenological philosophy. Because they are always historically located, they also tap into local and wider social conditions and social change. They are usually presented as illustrative of theoretical arguments or in a rich and descriptive way to challenge taken-for-granted assumptions in other literature (Becker 1998). They often include a thick description of context (Geertz 1973), and locate understandings of a life within a whole life context. Methodologically, life history research is based on relationships with participants that are built over time, often involving the researcher returning to the participants several times for ongoing conversations. We might thus call them longitudinal (O'Reilly 2012c). For a classic example, see Clifford Shaw's ([1966] 1930) *The Jack Roller*, which enables the protagonist, Stanley, to tell his own story of how poverty, crime, delinquency, and the justice system shaped his life. For a more recent example, see Tracie Harrison and colleagues (2023) who use life story interviews to explore the long-term perspectives of Mexican American men who suffer pain, depression and limited mobility throughout their lifecourse. Their iterative-inductive analysis yields interesting and useful insights related to cultures of machismo, among other things. Also see Erin Jessee (2018) for her fabulous discussion about how life history interviews can be an ethical and sensitive approach to interviewing in conflict situations.

FOR YOUR TOOLKIT

Put oral and life history interviews in your toolkit and ask yourself to what extent aspects of a participant's whole life, their past experiences, their personal stories, or memories of an event or time period might be valuable to your research.

Oral histories have their emphasis on a specific historical moment rather than a whole life. They often aim to include diverse voices in the retelling of historical accounts, and the interviewer will especially be interested in the participant's own perspective, their memory and its retelling, of an event, an era, a time period, or even a culture. Studs Terkel's (1970) *Hard Times. An Oral History of the Great Depression* is a good example. Also see Pierre Bourdieu and colleagues' (1999) *The Weight of the World* (*La Misère du Monde*), a series of short stories about factory workers and immigrants, struggling families, unemployed workers, and discrimination and prejudice in late-20th-century France. An updated version of this, with stories of how people experienced COVID-19, would make a marvellous book. For a more recent example of this method, and how it dovetails with others, Andrés Gomensoro and Raúl Burgos Paredes (2017) combine life history, oral history, and narrative approaches in their work with children of Albanian-speaking immigrants in Switzerland.

FOR YOUR TOOLKIT

Role or whole? Consider to what extent you aim to interview a role (a person who represents a specific role) or a whole person with a wonderfully complex life experience, or both.

You do not need to be doing full-blown life or oral histories to learn from these approaches. When interviewing a person because of a role they occupy rather than who they are as a complex individual (for example, when interviewing a doctor or a teacher), consider to what extent other aspects of their lives not directly related to your research might still be useful, interesting, insightful or at least might give them a voice beyond their role. Consider that they might be happier to talk to you when you see them as a whole person, not just a role.

Narrative and storytelling

Narrative inquiry overlaps with oral and life histories to the extent that participants are given the agency to tell their lives in the way they wish to. Phenomenologically, stories have the potential to reveal how participants understand and live their lives as agents of change located in societies and cultures. In a study of the experiences of living and dying with dementia, family carers were invited to tell their own stories as a narrative with minimal interruption from the researcher. This 'ensured events and issues important and significant to the participant were reported' (Crowther et al 2022: 3). Paul Statham also used narrative techniques to complement his more usual critical analysis, as he came to understand that, from the women's perspectives and over the longer term, relationships between Thai women and older Western men can be transformative, with some positive outcomes (Statham 2019; and see Chapter 9).

Many narrative approaches (and they are diverse; see Wertz et al 2011) go beyond basic phenomenology to view the person's narrative, account, or story as the unit of analysis. Stories, narrative inquiry understands, provide ways for individuals to make sense of the world, their lives, and their place in the world (see Squire 2008; Squire and Andrews 2014; Lumsden 2019). As Brett Smith (2010: 87, emphasis in original) has recognised in relation to elite sports people adjusting to living with spinal injury:

> [H]umans lead *storied lives*. In part, we live *in*, *through*, and *out* of narratives. We *think* in story form, make *meaning* through stories, and make sense of our *experiences* via the stories provided by the socio-culture realms we inhabit. We not only tell stories, but *do* things with them. Stories do things *to*, *on*, and *for* people that can make a *difference*. They help *guide action*; *constitute human realities*; and help frame *who we are* and *who we can be*. Further, stories are a key means by which we know and understand the world. They offer a way of *knowing* oneself and others.

Analytically, as we explained in our own book about lifestyle migrants in Malaysia and Panama (Benson and O'Reilly 2018), life stories are viewed as 'remembered lives' (Davies 2008: 206), and as people discursively account for their actions they often frame them retrospectively as if they were mindful intentions.

FOR YOUR TOOLKIT

Put narrative inquiry in your toolkit and think about how stories guide identities, and how in every interaction both parties take account of the other in the telling of lives.

Group interviews: two basic models

I discuss group interviewing in Chapter 5; here I simply compare two basic models to inspire you to put 'talking to people in groups' in your interviewing toolkit.

The archetypal focus group model includes between four and 12 participants, who have been intentionally selected because of their characteristics that relate to the research. These are usually strangers. The focus group, which is one of a series on this same topic, takes place in an institutional setting; moderators manage and maintain control of the discussion using a standardised topic guide. Participants may be paid some sort of compensation for attendance. This approach is commonly used in applied and policy-focused research, and research for external clients.

The archetypal ethnographic group model (see O'Reilly 2012a) includes any number of participants, depending on the situation (but small is more manageable). These are people who already know each other, and the conversation arises spontaneously in a familiar setting. Ethnographers might try to direct the discussion towards their own interests; they do not attempt to monitor or manage but learn from how the interaction naturally unfolds. An ethnographer may have the opportunity to have similar discussions with other groups or may pick up on the topic again with this same group, another time. Standardisation of approach is impossible. These interviews are collaborative and ethical, based on trust and rapport built up over time and familiarity.

In practice, group interviews and focus groups can occur anywhere along a continuum between these two extreme models. The opportunities are endless for talking to people as couples, parent and child, small homogeneous groups, large heterogeneous groups; you can walk and talk, take kids to the zoo, chat around a dinner table – whatever works best for your participants and for you (see Chapters 5 and 7). Groups can have power dynamics that are challenging to manage but alternatively some people, for some topics, feel safer in a group (see Chapter 5).

FOR YOUR TOOLKIT

Put group chats and ethnographic approaches in your toolkit and consider whether participants (and your research) might benefit from a more flexible approach as to who to include and how. Think about the extent to which we can learn by being there and being spontaneous and creative.

Interviews in ethnography

As you will find in Chapter 6, in ethnographic fieldwork a passive approach to interviewing usually works best, at least to begin with. Here enquiring, exploring, and listening take place within everyday conversations. We learn to ask questions opportunistically, as we find it appropriate or as we see things that sparked an interest. There are also things that are better learned from simply listening rather than asking directly. As Herbert Rubin and Irene Rubin (2011) suggest, we try to think of fieldwork as one long conversation with someone you are fascinated with. I find it odd that people seem afraid to consider conversations as data; conversations yield productive insights and we can use them as long as we have informed consent (even if after the fact).

To conclude this section, the toolkit approach asks you to explore different approaches to interviewing and to ask questions like: to what extent are the participant's personal life, or events around that time, relevant in my research? Do I need to think about the way in which this participant's story or account is constructed, and to what ends? Have I thought about who has the power to tell whose story, or to listen, or to be heard? Would it work better to talk to people in groups? Perhaps some participants are happier to share a conversation if they are with others like them. Can I ask questions spontaneously, while people are doing things? Would it be useful to include some participant observation, so that I can get a feel for these participants' life contexts? Can I get to know participants beyond the boundaries of the interview, to build some trust and rapport, to simply help them out a bit or to give something back (Chapter 3)?

Finally, of course, put the individual, in-depth, semi-structured interview in your toolkit. In what follows, I spend time addressing practical issues in semi-structured, in-depth interviewing, including designing a discussion guide, arranging the interview, navigating the interview sensitively and meaningfully, and dealing with some specific challenges.

The individual, in-depth, semi-structured interview

The individual, in-depth, semi-structured interview is the most widely used method in qualitative social science research. It is informed by interpretivism (especially phenomenology, see Chapter 1). It involves a small number of participants (usually one to one). It does not use random samples: what we aim to understand is what the different responses tell us about the participants and about the social world more widely (see Chapter 2). It focuses on a specific field or area to explore in depth and detail. It uses a semi-structured discussion guide designed to enable flexibility, creativity, and openness.

Designing the discussion guide

A discussion guide is a document that helps to guide the discussion: it is not a questionnaire or (just) a topic guide, and most of the questions asked should be open-ended. Indeed, you might consider simply listing potential topics rather than even wording specific questions. As William Foote Whyte (1993: 303) argued, when he was first learning techniques for coming to understand life in the Italian American slum town that was so far from his own experience of life: 'one has to learn when to question and when not to question as well as what questions to ask'. The discussion guide must be used flexibly, and you should be brave enough to jump around to different sections as you undertake the actual interview and in response to your conversational partner's responses. It is OK to have elements of a discussion guide that do not get used for every participant.

The guide might be amended as you work through your project. This is positive; it means you are listening, hearing, and learning as you go and are open to having made mistakes, forgotten, or misunderstood things. Development of the discussion guide marks the beginning of analysis (Chapter 8). Where changes are substantial you might need to reconsider initial aims and objectives and maybe return to funding and ethics committees. But normally changes are subtle, like when Nicole Westmarland (2001) was learning about what violence means to taxi drivers, or as with a PhD student of mine who was interested in elder abuse but found the Asian elders she spoke to had an entirely different perspective than she did on the meaning of the term 'abuse'. Similarly, quite early in my research with the British in Spain, I learned to add questions about burial and cremation plans when I realised how central these were to understanding (especially older) people's sense of identity (O'Reilly 2000).

When working in a team you will want to ensure you are working from the same, developing, guide, so have regular meetings to discuss any developments as you go. The discussion guide is often added to outputs as an appendix. Normally this would be the final version, but feel free to use the first and the last versions to illustrate how your insights developed and how they shaped the research.

You might also have to decide *not* to incorporate something that comes up – either because you are not trained to cover it, or do not have the relevant ethical clearance, or it is too different from your main area, or too late to incorporate in your iterative-inductive analysis. In such cases, feel free to say 'This was also interesting but I wasn't able to pursue it for this reason. It would be a fascinating area for future research.'

> ### FOR YOUR TOOLKIT
> The discussion guide is a document that guides the discussion. It should be used flexibly in practice and it might be amended as you learn more as part of iterative-inductive analysis.

Focused, conversational and discovery approaches

Before you design the guide, think about the extent to which your approach is one of focus, conversation, or discovery. *Focused* approaches are used more often in applied and policy research, in evaluations, and assessment-type interviews. They investigate what is going on or what happened in detail. They require careful planning and may need to be more deductive than inductive (see Chapter 1). This is what Steinar Kvale and Svend Brinkmann (2015) term the 'mining approach'. *Conversational* approaches are more interested in how a particular topic or area affects a person's life. They ask for the person's story or perspective with minimal interruption from the interviewer. The guide uses a potential list of topics and open, follow-up questions, with a loose structure. The approach here is more inductive. *Discovery* approaches come somewhere between the two. There is a specific field or area or experience to explore in depth, but you also hope to understand the participant's experiences from their point of view, in the context of their life. This is a more iterative-inductive approach, and comes closer to what Kvale and Brinkmann (2015) mean when they talk of the traveller approach in *InterViews*.

FOR YOUR TOOLKIT

Put discovery, conversational, and focused approaches to interviewing in your toolkit to use as appropriate, even within one interview.

In practice, interviews vary in the extent to which they are discovering, open, discursive and exploratory or more focused and structured. You need to know, for your own research, what needs to be asked in a specific way and a specific order and where it is better to leave topics vague to explore using language that feels right at the time. Readers working in applied and policy fields must consider how much factual detail they need compared with how much fluid discovery. Is it worth asking some things in a different way? Might a survey-type questionnaire be more useful for some aspects of the interview? Or could you focus more on some details in other ways, through a pre-interview or an email? If your interview is swallowed up with asking questions that require simple answers, or that require a participant to collect factual or written information, then a qualitative interview is probably not what you want – at least for these aspects.

Elements of a discussion guide

The discussion guide includes an introduction, some orienting questions, a list of main discussion areas (or topics), prompts and probes, topics you add during the interview, explanatory statements, ending statements, and creative techniques. It might be useful to sketch out a long discussion guide full of everything you want to know or think might come up, then make a shorter version that you take into the interview with you: the version used in an interview should be no more than a couple of pages so that you are not flicking through lots of paper while trying to have a conversation.

Sketch out in detail a brief *introduction* to your research, its aims and objectives, how long the interview will be, what will happen to the material, that it is confidential and so on. This can be designed to be read to participants but use language that works best at the time, depending on who your participant is: a professor working in your field would require a very different type of introduction from one for an eight-year-old child. This can also be a useful opportunity to verbally confirm and to record informed consent.

FOR YOUR TOOLKIT

The discussion guide might include an introduction, some orienting questions, a list of main discussion areas (or topics), prompts and probes, topics you add during the interview, explanatory statements, ending statements, and creative techniques.

Then start with a few *orienting questions* for which you need direct answers (for example: how long have you lived here? How old are your children? How long have you been taking this medication?). Targeted and shorter questions like this can help get the participant in the mood for talking. But if they have already started to talk at length about the topic, do not insist on using these, and if you still need them answered deal with them at the end, or even after the interview. They cover detail you may already know and may ask for the sake of clarity, or they help you get to know participants a bit more. Do not have too many of these, otherwise you might be better to use/add a survey.

The *main discussion areas* (topics) do not need to be written in any specific order and do not have to be written as questions; that way you will be more spontaneous and responsive. Indeed, your discussion guide could make use of mind maps or visual prompts. Or you could simply design a visually appealing interview card with a loose structure and a few topics (Mason 2018: 121). Use your own experience or knowledge, prior literature, preliminary research, and general informants to learn about the field so that you have an idea of what to cover. Start with areas of broad scope so that you gradually learn more about the participant and know how to word other questions in situ. A common opening question is 'Just to start, can you tell me a bit about yourself?' (Yeo et al 2014: 188). Questions should be open to encourage discussion. Try phrases such as: 'How did you …' (to tap into past experiences, details); 'How do you think one should …' (to explore norms); 'How do you think others would …' (to explore assumptions and attitudes); 'Talk me through …' (to examine processes); 'Tell me about …' (to obtain more detail); 'How do you think you would …' (for forward thinking); 'Imagine if …' (for imagining alternatives).

Discussions are pursued using *prompts and probes* (Yeo et al 2014), which you might sketch out in advance or think of in the spur of the moment. Prompts encourage people to keep talking and thinking, and include phrases like 'Tell me a bit more about that. How did that feel? And then what?' Even saying

'That's interesting' or 'Hmm, go on' works as a prompt. Probes, alternatively, encourage participants to think about various other specific aspects and include phrases such as: 'How about smoking? Some people have said that is important, what do you think?' or 'Are children affected by that?' or 'How about obtaining citizenship, have you thought about that at all?'

> **FOR YOUR TOOLKIT**
> Prompts encourage participants to elaborate; probes encourage participants to think about something specific that you have identified (Yeo et al 2014).

In an iterative-inductive approach, you are trying to learn from your participants and therefore if they tell you something which is a surprise to you, or that you had not thought of before, you may want to incorporate these *new topics* or *new directions* into the research, as discussed previously. Maybe you can even return to explore these new issues with earlier participants if you have kept the door open, even by email or a subsequent short conversation.

It can be helpful for your discussion guide to include some *explanatory statements* or factual details to read out to participants where a topic is very complex. Certainly, consider planning your final *ending statements* and questions. Sometimes it is easier to give a sense of an ending if you look down and read your final question and/or statement about what will happen next. Have 'thank you' written in big writing so that the participant can see it. Also, use body language to indicate that the interview is coming to a close.

Plan any exercises or *creative approaches* so that you know what materials to bring along. There are numerous ways an interview can be made more interactive, co-productive, or creative: bringing along photos; drawing maps; taking a transect walk; making a short video; filling in an imaginary form; vignettes; tours ('Talk me through how you would do this'); bringing or making diaries; drawing; making things with play bricks or dough (these are more commonly used in focus groups, or with children, but can be very useful at different stages of any interview – see Chapter 7). Think carefully about their roles in your interview and put them in your toolkit.

> **FOR YOUR TOOLKIT**
> Having creative or interactive techniques available can be useful for when an interview stalls or needs some prompting, for challenging topics, or just for fun.

Arranging the interview

Having designed your discussion guide, it is time to set up an appointment and choose an appropriate place and time.

Obtaining consent

The first step is to get the interest and then obtain the consent of the participant. People are often busy; they may not know you or understand about your work; they may be nervous of the idea of an interview, perhaps the word invokes job interviews or police or border force interviews. Tell them you would love some time to talk with them in depth about something, to share a chat or a conversation. If you do not have face-to-face contact then use a phone call, email, social media, or other means to explain about your research first. Make use of your participant information sheet, but as a backup not as a replacement for a detailed verbal explanation (Chapter 3). If even asking for an interview, chat or conversation is difficult, consider asking to meet (online or face to face or on the phone) for just a few minutes to explain more about the research. Think about how to build trust and confidence; give them a chance to ask questions; be sure you have a good reason why participants might want to contribute. Combine professionalism with empathy and interest. Consider designing a web page, even a static one: curiously, people now seem to feel something is more real when it has a virtual presence. Make the participant feel worthwhile (they are!). Think carefully about how you appear to them, visually and in terms of status, body language and so on. Although we normally advise that qualitative interviews should have an informal feel, I once advised a PhD student to power dress when interviewing bank managers, and I certainly took a less informal approach when approaching solicitors, teachers, lawyers and so on. You want your participants to feel, given the topic and given the situation, comfortable to talk to you frankly and openly.

> **FOR YOUR TOOLKIT**
> You may not want to use the word interview when asking to arrange an interview: ask for a chat, or a conversation or more time to talk instead.

Taking your time

An individual, in-depth interview normally lasts between 45 and 90 minutes. This is long enough to explore, relax, think, without getting bored or uncomfortable. They are best accomplished in a small and comfortable setting that gives the right message, permits the participant to relax, and ensures you are not overheard. Of course, an interview can be longer or shorter but if you only need (or have) 20 to 30 minutes are you certain you have time to explore, in depth, the participant's meanings and experiences and to get the rich detail with which to make sense of the complexity of their life? Could a short survey be used for supplementary material? If the interview takes longer than 90 minutes, have you checked the participant hasn't got a commitment to be somewhere else? Are you sure you are still paying attention, that they are not tired, that the parking meter isn't running up a huge bill, that they are not thirsty or aching? Have a watch or clock in plain sight so that you don't have to keep looking at your wrist or phone. 'A qualitative interview usually lasts 45 to 90 minutes' is a guide not a rule, but it is a guide based on a lot of experience.

FOR YOUR TOOLKIT
Ensure you have enough time for a good conversation but not so much it starts to get uncomfortable.

Do not plan to do too many interviews in one day. I recommend two or three at the very most. Allow time for the interview to take longer than you had expected. You don't want to have to cut someone off as they start to open up just because you have to rush off. You need time to explore new topics that arise in the moment. And you will need time after the interview to check the recorder worked properly, to gather your thoughts, to make some notes to help you remember anything relevant when you listen back, and to begin your iterative-inductive analyses (Chapter 8). There is much more to interviewing than just the interview.

Choosing a good spot

If possible, choose a small comfortable setting with few distractions. Think about how participants feel about the place they are in and how they will get there. Ask how much time they have got and whether they need to leave exactly when planned (maybe they have childcare or an appointment). Try to find somewhere where the recorder will pick up the sound well. Make it a treat for the participant; ask if they can find time when there will be no distractions so they can relax and enjoy it. Consider walking, sharing a coffee, or doing things together. I did a great interview in the back of a charity shop, hanging clothes as we chatted (until the shop manager nagged that there was a lot to do, and so we decided to finish another day at the participant's house, which then turned into a group interview as her friends turned up). Take a pen and paper to make notes but explain to the participant what you are doing and be careful what you write and when; and I personally like to sit next to a table as long as it feels relaxed and comfortable.

FOR YOUR TOOLKIT
Think carefully about whether the venue you, or they, choose is appropriate and feels welcoming.

All that said, it is both ethical and insightful to ask participants what time and place would work for them. I have done an interview outside a noisy cafe with people playing dominoes loudly at the next table; with loud motorbikes whizzing past; with workers popping in and out for the menu of the day. But these were the participants' choices; it was where they felt comfortable and anonymous, and in truth, no one took any notice of us chatting away in the corner (and recording technology is so good now, my voice recorder picked up our conversations beautifully).

Navigating the interview

Qualitative interviews are exciting and exhausting. You are listening carefully, thinking about what was said, planning what to say next, maintaining good eye contact and body language, all while keeping an eye on the time and on your discussion guide. Every stage, from start to end, needs careful thought and planning: begin sensitively, tread lightly, keep it going, and finish gently.

Begin sensitively

Start by reminding people why they are there, and what your goals are. Hopefully, you have had time to explain all the terms and conditions; here they should be reiterated. If you do this when the recorder is on, then you have the added advantage of having verbally recorded consent. I usually say something like: 'Just to check before we start, you've seen and understood the participant information sheet? You know you can stop, change your mind, refuse to answer, add new topics, anything you wish. I'm hoping this will be a nice conversation, not an interrogation. And at the end I will get you to confirm as well. Is that OK?' Then begin the interview (or chat or conversation) with a pleasant, informal, topical discussion and gradually move on to the various topics you have planned or that arise.

> *As an aside,* I have usually shown participants the consent form and the participant information sheet before the interview (Chapter 3), but I ask them to sign the form afterwards, when they know what they are agreeing to. For online interviews, I send a message afterwards with the consent form as an attachment and ask them to read the consent form again and simply reply to me by a given date with the words 'I have seen and consent to everything that is on the consent form.' We will have spoken about all this in advance so it will not come as a surprise. The date gives you an excuse to chase them up if they forget to reply.

Tread lightly

Gently encourage openness and frankness by showing you are listening and not judging. Wait until it feels appropriate to raise any sensitive or provocative topics. Sometimes it is easier to be more abstract or to start by talking about other people (in general, not specific). For example, you can say something like: 'Some people have told me they feel angry that their medicine is so expensive. How do you feel about that?' This gives the participant the opportunity to talk about others beforehand or instead of themselves, but you still learn how they feel. Vignettes, photographs and creative techniques can help with difficult topics (see Chapter 7).

Think about how you will present yourself and how this will affect the interview. You are taking on the role of empathetic listener, not judging, not condemning, and not even agreeing – just listening, hearing and enquiring. Do not be afraid to remind people, when it is appropriate, that you respect their confidences, that you can delete any bits they regret, or that you can stop any time. In my research for the Brexit and British People Abroad project (Benson and O'Reilly 2020b), one man kept putting his hand over the voice recorder when he said things he felt he shouldn't be sharing (he was grumbling about people who lived in Spain but had voted for Brexit). I asked if he would like me to pause the recording or delete those parts and he said 'No, it's fine,' then luckily stopped doing it, otherwise it would have been a challenge for transcribing. Note at this point that I laughed gently at his behaviour. It felt right at the time; he was enjoying being gossipy and I was enjoying letting him. If things do get difficult, be prepared to stop, don't just offer to stop. And even if you are a therapist, this is not your job right now, so don't turn it into a therapy session.

> **FOR YOUR TOOLKIT**
> Begin sensitively, tread lightly, feel your way, listen, respond, allow the participant to guide you, but stay in control.

It might be relevant to prepare materials or information to share with participants after the interview, such as phone numbers for helplines or published advice. In our Brexit and British People Abroad project we found people were asking us what the latest rules and regulations were. It was interesting, from a research point of view, that people were so confused and helped us to understand them and their decision-making practices. But from an ethical point of view, we felt we ought to help where we could and so we started to compile information that we could trust and share.

Keep it going

Being a good qualitative interviewer is a highly skilled job: to keep the interview going you need:

- genuine curiosity and fascination
- to surrender some control

- naivety and knowledge
- patience, resilience and composure
- endless attentive listening and concentration and a good memory
- flexibility and quick thinking
- a sense of humour and plenty of humility

If you start to lose interest in your research, or feel jaded (it can happen, I know), take some time out to get inspired again; read some of the research literature, listen back to transcripts, talk to colleagues, begin tentative analyses (Chapter 8), remind yourself about that initial intellectual puzzle in all its complexity (Chapter 1), and rediscover that genuine curiosity.

Allow the participant to guide the interview with their responses but keep control of the topics you need covered and watch the time. Listen and learn about the participant's life as much as you can (either in advance or during the interview) so that you understand their time pressures, or how much they are likely to understand of any technical jargon or specific details of an event, and how to respond to them.

Naivety is a wonderful tool to use: the participant is the expert, and you are there to learn from them. If you are an expert in the field (perhaps a teacher or a nurse) try not to let that shape the interview too much. On the other hand, showing you understand the context and their lives a little shows respect. Work with not against your own personality: I am not suggesting you chat away, take over the conversation, talk about yourself endlessly, but don't try to be someone you're not either.

As I will go on to discuss, there will be times when you need to be patient and composed, and times when you will need to reflect on your own language and body language and be prepared to admit mistakes, to reword questions. Over time and with practice, you will learn how to hear what is being said, think about how to respond, and remember what else they said that you may need to come back to. Don't be afraid to say 'Hang on a minute, there's a lot there, I just want to write a few things down so we can come back to them.' They will love that you are listening so well.

This of course requires flexibility and quick thinking. You must judge when to jump ahead to a topic you had planned to address later, when to drop a topic altogether, when to reword something to address a misunderstanding. When all else fails I often blame myself and/or laugh at myself.

During the interview try to guide rather than lead, make space for silent reflection, and remember to listen and to hear. Leading is asking a question in such a way that an answer is implied or suggested (Yeo et al 2014). Try to avoid agreeing or disagreeing. Be empathetic but neutral: 'That's interesting, yes, I can see that, that makes sense, that must have been difficult, Mmm hmm.' But even a tone of 'Hmm' can affect the participant. I made this mistake when I returned to fieldwork in Spain ten years after my first ethnographic fieldwork there (O'Reilly 2012c). Listening back to recordings, I realised people were not talking much because I kept saying 'Hmm' in a way that implied 'Oh yes,

I've heard this before.' You do need to keep sounding (and being) interested, as if you are hearing everything for the first time.

> **FOR YOUR TOOLKIT**
> During the interview try to guide rather than lead, make space for silent reflection, and remember to listen and to hear.

Give space for silent reflection; the tone of an interview should be peaceful and reflective as well as animated and excited. If you are afraid of silences, you will rush to fill them, so practise on friends, learn to stay quiet, and give people time to think. A trick I learned many years ago was to look away gently, count to five slowly in your head, perhaps look down at your notes, or do anything that gives the message that you are not in a hurry and it is OK for you both to sit and think and not talk.

Remember that a qualitative interview aims to be rich, meaningful and insightful. We want to begin to understand what compels and constrains people to develop the patterns of behaviour that follow complex pathways that might enable us to see inside their worlds better or even design interventions (Chapter 1). Our data are not numbers but details, examples, quotes, accounts, and stories. Try to ensure, as you listen, that you have heard and collected the detail that is going to be able to illustrate a point you might want to make later, that you have understood the complexity of an answer and not accepted a superficial response.

> **FOR YOUR TOOLKIT**
> Try to ensure, as you listen, that you have understood the detail and complexity of an answer and not accepted a superficial response.

Finish gently

With practice, you will get the sense of how much you can cover in each interview and will learn when a discussion guide is too long or detailed, or perhaps the opposite. Feel your way: ethical and interpretivist research should be sensitive to the participants and their feelings, thoughts, and experiences. But do plan how to end the interview.

> **FOR YOUR TOOLKIT**
> Finish an interview gently by moving away from sensitive topics, ending on a positive note; ask if there is anything you forgot to cover, leave open the chance to get back to each other, and remind the participant what happens next.

One way to end a difficult or sensitive interview that has raised painful memories is to conclude with some positive takeaways that your participant helps you summarise. You could say something like: 'Thank you so much for sharing all that with me. I think it is going to be really helpful for me to take away these key messages [agree on what they are]. We all need to think more about this kind of experience. What do you think?'

Always ask if there is anything you forgot to cover or anything else the participant wishes to share. I say something like 'We've got a few minutes before we need to go. I wanted to check if there is anything else you wanted to talk about' and/or 'Is there anything you think I should be covering in future interviews?' Sometimes people reach the point where they have no more energy to talk about themselves but asking them to think more generally about the research can be motivating and can lead to some wonderful new insights.

If possible, leave open the opportunity to get back to participants to ask anything you are not sure about or even about anything new that arises, and give them the opportunity to come back to you if they wish to. This can be difficult to manage in practice and you may need to mention that this would just be for clarification, not to revisit the entire interview. You might also need to have a cut-off date from which changes can no longer be made. Some researchers offer a quick five minute debrief a week or so after an interview, or a short email exchange.

Check any points of confidentiality, clarify where you were unsure whether participants wanted to keep the material in the interview or maybe delete or anonymise aspects. Remind the participant what will happen next, whether and how you will send the consent form, what updates about the project you will share, whether you will send the transcript to check. In the Brexit and British People Abroad project (Box 1.3) we offered participants the opportunity to read and comment (briefly) on their transcripts, but we gave a deadline for responses so that we had some control over how long this ongoing communication could continue.

Hopefully, you both enjoyed the interview and will be able to part with a smile on your faces and some optimism for the future.

Dealing with challenging issues

I'd like to end by addressing some of the challenging issues I have been confronted with over the years: namely, how to respond if a participant gets upset or angry, is shy or reticent, rambles too much off topic, is wary or suspicious, has challenging opinions, has their own agenda, is very short of time, or is higher status than us (also see Yeo et al 2014). Our response must always be both ethical and interpretivist and requires us to draw on the skills outlined earlier.

When faced with any queries or dilemmas always remember the key principles that guide your research. Interview partners should feel relaxed and able to interject, wander off, pick up with you again later, change their minds. We are interested in trying to understand (and help them think about) their feelings and experiences, hopes and desires, fears and challenges; we hope they will expand, digress, discuss, explore, imagine, go into detail, explain, ponder, and even contradict themselves. Our research should always be ethical; we want them to feel empowered, to enjoy, to dare to tell us we asked the wrong thing or left something out; and at the same time, we hope they will answer (most of) our questions.

Ensure that, when you started, you reassured your participant that you wanted to hear their opinions, that there are no right or wrong responses, and that they can refuse to answer any questions. Then if a participant angrily says something like: 'Why do you ask me that?! I just want to forget about that. I'm not discussing this with you,' there are various ways you can respond, but try always to be in tune with the participant and the feelings of the moment. Never overreact or react against a participant, but reacting *with* a participant can be comfortable, as long as you are not leading them. Pause the interview for a while, turn the recorder off, talk about something else. Perhaps say: 'That's OK, we can move on, I'm sorry if I made you feel uncomfortable,' and then move on to a less emotive topic (surrendering some control). If it is crucial, return to the sensitive topic later and approach it a different way, or ask how you could approach this sort of thing in future, with others, so that you don't make the same mistake again (using naivety and quick thinking).

If a participant is shy or reticent, giving very short answers, or seems reluctant to take part, make sure you are being encouraging and approving, and smiling where appropriate, with genuine curiosity and fascination. Check you are not being interrogative: looking at your notes; breaking eye contact and slowing the pace of the interview can make for a more comfortable interaction than staring and waiting for a response. Use phrases like 'tell me about' or 'what happened when' that invite a longer response. Alternatively, spend a bit of time asking direct or descriptive questions rather than opinion ones until the participant is more forthcoming. Some of the creative techniques in Chapter 7 can help a participant be more engaged. But, also, accept that some participants are taciturn while others are garrulous.

What can be done when participants go off topic or spend too much time on apparent irrelevances? First, allow some rambling before trying to rein them back in (surrender control). Then think about your body language: are you inviting them to continue, or to move on to something else? Look down at your topic guide to indicate that you still have things to cover. My response to many challenging situations is to blame myself (using humility and humour). Here I might say something like: 'Oh dear, my fault, but we've gone right off track here. I wish we had longer, I'd love to hear more about that, but I'm going to have to get back on track.' Then ask them about something they are interested in, or have mentioned, that is also relevant to you. Participants like to be guided and are often concerned that they might be going off track, so do not be afraid to regain the initiative. On the other hand, don't forget to listen because sometimes when somebody has apparently rambled completely off topic, they are saying something relevant, important and insightful. This was how I learned to include questions about burial and cremation in my interviews with British people living in Spain.

Participants can be wary, suspicious or even challenging. Try to pre-empt this by sharing enticing, interesting and informative information about the project (Chapter 3). If it still happens, draw on your patience, resilience and composure; ask what they would like to talk about next, what is important to them. But, in the end, their participation is voluntary and they can withdraw if they wish. I once interviewed a man who was being very difficult, looking me straight in the eye and giving very simple one word answers. I tried every technique I could think of until I finally put down my pen, looked him in the eye, laughed gently and said 'This isn't working is it? What am I doing wrong?' He laughed and said 'No, I'm sorry, it's me. I was giving you a hard time. Go on, let's start again.' After that, everything was fine (though it required some reflexive practice later).

We might come across participants with opinions we do not agree with. Never lie; you do not need to give your own opinion unless asked, but neither do you have to agree with them. Responses such as 'I see, interesting, I understand,' show empathy but are non-committal. You can even explore the opposing opinion by gently suggesting: 'Some people would not agree … what do you think about that?' We used this in our interviews about Brexit when we (occasionally) found people who had moved to live in Europe and were in favour of Brexit (O'Reilly 2017b, 2018a; Benson and O'Reilly 2020a). The important thing is to genuinely be curious, not to pretend to be.

It can be challenging when participants have a personal agenda they wish to impose on the interview, such as grievances about their organisation, which may not be directly relevant. Ethically, they have a right to give their opinion and to briefly share these things with you, and you have a responsibility to understand this need. But where you are aware of such concerns, it might be useful to clarify in advance that though you empathise with their position the interview is not the space to go into this in detail. Or during the interview, you can give them a little while to air these things but then try to bring them back to your own agenda.

FOR YOUR TOOLKIT
If things don't go as planned, take time out to reflect and learn, talk to colleagues, and perhaps to participants; ensure you are being ethical and reflexive, humble and kind (including to yourself).

If potential participants are short of time and can give you maybe 15 or 20 minutes only, you may still want to take the opportunity to have a qualitative interview, but you can achieve more by being flexible, organised and focused. Although I would not normally recommend doing this, you could show them a version of the discussion guide in advance to initiate a discussion about which elements they might have time to focus on. Ask if they can answer a few further quick questions by email or other media before or after the interview. Perhaps turn a few questions into a short survey questionnaire that can be dealt with at a different time or online. On the other hand, there have been several occasions where somebody has agreed to meet me for a short period of time, but where in the end the interview continued far longer than expected. I like to think this is because they were enjoying it. Whatever the reason, I was happy for that to happen and grateful that I had not scheduled something in my diary for right after the interview: always leave space for the interview to take longer than expected.

Finally (and this is not as an exhaustive list), there are some useful published discussions about interviewing elites (see Mbohou and Tomkinson 2022), or people who are (seen as or feel) powerful in relation to the researcher. The power dynamics here challenge much of what we have learned about doing interviews, about putting people at their ease, helping them relax, giving them time to talk and so on, because some participants can be directive, forceful, or controlling. However, all relationships are complex, shifting, changeable and dynamic and, as Mbohou and Tomkinson remind us, it is often in moments of discomfort that we learn the most.

We all make mistakes in our interviews: human interaction is unpredictable. Please do not be too self-critical when things go wrong. Take some time out, talk to a colleague, listen back to your recordings, and use reflexive practice to think about how you might do things differently next time. But also, try to make sure you know a little about your participants before you start, that you understand their life and work situation, the complexity of the job, the extent of their experiences, and so on, so that you are not caught in too many difficult situations. Above all, when done well, interviewing is an enlightening and heartening experience. I hope you enjoy it.

Final thoughts

Interpretivist qualitative interviews are conversational-style exchanges of communication where one person in the exchange has a specific purpose and the other person's role is to freely participate, engage, assist, and respond. They are usually conducted with individuals who have taken time out of their normal lives to share a focused conversation, but this is not the only approach. A guide to the discussion is used flexibly and might be amended as you learn more as part of iterative-inductive analysis. When confronting any challenging situations, remember why you chose to do qualitative interviews, that you are trying to understand their point of view, that you wish to be ethical, not exploitative, to give them a voice, and to remain open to their stories and their experiences.

Speaking of interviewing

'If I act like a robot, I will be sure not to affect the interviewee, but they won't be very open or honest with me, will they?'

'We were in a bar. Those at the next table were talking so loudly I thought they might be arguing, and at another table they were playing dominoes. But it felt comfortable and private, and we chatted for ages.'

'She was really busy, but I wanted to give her time to talk to me in depth, so we met briefly a few times in different places, even over the phone a couple of times.'

'I was a bit nervous when we first started but I'd prepared an opening statement to get me going and once we started listening to each other and sharing our thoughts, I learned a lot.'

'He got a bit upset at one point and I had to turn the recorder off and take a little break. We got a cup of coffee and talked about other things, and then he said "Right, shall we get back to it." I was so pleased he felt able to do that.'

Taking things further

Kvale and Brinkmann (2015) and Rubin and Rubin (2011) are my favourite books on qualitative interviewing. For a more extensive consideration **of life history research**, see Cole and Knowles (2001), Plummer (2001) and Thompson (1988). See Mbohou and Tomkinson (2022) for a great way into the literature on **elite interviews**. The chapter by Yeo et al (2014) on in-depth interviewing has more on their great distinction between **probes and prompts** as well as lots of practical advice and references to pursue. Wertz et al (2011) is a useful reference for learning about **different approaches** to interviewing and analysis.

Listen to the related episode for this chapter on
Qualitative Research Methods for Everyone podcast:

5

Group discussions

What this chapter is about

This chapter inspires readers to think outside the box of individual semi-structured interviewing and to consider what happens when people talk about things together, in groups. It should be read in conjunction with the previous chapter as there may be further relevant advice or insights there. I start by discussing a traditional approach to focus groups before moving on to consider how this can be adapted for different purposes and populations, especially to avoid 'methodological hegemony' (Pink et al 2022: 161). It is important to learn from the past, not discard it and not be determined by it. I use the terms 'focus groups' and 'group discussions' almost interchangeably, but 'focus groups' tends to be used in more conventional approaches and 'group discussions' for more creative approaches. The chapter, as with the previous one, is a basic teaching tool that lays the groundwork for innovative approaches.

A bit of background

As far as we know, focus groups began in the 1920s as a method used by market researchers to garner opinion from the public quickly, cheaply and fairly easily. I remember being enticed into one myself as I was out shopping. It was a discussion about the colour that Cadbury's chocolate wrappers could be – I chose deep purple – and we were 'paid' with free chocolate. Focus groups were adapted for academia in communications and media studies as a useful way to understand audience reception of, for example, television programmes and newspaper articles. By the 1980s they became popular across academic disciplines, and are now also used in all political, policy and applied areas, such as political campaign planning, product design, user involvement in public services, and citizens' juries that give people access to government debates and decision-making processes (Morgan 1988; Krueger and Casey 2015). Their usage has become increasingly diverse and creative over recent decades.

> **FOR YOUR TOOLKIT**
> The use of focus groups and group discussions has become increasingly diverse and creative over recent decades.

Focus groups are now used in policy research to garner opinions about policy or political issues, in organisational research to gather staff members' opinions, in consultation or evaluation to examine user demands and responses to services, in media studies to look at audience reception. They are used in the interpretive study of culture and interaction, and with children and with other groups to create a comfortable and safe environment, a sense of group belonging, or to correct power imbalances compared with one-to-one interviews (Madriz 2000).

A conventional definition

Traditionally and conventionally, focus groups are a qualitative research method for generating fascinating insights from a group of people over a short period of time using a discussion guide. The convention is for between six and ten participants (seven is my magic number) to discuss a range of related topics for one to two hours. Group members are carefully chosen for their relationship to the research aims. The group composition requires careful planning to facilitate a comfortable and lively debate. Participants share an implicit contract that they will come together to discuss given topics. Traditionally, focus groups would meet just once but they can reconvene longitudinally where possible or interesting.

Key characteristics of a focus group are the role of the moderator and the generation of insights through group interaction. The moderator sets and manages the agenda using a discussion guide, facilitates and steers the discussion, keeps participants focused, and tries to ensure balanced contributions from the group. Spontaneity is also encouraged so that the data that emerge (or are created) are interactive and dynamic (Finch et al 2014). When discussing something in a group, participants will listen to others, consider, respond, and react. Views and opinions may develop or change.

> **FOR YOUR TOOLKIT**
> The conventional model of a focus group is of six to ten people, often strangers, who discuss a topic for one to two hours, in an institutional setting. Key characteristics are the role of the moderator and the generation of insights through group interaction. Spontaneity is encouraged so that new insights emerge interactively and dynamically.

When to use focus groups

Focus groups should be used when your goal is to get a broad understanding or an overview of the topic. They are useful for clarifying perceptions, definitions, and social conventions, for comparing and contrasting views and experiences, to generate new ideas and test alternative strategies. They are particularly useful when the group share something in common, a similar status or circumstances, or at least are not too different, and are happy to bounce ideas off each other, sharing some things and content to have other things they disagree about. It is preferable if the topic area is not overly complex or sensitive or bound by rigid social norms and conventions.

> The most compelling reason for using focus group discussion is the need to generate discussion or debate about a research topic that requires collective views and the meanings that lie behind those views (including their experiences and beliefs). Researchers can hugely benefit from the group context since it provides insight into social relations, and the information obtained reflects the social and overlapping nature of knowledge better than a summation of individual narratives through interviews and surveys. (Nyumba et al 2018: 28)

Focus groups should not be used when exploring in depth, individual attitudes, experiences and decision-making processes. It can be uncomfortable if the moderator spends too much time focusing on one person, both for the participant and for others in the group. Nor are they suitable when your desire is to set views and experiences in the context of individual biographies or detailed case studies. If your research needs a lot of in-depth or intimate detail from individuals, use individual interviews instead (or as well). Note that it can be interesting to compare what people say in groups with what they say individually (Reay 2004; Jakobsen 2012). Focus groups are not usually appropriate for overly sensitive, personal or political issues. However, as I discuss later, it is worth giving people a choice as sometimes sharing a conversation with others with similar circumstances can be a better or more comfortable way for people to talk than an interview (Barbour and Kitzinger 1998). Focus groups are not useful for detailed content or for complex, factual or contextual material. Of course you can, and should, gather some contextual detail: we always want to try to relate what people are telling us to the wider context of action, but the idea is to have a group discussion not a series of one-to-one interviews. Finally, the emphasis is on how people talk about things rather than what they do in practice. But again, it can be interesting to compare the two. In my first ethnographic fieldwork I noted that British residents in Spain who ran a theatre group told me, in a group discussion, that they were open to all nationalities; in practice, the group advertised all its events and ran the entire operation in English (O'Reilly 2000).

FOR YOUR TOOLKIT
Discovery approaches are inductive, opening, and seek diversity and breadth. Focused approaches begin inductively, but work towards reaching a negotiated consensus, by closing. These approaches can be combined.

It is useful to distinguish discovery and focused approaches to running and analysing group discussions. A discovery (or opening up) approach to a group discussion asks, for example, how people feel about or understand health issues, to generate dynamic and diverse responses. Or it might aim to explore the discussion process itself, the 'formation and negotiation of accounts, within a group context, how people define, discuss, and contest ideas through social interaction' (Tonkiss 2012: 238). A more focused (or closing down) approach is specifically designed to generate shared conclusions or an agreed consensus; the method overlaps with the concept of a workshop (Finch et al 2014). This is related to the extent to which the research is at a more inductive and discovery stage, or perhaps has already generated some insights and now aims to be more deductive in asking a group to compare, rank, or test out ideas together. It is also possible to combine approaches within a single project (being iterative-inductive; Chapter 1). This methodology is used by researchers assessing the Minimum Income Standard in which groups first spontaneously and openly explore what might be required for a minimum standard of living in the UK and then the group is guided to work together to achieve a 'negotiated consensus'. Regular research on the Minimum Income Standard (MIS) produces budgets for different household types, based on what members of the public think is needed for a minimum acceptable standard of living in the UK. It is carried out by Loughborough University's Centre for Research in Social Policy.

Focus groups are therefore relevant for applied social research with a strong policy or practical orientation, as well as formal, theoretical, exploratory, or basic research that explores shared social and cultural meanings, discourses, and so on. They are useful at the start of the project to refine and clarify the concept or approach to be used in the study. They are useful with other methods to generate a rich, complex and multimethod understanding of an issue. They are helpful as the core of a project, and can be conducted in a series or longitudinally to explore social change (McLeod and Thomson 2009; Finch et al 2014). Online versions (see Chapter 7) are becoming more common because they can quickly and cheaply access people across the globe, including those with travel or access difficulties, and because this is becoming a more common way to share thoughts and conversations in everyday life. Such choices will depend on your aims and objectives, as discussed in Chapter 1.

FOR YOUR TOOLKIT

Focus groups can be used at the start of a project, as the core of a project, or as a mixed-method design. They are relevant for basic exploratory, and policy and applied research. They can be done in a series, with different participants, or longitudinally, returning to the same participants over time.

Who is going to take part?

First consider your target population and think about who you are hoping to represent thematically with your focus groups, for the entire study and for the focus groups aspect of it. Turn back to Chapter 2 to learn all about interpretive sampling. Recruit approximately two weeks beforehand for the general population, but you need a longer lead time for professionals and specialist populations. Over-recruit by one or two in case some do not show up. Monitor the composition as you go and consider to what extent you need to adapt the make-up of future groups. Send people personal and friendly reminders in advance of the focus group: make them feel special.

> **FOR YOUR TOOLKIT**
> Begin with purposeful sampling but learn as you go, monitor who and what ends up being included; amend it if you can, to achieve final sample fitness (Chapter 2).

Who can we put together?

When thinking about who to put together in which focus groups, consider characteristics relevant to the nature of the method, such as literacy, language abilities, geographical location, and accessibility. Think about who can travel where, who can sit, for how long, who will work together in what ways in a group. Also consider characteristics relevant to the topic. For example, will you put parents with children, or parents of different social classes together or separately? It is worth sketching this out in advance as far as you can in planning your initial sample, and to some extent this will inform how many focus groups you want to run and how many participants will be in each group.

Try to achieve a group that is comfortable but not too comfortable. This will depend on the nature of the research topic as well as the nature of the group and whether they know each other already. I learned after one focus group with British people living in Spain that it was not a good idea to put people who were in favour of Brexit together with those who were opposed (Benson and O'Reilly 2020a). It was my first experience of navigating a full-blown argument. There are times when people can provide comfort by sharing experiences (Gram et al 2023), but if people know each other too well they may have already discussed the topics and even reached established positions on it. If people have strong views on a subject think about whether some would be upset to hear from others in the same group; if views on the topic are likely to be jaded, think about how to ensure the discussion is lively. Overall, it tends to be easier to combine people who differ in terms of the research topic than differences in sociodemographic characteristics. That is to say, power, class, status, and gender may be more uncomfortable than differences of opinion on the given topic. But with Brexit I found the opposite was the case.

> **FOR YOUR TOOLKIT**
> Plan who to put together in a group and monitor this as you go. Groups should be small enough that all participants feel comfortable to speak and large enough to bounce ideas off each other and generate a variety of perspectives.

How many focus groups?

The number of focus groups you run will depend on the number of selection criteria in your research, the diversity of the target population, the contribution your focus groups hope to make to knowledge (and whether it will inform a chapter, a short report, an entire PhD thesis, or several papers), as well as who you can put with whom in one group. Diane Reay's (2004) research with Helen Lucey in inner-city schools in London involved 77 focus groups, with 454 children. The study found that children together spoke negatively about inner-city schools, often drawing on derogatory representations of race and social class. The study then used one-to-one interviews, and these explored how individual children negotiated these group discourses. Hilde Jakobsen (2012) held 40 focus groups in Tanzania on the broad topic of violence against women and corruption (and she suggests five to ten participants in a group is usual). Kate Legge and colleagues (2006), exploring people's spending choices and management of resources for the Joseph Rowntree Foundation, held 11 focus groups in a first stage, with people who had made applications for a Social Fund loan; five focus groups at stage two, with people of different income levels; and a workshop in stage three bringing together participants from the first two stages to draw some conclusions. Owen (2001; see also Chapter 7) conducted five focus groups with women with serious and enduring mental health problems. For more on sample size and sample fitness see Chapter 2.

How many participants in a group?

The number of participants in a focus group usually varies between six and ten. Too small a group stifles discussion and is less interactive and dynamic; too large and some people inevitably become quiet or passive. That said, I did one with over 30 children in a classroom. It was exciting and dynamic, and I learned to think about the role of clothing in identity (O'Reilly 2012b), but the discussion was brief and after ten minutes I resorted to more creative exercises (Chapter 7). I regularly talk to people in small groups of even two or three (more on that later). Social researchers often prefer smaller sizes and market researchers prefer larger ones. This is probably because market research approaches are often less exploratory and more focused. The overall aim is to have small enough groups to allow all participants the chance to speak and to work well together, and large enough to bounce ideas off each other and capture a variety of perspectives.

Organisational issues

Let's briefly think about the venue, refreshments, incentives, seating arrangements, recording equipment, and anyone other than the participants who might be in the room. Be sure the venue gives out the right message and feels comfortable and welcoming. I once tried to have small group discussions with two to three children in a room allocated by the head teacher but soon discovered it was the same room they used for detention! The children were giggling, looking embarrassed, and talking very little (O'Reilly 2012c). I asked them where they thought we should talk, and they told me we should go round by the bike sheds, so that is what we did, then and for future groups (with permission, of course, and in Spain it was warm and bright and there was a bench).

Think carefully about when to give any refreshments. At the beginning is usually best, unless there is a natural space in your discussion guide where taking refreshments might work, maybe as part of an exercise.

Whether or not to give incentives is a thorny issue and will depend on where you work and what funding is available. As a general rule, your research should not leave participants out of pocket: it should not cost them to come along. There is some consensus for ethical reasons that payment should be made to anyone in severe poverty and, paradoxically, a reluctant acceptance that people with very high earnings will not agree to take part unless they are adequately compensated for their time.

It is usual for focus groups to take place around a table. Aim to sit in a horseshoe shape with you at the top, rather than a circle. You and your facilitator (if you have one) want to be able to see everyone easily, without having to turn your heads. A table is useful for you to rest your discussion guide on, to lean on as you take any notes, for your participants to engage in any creative activities, and to display name labels if you use them. Have a watch or clock in plain sight so that you don't have to keep looking at your wrist or phone.

Audio record your focus group if you can. Some use video recordings or photographs too, but be sure consent is fully informed, and consider how intrusive such equipment might be. Test any equipment for quality before you start. Take along note paper and pens for yourself as well: it can be difficult to remember everything when there is a lot going on. You might find a flipchart handy for noting themes at the content mapping stage (discussed later), for writing down anything you'd like to come back to, or for concluding takeaway messages at a more focused stage. I like to give all the participants a pen and paper too, so that they can note down anything they want to remember or come back to. I also sometimes give them play dough to fiddle with (if they want to).

> **FOR YOUR TOOLKIT**
>
> Think carefully about the venue, refreshments, incentives, seating arrangements, recording equipment, and anyone other than the participants who might be in the room.

Think carefully about anyone other than the participants who is in the room. If participants are attended by carers or helpers, for example, these should be introduced, it should be clear whether they will participate, and that confidentiality rules and group norms apply to them. Try to avoid others coming into the room (perhaps delivering refreshments or materials), as this can be awkward for those involved and can raise issues of confidentiality.

Setting the agenda and getting started

A focus group needs to have a shared agenda so that you and the participants all know what to expect and the best way to achieve this is to discuss it with your participants in advance. Turn back to Chapter 4 for more on this, as the same issues apply with regard to obtaining the participant's consent to take part. Prepare participant information sheets and consent forms and think about how and when they will be used (Chapter 3). Prepare a discussion guide and any additional materials you might need such as handouts or photographs that you will be using for creative approaches. As with individual interviews, I like to make sure participants have (1) seen the information sheet, (2) had the opportunity to read it and ask questions, (3) seen the consent form and understand it. I then clarify at the beginning of the focus group (verbally and with the recorder on) that they have understood what is going to happen and what consent means. I then ask them to sign the consent forms as they leave at the end of the focus group, or if it is online I send the forms and ask for consent (as in Chapter 4).

> **FOR YOUR TOOLKIT**
>
> Obtaining the consent of the participant to take part can go through several stages, including designing information sheets, discussing the project with them, clarifying formal consent, building trust and rapport, and helping them feel at ease.

Discussion guides

Design the discussion guide thoughtfully (see Chapter 4). It is an important tool in setting the agenda and helping focus the discussion. It also provides an important comparison across groups and between moderators and facilitators. It might end up as an accountable document, and it will be the framework or starting point for your analysis.

The goal of any focus group is to achieve a creative discussion rather than answers to a list of questions. A semi-structured discussion guide includes a set of fully worded questions to be asked, perhaps in order, and some open-ended follow-up probes to be used as and when required. In practice, the moderator must decide how rigidly or flexibly to use the document, when to ask the questions exactly as written, and in which order, and when to adapt them, depending on previous answers. The moderator also needs to decide how much probing to do. In a discovery approach, the guide might simply have a list of themes and sub themes to be internalised by the moderator, rather than specific questions. The guide acts to shape the focus group but not to direct it. Here a shorter guide is more useful than a lot of detail.

In practice, you will usually combine these approaches within one focus group. Referring to the distinction above, between more discovery or more focused approaches, the design will depend on the level of detail and specificity you need for different items at given times. With time, you will learn to ensure the guide is not too ambitious. The number of topics needs to be modest enough to permit reflection and consideration but extensive enough to encourage animated discussion. Remember, not everyone will express a view on every aspect of the guide (it should be a discussion not a question-and-answer session), but you do need to allow time to check out other views on a regular basis by asking questions such as 'Are there any other thoughts on this? Did I miss anything?' It is better if you can memorise most of it and not rely too much on looking down and flicking through an extensive document. Finally, you may need discussion guides designed in different ways for different constituencies. For example, if your research includes separate groups for parents and children, or patients and doctors.

FOR YOUR TOOLKIT
Be familiar with the guide and use it as a guide not a crutch. In practice, decide how rigidly or flexibly to use the discussion guide, when to ask the questions exactly as written, and in which order, and when to adapt them in response to previous answers.

Any creative approaches (see Chapter 7) need to be planned and scheduled into the discussion guide. Think carefully about accessibility and usability; you cannot assume people will read things in advance and people often do not like to read or draw or make things in front of others or under pressure. Divide any reading (or viewing) into bite-size pieces, remove jargon, and if you are asking participants to draw or paint always give them alternative options such as noting down a few words.

Navigating the discussion

I usually begin with a brief prepared statement (Chapter 4) and then move on quickly to an activity that involves all participants, such as asking each a short question in turn. This way they have all started to contribute. Try to pace the discussion to cover the agenda. If you are familiar with the guide and have memorised the key themes it becomes a guide not a crutch. Instead of looking down at your notes, you can look at the participants, maintain good eye contact, watch for non-verbal signals, show interest, and respond appropriately.

Try to avoid summing up too much. A comment like 'OK, so everyone agrees [x]' is closing and will thwart the discussion. A comment such as 'OK, we've had some great responses to this now, such as [x] and [x]. Is there anything else before we move on?' is opening and gives people the opportunity to challenge the consensus or 'group think' (Busetto et al, 2020), to contribute further detail, and to feel heard.

Questions and probes should be opening, simple, single, and (usually) non-directive. Allow time for people to answer, do not rush to fill silences, and try not to finish people's sentences. I, like many people, do not feel comfortable with silences, so if I feel the urge to press on rather than wait patiently, I quietly count to five in my head without staring at anyone in particular. This slows down the pace, gives people a chance to think, and sets the tone as one where we are allowed to reflect and not answer quickly.

Probing and prompting

Probing means to explore, examine, or enquire. In a focus group, probes are open-ended, follow-up questions that are used to elicit more detail based on what has been said. A prompt on the other hand puts forward a suggestion or idea or word that maybe hasn't arisen. Probe fully: don't accept a passing mention, don't assume you know the context or motivation or background story. Probe for richness and detail; prompt to elicit or engender a response (Yeo et al 2014).

> **FOR YOUR TOOLKIT**
> Probes encourage participants to elaborate on a response; prompts encourage participants to think about something specific that you have identified (Yeo et al 2014).

Probes can invite further responses by nodding or just listening, or by asking: Does anyone else want to come in on this? Have we missed anything? We have discussed [x] and [x], is there anything else I missed? Probes can seek rich description by asking: Can you tell me a bit more about that? Then what? What was that like? Can you talk me through that a bit more? When was that? Probes can seek clarification: 'What do you mean by that? Have I got this right? Probes explore reasons and motivations: Why do you think that is? Why do you think people believe that? Probes can explore consequences and impacts: Then what happened? What effect did that have?

Probes are useful for clarifying diverse perspectives with questions such as: What were the advantages of that approach? What do others think? Are there any other thoughts on this? Is there anything we've missed? Probes can return to earlier issues with: I noted earlier you said you felt embarrassed, would you like to talk about that? We had a heated discussion about [x] earlier, but some were quiet so does anyone want to return to that? Probes can challenge opinions or give permission to express controversial views: Some people (or *I have read in the literature*, or *Other groups*) have said [x], what do you think about that? Does anyone want to disagree?

Prompts are used in more focused aspects of a discussion (Finch et al 2014; Yeo et al 2014). You may need to direct the conversation along certain lines or inspire a reaction to a given topic or suggestion, policy or political opinion. These questions are more likely to be pre-scripted, at least loosely, such as: How would you feel if you were told coffee is good for you? How about making lists to get through the day? What are your thoughts about applying for Spanish nationality? Some people are surprised to know you live in Spain and yet voted for Brexit; how do you feel about that?

Mapping and mining

The focus group swings constantly between content mapping, or getting a breadth of responses and content mining, or exploring the depth and detail behind responses (Legard et al 2003). The early stages of a focus group tend to involve more content mapping, and content mining tends to follow. Relatedly, as each new topic is raised it will usually generate quick, off-the-cuff, diverse (mapping) responses that can then be explored (mined) in more detail. Of course, we may return every now and then to an earlier topic or to the beginning of a theme to check that we have covered the breadth as well: focus groups tend towards overt consensus if we are not careful; it is generally easier to agree than to disagree.

Content mapping questions ask for a variety of perspectives and experiences before moving on to explore them. Questions such as: Who has ambitions, what do they look like, what other words come to mind? Why do people go to university? What else might they want from the experience? What examples have you got of people choosing/not to go, where to go? Content mining questions take the responses and examine them more closely with questions such as: Tell me more about your plans, for next week, for next year. Have you been to university? How did you make your choices? What conversations did you have, with family, friends, tutors? Content mining questions depend on you listening, hearing and thinking, and then responding.

FOR YOUR TOOLKIT

Content mapping involves getting a breadth of responses and content mining involves exploring the depth and detail behind responses (Legard et al 2003). You need to do both.

As discussed in Chapter 4, you should avoid leading questions. Leading is a way of asking that suggests an answer or does not easily permit the opportunity to say no, or to discuss other things. Closed questions such as 'Should you have five a day? Is it good for you?', 'Do you have ambitions?', 'Does everyone agree?' are more leading than open ones such as: 'How do you feel about five a day?', 'Are there some other opinions on this?' If in doubt, listen back to your recordings and ask yourself if participants were able to disagree, contradict each other (and themselves), to reflect, to ponder, and to deliberate. Often it is more about the tone used than the actual question asked. We all make mistakes but try to learn from them using reflexive practice (Chapter 3).

Moderators and facilitators

It is useful to have a moderator to run a focus group and a facilitator to offer support. I don't think it matters what words you use – you are moderating or facilitating or doing a bit of both. What is important is that you and the participants understand your role in facilitating, moderating, and navigating a good discussion. Introduce yourselves and explain to the participants what you will each be doing. It works well for one to have a more dominant role and the other one to listen, make suggestions, pick up on things the moderator missed, take notes on the board, and maybe take over after a while. But this is just a suggestion; in practice do what works best for you. Generally speaking, not enough attention is paid to the skills needed for a good moderator or facilitator (Nyumba et al 2018). Managing a conversation, remembering what has come up that you might want to return to, deciding what to address next, thinking about people who were quiet or noisy and how to deal with that, remembering to allow time for people to change their minds, and to ensure you gather details, richness and complexity, is exhausting. You will need to be responsive, flexible, confident, adaptable, sometimes assertive, and always tactful and kind.

FOR YOUR TOOLKIT

Moderating and facilitating focus groups is a skill that requires responsiveness, flexibility, confidence, adaptability, sometimes assertiveness, and always tactfulness and kindness.

Getting started

Welcome people as they arrive, with refreshments perhaps. Find the right opportunity to introduce yourself, to restate the purpose of the focus group, and any norms you expect everyone to abide by. Remind participants that there are no right or wrong answers, that they should respect each other's positions, that it is a discussion, that everyone is expected to join in, and that they should try not to interrupt each other. Take this opportunity to mention that if people talk over each other, or have side conversations, the recorder (or you) will not be able to pick it up and you might miss something important. Remind them about the consent and confidentiality agreements, as outlined in the participant information sheet. For example, remind them that you will be recording and just check that they are all in agreement, and alert them if a colleague or you are also taking notes. Explain what will happen to the notes as well. Explain feedback arrangements. Maybe tell them a bit about why you chose this particular group of people in order to begin to introduce them. While I am going through all this, usually with a prepared statement, I often simultaneously share blank name cards on which participants can write how they want to be known during the discussion. They can even use coloured pens and decorate these if you feel that would work.

Group dynamics: from forming to mourning

For many focus groups, the participants will need to overcome a degree of awkwardness and anxiety before they feel comfortable to talk in front of, and then to, each other. Your job is to facilitate this through building trust and rapport within the group. Helen Finch, Jane Lewis and Caroline Turley (2014), drawing on previous research from Tuckman and Jenson (1977), have identified a number of stages that group formation goes through and found this a useful way for thinking about focus groups. In the *forming* stage, participants are somewhat anxious and guarded, slow to talk much, unsure of how they will be received, often trying not to dominate the conversation or nervous to speak up at all. In the *storming* phase, there is some tension and aloofness from some members of the group, while others are keen to get their voices heard as soon as possible. The *norming* phase happens when the group begins to settle down, they have learned the rules and norms via your moderating practice, are listening to each other, being kind, giving space for each other and no one is dominating too much. Things start to settle down.

The *performing* stage is interactive; participants have forgotten they are in a focus group and are simply enjoying the conversation. Here the responses are directed to each other rather than all being aimed at you. This is the stage when the most challenging topics can be tackled. Finally, the *adjourning and mourning* phases occur as you move towards a sense of an ending (Finch et al 2014: 215–17). Your role here is to create a sense that this is not the time to start whole new discussions. You also need to think about how to manage the departing. Participants often find it difficult to relinquish their role in a focus group, so have a clear sense of how you will end and address the fact that people may have questions or want to talk to you or each other privately. Maybe give them an email address so that they can come back to you within a specific time period. Or have a five-minute call back a week later where you ask them if there is anything else they need to address. However, this should not be an opportunity to revisit the whole discussion unless you are designing it as an interview (see Chapter 4).

FOR YOUR TOOLKIT

Groups may go through stages of forming, storming, norming, performing, adjourning and mourning (Finch et al 2014). During the focus group, and when you interpret the data, be conscious what dynamics are shaping the discussion at any time.

In practice, of course, the phases will overlap or not occur at all. They are a heuristic device for thinking about the extent to which the focus group is yielding diverse insights, reflections and detail, dynamic responses and spontaneity, disagreement or consensus. When you interpret the data later, be aware of the dynamics of the group at the time. You cannot conclude, for example, that everyone agreed about something unless you gave them a chance to give alternative opinions. You cannot conclude that they did not have much to say on a particular point if you only raised it at the beginning, at the forming stage, and not again when they had started to talk more, at the performing stage.

Creating and maintaining a dynamic group

Our experiences in using the technique indicate that restricting participants to the topic of the researcher's interest constrains creativity and encourages conformity and strategic biases. (Nyumba et al 2018: 29)

To facilitate a discussion, as opposed to what can feel like a collection of one-to-one interviews, address the whole group when introducing each new topic or section. Always look at the person speaking, but also look around from time to time using body language to illustrate that you were hoping for a response from others. This way you can use the group dynamics to explore emerging themes, to examine the diversity of views and experiences, and to challenge consensus and social norms. Keep an eye on the body language of the group and judge when it is appropriate to do more content mapping (maybe asking other members of the group for more insights) and when to do more mining, to explore in detail the response from one person. You will need to judge when to move on to a new topic or exercise, when to follow the participants' lead, or when to stick to your agenda.

> ## FOR YOUR TOOLKIT
>
> Try to enable fairly balanced participation, without destroying the natural dynamic of the group, and work gently towards the sense of an ending.

If one person tends to be talking too much or is disruptive, there are several techniques you can use, such as leaning back, looking away a little, appealing to other participants using hand gestures and eye contact. Eventually you may have to remind people that you are here to get everyone's views; perhaps tactfully say something like: 'I could listen to you forever. It is really fascinating but we must give other people the chance to come in on this, I think.'

Some people will say more than others, and it is important not to kill the dynamic by imposing equal time for responses, but try to ensure everyone has at least been given the opportunity to regularly contribute. It is also important not to let someone stay silent for too long, as it can become a habit. Given the implicit contract to take part in a discussion and that people can be nervous about speaking up unless they are addressed, it is OK to turn to people and say 'I just want to give you the opportunity to come in on this,' or 'Is there anything else that you wanted to go back to?' I will often randomly name a few participants and ask 'What do you think?' This would include both those who have spoken and those who have spoken less, so that it is not too obvious that I am addressing the ones who have been quiet. In my focus group training workshops, quiet people almost always tell me they appreciate being given the explicit opportunity to speak up.

As with one-to-one interviews (Chapter 4), you will need time to bring the conversation to a close. Try to end on a positive or constructive note that focuses on what the focus group has achieved. Use phrases such as: 'This has been great, thank you. We've had a fascinating discussion and we've explored some really interesting areas, such as [x], [x] and [x]. Is there anything that I've missed here that's really important?' Or perhaps ask, in a more directive way, 'What are the key messages from today that we can build on or work with?' It can be useful to do this as an exercise. It is important that this final discussion uses examples and is not a summary of the entire discussion, otherwise people whose points you overlooked will feel left out. If you invite final questions or comments, make sure you allow time for the responses. Finally reaffirm what will happen next, confidentiality and feedback arrangements.

Creative and participatory exercises

Creative approaches are covered in full in Chapter 7; here, I consider their role in focus groups and suggest a few examples. Exercises can be fun, enlivening a discussion and getting everyone talking. They can help to focus a discussion on a particular topic, especially one that is abstract, sensitive or difficult to talk about. They can be a useful way of gathering rich detail, as participants dig deeply into the complexity and diversity of an issue. They can also simply be a way of making sure every participant has an opportunity to take part. If you use any, please be clear what its role is in your research. Perhaps have some in your discussion guide toolkit to use if you need to, but don't use them if the need doesn't arise. Here are some examples.

Vignettes are hypothetical situations, or fictitious cases, short stories or accounts, that participants discuss in detail. They are an elaborate way of starting a discussion with 'Imagine if …'. They provide a common focus for a discussion that might otherwise have been too emotive or abstract or complex, such as prostate cancer (Gram et al 2023). Talking about other people can help overcome taboos or discomfort. Alice Dutton and Kandazi Sisya (2024) used vignettes in their focus groups with young people to explore which situations were recognised as abusive and what they would do about it. Vignettes are good for focusing on norms and to encourage reflection. But, we cannot conclude this is actually what people *would do* or *did* in these circumstances. For that, attention must return to the participants in the group.

Projective techniques enable participants to voice things that were implicit, hidden, or subconscious. They lead to some fun and imaginative discussions. Examples include: What kind of image comes to mind when you think of your illness? If you were asked to describe your organisation as an animal, what animal would you choose? What does this image make you think of/feel? Draw me a picture of a politician. Write down three words that come to mind when you think of a politician (perhaps use sticky notes that can be clustered into types).

You can ask participants to work in small groups of two or three and talk to each other while making something relevant out of play bricks or dough or drawing on sticky notes. You can ask participants to draw and talk about geographical maps, life maps, timelines. You can make posters together. You can ask people to write something on a sticky note and then together put them into themes; watch videos and discuss; do a quiz, usually for fun. You can do brainstorming, in the mapping stage. Use sticky notes to write down what they think you forgot to cover today. Whatever you do, the goal is usually to generate discussion not to assess their performance or analyse what they produced in the moment (see Chapter 7).

FOR YOUR TOOLKIT

Creative and participatory approaches can be fun, can help focus discussion for a specific topic, can yield rich detail, can ensure participants all take part, or can be useful for abstract notions or sensitive topics. Use them purposefully.

A word of caution: if you go round the group asking a question in turn, participants may follow each other's lead. Once the first person describes their organisation in a negative way, for example, the others will be primed to follow. You can either do it again asking next for a more positive angle (for complexity's sake), or you can ask everyone to think and note down something before they speak, to rule out some of the influence of others. Either way, your job is to explore balanced views, complexity, richness, contradictions (and perhaps taboos, norms, and ambivalences), not just off-the-cuff responses.

A note on transcribing and analysing

Focus group discussions can take six to eight times as long to transcribe as to record, although new developments in technology are making this easier all the time. Remember to cost in time for this when quoting for your project. Transcribing is a useful time for you to reflect on what has been said. In the spirit of the iterative-inductive approach that I have advanced in this book, I recommend transcribing as soon as possible so that you can learn from each group in terms of emergent themes, as well as what is working well and not so well. Transcriptions normally should be verbatim not paraphrased and should include silences, laughter, hesitations, ers and ums, but not usually timed pauses (as in conversational analysis). Include the words of the moderator and facilitator and anyone else who participated. It will probably be difficult or impossible to attribute individual quotes to identified participants but at least mention what you can (for example male, female, patient, carer, or whoever). This is when blended accounts and free direct speech become useful (Chapter 3).

FOR YOUR TOOLKIT
The group is more than the sum of its parts and therefore the group and its dynamic and progress must be the unit of analysis.

Analysis is discussed at length in Chapters 8 and 9. A key point with focus groups is that the group is more than the sum of its parts and therefore the group must be the unit of analysis. By that I mean, whenever making sense of anything that has come from focus group discussions, one needs to note the moment at which this arose. Was it a time when people had reached consensus, was there a lot of disagreement, was it a period when people were saying very little and just a few strong voices were able to be heard? Had you given the opportunity for people to change their minds or the direction of the discussion, to explore alternative viewpoints for balance and complexity? Focus group analysis needs to recognise that opinions, attitudes and accounts are always somewhat socially produced (Tonkiss 2012).

Doing things differently

Despite all that has been said, focus groups can be used differently: with larger groups, with small groups, to create a comfortable and cosy atmosphere, to correct power imbalances, to be respectful, and to create a safe space for listening and hearing. This is especially important when doing research with vulnerable groups, with children, and on sensitive and emotive issues (for example, Dutton and Sisya 2024). Here discussion group methodology is more collaborative and participatory than described earlier (see Chapters 6 and 7). Sara Owen (2001), in addressing 'practical, methodological and ethical dilemmas of conducting focus groups with vulnerable clients', elucidates this in more detail than I can achieve here, but I will try to do justice to some of her main points.

> **FOR YOUR TOOLKIT**
> Focus groups can be used to create a comfortable and cosy atmosphere, to balance power imbalances, to be respectful, and to create a safe space for listening and hearing. This is especially important when doing research with vulnerable groups, with children, and on sensitive and emotive issues.

First, you may not have a choice about who to include; access may be limited to already existing groups. Or you may choose to talk to people who already know each other, or at least know *of* each other, to help create a comfortable atmosphere where participants feel safe (O'Reilly 2012a). You might prefer to have smaller numbers of people in the group. In ethnographic research (Chapter 6), we often share conversations in small groups without needing to ask ourselves 'Is this a focus group?' We free ourselves up from the constraints of what we might call a traditional market research approach by simply thinking about what works for whom under what conditions. Certainly, when working with children, small groups are preferable to one-to-one interviews.

How you gain access to your participants is another issue. Much research uses gatekeepers, which can be both useful and problematic. Think carefully about who has given you access and how they introduced you. Try to make sure that the group understands what you are doing, what you hope to achieve and your ethical and participatory approach to research. Owen (2001) used focus groups to explore the perspectives of women with serious and enduring mental health problems who were currently receiving care and support within a specific service. She found it difficult to persuade women to take part, and had to rethink seating arrangements, who could not be included because of access issues and unwillingness, venue, and how to navigate the focus groups in practice.

Be realistic about how long access will take and get advice from those who understand the situation well. Previously established groups of people can have their own internal power dynamics and norms shaped by old arguments, long-held assumptions and hard-won agreements. How dynamic and interactive can a focus group be in such circumstances? Try to meet your participants before the discussion group and get to know them a little, to build trust and rapport (Owen 2001). Take from your toolkit the method of casual conversations (Chapter 6). If you can't do that, then try to get to know participants another way, through phone calls or online media, or at least to get to know *about* their lives via someone who knows better. Familiarity lends a feeling of security. Owen (2001) said that because of the nature of their social disabilities, many women she talked with had a poor concentration span, were experiencing auditory hallucinations, and had low self-confidence and self-esteem – all factors that made eliciting their views difficult. She kept direct questioning to a minimum and let the companionship within groups do its work where possible.

When working on sensitive topics or with vulnerable groups or children, consider the venue carefully. Is it familiar and comfortable? How will they get there? Think about how and where people will sit, and how comfortable they will be. There are those who may want to get up and stretch or move around or even want to stand for the duration. Will you have support staff or carers in the room? Have you thought carefully about their role in the discussion? You can always take your discussion to a natural setting, as when Melisa Duque (Pink et al 2022: 169) organised a workshopping event in a charity shop with volunteers making explicit their practices of sorting and revaluing the second-hand donations.

Market research groups and traditional approaches can feel rather detached, trying to be naively objective, and they use language that reflects this. Even the word 'focus group' can sound somewhat daunting and controlling. Similarly, words like 'moderator' and 'facilitator' might need thinking about, as well as the wording in your discussion guide itself. At all times, take advice from those who are more experienced than you. Think carefully about how you approach people; consider asking for a chat or a get-together to talk things through in a bit more depth. Make it clear it is your participants who are the experts and that you just want to hear from them in the way that suits them best. Design the discussion guide to include more creative and participatory approaches that treat the participants as active in the research, rather than as subjects responding to your questions.

When navigating the discussion itself, try to make it feel more like a friendly sharing of views than an extraction of information. If you have put some effort into getting to know your participants or at least about them and their experiences, then you will be able to empathise without being patronising. If working with particularly vulnerable groups or on particularly sensitive topics, then be sure that you have relevant experience and training. It is also becoming more common, especially in applied research, to train participants with lived experience to run the discussion groups themselves (usually with the researcher also present).

The sort of group discussion we are talking about here is more about security and safety and creating a comfortable environment than it is about having a group conversation. You are using a group as a way to learn from and with participants rather than generating a creative dynamic situation that focus groups normally offer. Do not expect to reach the performing stage:

> In all the focus groups the women mainly directed their comments to me and were often reluctant to discuss issues amongst themselves. This was possibly a reflection of the women's poor communication and social skills, and their lack of experience of sharing ideas in a group. (Owen 2001: 655)

You might need to be even more responsive, reflexive, and flexible than described in the earlier sections of this chapter. Remember that it is OK for people to change their minds, to have diverse views, to be contradictory, and even to be emotional at times. However, try to avoid distress and try to avoid too much disclosure where it is not relevant, or shared. Move on quickly where you need to, perhaps by introducing a creative exercise, and try to end on a constructive note, as discussed earlier. But remember, even silences, jokes and dismissive responses can be revealing: they tell you what matters to people and help you do a better discussion group next time (using reflexive practice; Chapter 3).

As Owen (2001) describes, you may need to permit some unexpected behaviours like people leaving the room, or withdrawing for a while and becoming passive. You should not force interaction if the group doesn't work as a group. It is OK to go around the group in turn to encourage contributions from reticent people, but always be sensitive and careful. Always observe behaviours and learn from them. And remember that the power balances do exist and you will not be able to entirely cancel these out, but losing control of the discussion a little bit can be a positive thing.

Finally, you should not try to be a therapist. By all means have advice to give people when you are finished, know who they can turn to, and know of any regulations you must adhere to. But you should try not to turn the session into a therapy session.

FOR YOUR TOOLKIT

Do not be constrained by the conventional definition of a focus group; sampling, group size, access, venue, navigating the discussion group, all require extra thought when working with some groups and topics.

Given the plethora of research and writing on doing research with children, I raise a few key issues here before directing you to further reading at the end of the chapter. It would be unusual to interview children one-to-one until they have reached 16 to 18 years of age. Groups work well with children but usually they would be much smaller groups than described earlier (O'Reilly 2009, 2012a). As a rule, the younger the children, the smaller the group, and the shorter concentration span they will have. With children, you will always gain access through gatekeepers and therefore must be careful what consent has been given on their behalf and what understanding the children themselves have. You will always appear somewhat powerful and will need to find ways to put children at their ease and give them a sense of control in the situation. Children are unlikely to understand words like moderator, facilitator, and focus group. Creative and participatory methods are useful when working with children. As I said, they will have a shorter concentration span than older people and so mixing it up with a different variety of exercises and activities is a good idea. The British Heart Foundation has a lot of experience of research with children and will take children on trips and combine doing fun things like going to the zoo with spending time in a classroom talking about things that are relevant to them and doing short creative exercises. Think about how long you can expect children to sit and think carefully about the language you use.

Final thoughts

Overall, running a focus group involves managing a conversation, remembering what has come up that you might want to return to, deciding what to address next, thinking about people who were quiet or noisy and how to deal with that, remembering to allow time for people to change their minds, and to ensure you gather details, richness and complexity. It is exhausting and requires considerable skill. But focus groups and discussion groups are enjoyable when they work well; they are animated, sometimes moving, often revelatory (perhaps even revolutionary), as participants get lost in the conversation and forget they are taking part in research. Enjoy them.

Speaking of focus groups

'The stuff that came up in this group discussion was amazing – lots of things I hadn't even considered before.'

'One person started to tell me her life story and the others were getting bored so I told her she has a fascinating life and I wish I could hear more but we must get on with the discussion because we've only got a certain amount of time. Maybe I could also do one-to-one interviews with some people.'

'Given some of the things I wanted to ask only required short answers, I decided to add a little survey to my project design – that way the discussion group could focus on sharing views.'

'That ended up in an argument! I'm going to have to think a bit more carefully about who I put together.'

'I think I've done enough focus groups. I've got a good sense of the broad diversity of responses now.'

Taking things further

Key sources on focus groups include, in date order, Morgan (1988, 1993), Krueger (1994) and Kitzinger (1995). Busetto et al (2020) offer a compact **introduction**. Krueger and Casey (2015) bring everything up to date with lots of practical advice including emerging areas such as **internet** focus groups. For a more in-depth **origin** story see Berg and Lune (2012). To read more about **empowerment**, feminist research and focus groups see Madriz (2000) and Wilkinson (1998, 1999). There is a wonderful project in Wales called Lleisiau Bach Little Voices (2022); visit their website for more about participatory action research and **child-led research**. The chapter 'Focus Groups' by Finch et al (2014) is a fabulous resource for **practical** issues. I am indebted to them for when I first designed my own training courses. For an interesting discussion of methodological issues that arise when conducting focus groups in **the majority world**, developing countries, or the global South, see Jakobsen (2012). For exciting new directions see Pink and colleagues' (2022: 160–75) long discussion of **workshopping**, including workshops as small 'kitchen-table' type gatherings, workshops framed by uncertainty, and collaborative workshops that fully engage reflexive practice. Samardzic and colleagues (2023) discuss **online focus groups** for **sensitive issues**, and cover platform choice, security, connection and communication issues, and end with recommendations.

Listen to the related episode for this chapter on
Qualitative Research Methods for Everyone podcast:

6

Being ethnographic

What this chapter is about

The aim of this chapter is to give you the tools to draw on ethnographic methodology and methods as and when required to pursue good, interpretive, qualitative research. I start with a brief review of where ethnography began, its foundational narrative, and then examine its many developments and adaptations through visual and sensory ethnography to applied and focused approaches. I then revise ethnography's basic key principles and emphasise what is important to hang on to when adopting and adapting ethnographic methodology. I am expecting most of my readers to *not* have time to commit to a conventional (long-term, fully immersive) ethnography but to adapt the approach. I therefore discuss what remains important despite the methods chosen and think about how conventional approaches can be adapted for contemporary themes and research contexts.

> **FOR YOUR TOOLKIT**
> Ethnography evolves in design as the study progresses, but always involves sustained personal interaction in human lives (listening, hearing, and sharing); draws flexibly and creatively on methods as appropriate; takes time to build trust, rapport and understandings; and recognises the role of structures and agency and their intersection in practice over time. It is ethical and reflexive (O'Reilly 2012a).

Early ethnography was inspirational and revolutionary in terms of introducing us to the ground-breaking notion of participant observation as a social scientific research method. The ethnographers were conscientious, devoted scientists who contributed a great deal of time and effort in their pursuit of rich, complex understandings of communities and lives that were previously strange to the Western world. But they also made mistakes or overlooked issues that now rightly concern us (they were often positivist, lacked reflexivity, focused on the exotic other, ignored wider powers and geography, and shared some deep-seated biases; Asad 1973; Clifford and Marcus 1986; Clifford 1988). They established a tradition that is difficult to challenge: the tradition of the lone (often male) traveller making an arduous journey to a distant land where they remained for years to understand an entire (isolated) community (Wall 2015).

There have been numerous advances. Ethnographers have learned from interpretivist philosophies, attend to wider influences, and aim to be reflexive and ethical. We have seen the development of adjectival ethnographies (such as auto, sensory, visual, and internet ethnographies; see Box 6.1), which in turn have caused us to think about the role of each in people's lives, as well as their role in our interpretations and thus in methodology and methods.

FOR YOUR TOOLKIT

With the development of a plethora of adjectival ethnographies (such as visual, mobile, internet, and focused ethnographies) it is crucial to recall ethnography's key principles and their basic logic.

More recently still, we have witnessed the adaptation of ethnography for contemporary settings and issues. First anthropology (or ethnography) 'came home' to analyse their own societies and cultures, then it was used in part-time, temporary settings for issues and interests that cannot be attributed to an entire community or group. Ethnography became mobile and multi-sited (Box 6.3). We saw the rise of more adjectival ethnographies such as focused ethnography, and corollary criticisms that some of this cannot even be considered ethnography (for example, Marcus 2012). It is essential now to consider what remain the key principles and the logic behind them, and how they can be addressed for contemporary settings.

Where we started: the foundational narrative

Early ethnography was founded on a desire to challenge received approaches to knowledge and to yield more complex and contextual understandings of other ways of life than those proposed by missionaries, travellers, adventurers, and scientists. Much has changed since its inception but, in a literal sense, the key principles of ethnography within anthropology remain *fundamental* and it is these principles I want to begin by emphasising. Further, despite the acknowledgement that Bronislaw Malinowski was by no means the only or first anthropologist to travel to distant lands, his work has become something of a foundational myth for anthropological ethnography (O'Reilly 2015), especially because of the elaboration of his methods in *Argonauts of the Western Pacific* (Malinowski, 1922).

FOR YOUR TOOLKIT

Bronislaw Malinowski's renowned chapter in *Argonauts of the Western Pacific* (1922) is an eloquent, thoughtful and didactic way to recall ethnography's roots, and has become something of a foundational myth for anthropological ethnography.

Malinowski was a Polish aristocrat born in 1884, who studied maths, law and physics before going on to study anthropology at the London School of Economics and Political Science in the UK. He embarked on fieldwork in the Trobriand Islands, Melanesia, in 1914 and famously spent years there learning the language and studying those he called 'the natives'. This was a time of, usually male, adventurers travelling the world discovering new peoples and places, missionaries spreading the gospel in far lands, and colonial administrators travelling to distant places to help acquire them. In this context, Malinowski, while conditioned into a certain positivist, masculine, Western elitist way of thinking, was radical in arguing that rather than merely sensationalise and exoticise the peoples they were meeting, it would be better to spend time among them to witness and share in their lives, habits, and practices within the context of their own worldview and environment.

FOR YOUR TOOLKIT

Malinowski was radical in arguing that we could best learn about other lives by spending time with them, witnessing and sharing in their lives, habits, and practices within the context of their own worldview and environment.

Malinowski argued that rather than analysing exotic artefacts from a distance (known as armchair theorising) ethnographers should spend time with 'the natives' personally to understand their lives within the context of their cultures and how they feel and think, because: 'Every human culture gives its members a definite vision of the world, a definite *zest* for life' (Malinowski 1922: 517, emphasis in original). He says that the White residents who had 'lived for years in the place with constant opportunities of observing the natives and communicating with them ... were full of the biased and pre-judged opinions inevitable in the average, practical man' (Malinowski 1922: 5). Philosophy of social science has helped us understand this using the language of interpretivism, and descriptive, interpretive and structured phenomenology. We also understand the centrality of time. Contemporary ethnography does not seek the faddish news story; it is long, arduous, committed and engaged (Scheper-Hughes 2004; Puddephatt et al 2009; O'Reilly 2015). Ethnography, Christine Hine (2000: 21) says, is sustained and involved, 'a way of seeing through participants' eyes'.

What we now call 'participant observation' (the sine qua non of the ethnographer's toolkit) was proposed by Malinowski, although he didn't use that term. Instead, he spoke of taking your time, 'camping right in the village' and sharing in the 'natural discourse' of others, as well as observing the daily rituals and intimate details of life such as 'toilet, cooking, taking of meals'. His method was about being there and sharing in the atmosphere of life. It took time, and commitment, and was sometimes uncomfortable. But its purpose was to avoid superficial and subjective understandings. Ethnographers today would still emphasise the role of both observing and participating, of taking time for participants to get used to you, of learning through sharing, and being free to ask questions as and when they arise.

We might well criticise Malinowski (as with other anthropologists of his time, some of whom spread diseases) for his total lack of awareness of any effects of his presence on the community. He had what we would now understand as a naive understanding of objectivity in his pursuit of independent facts. Later amendments to the ethnographic gaze have included attention to reflexivity as practice (Chapter 3), and to the embodied and immersive nature of the endeavour (Boellstorff et al 2012: 1). There is also a somewhat denigratory tone in Malinowski's work, that became even more noticeable when his diary was published posthumously in 1967. We can critique, and try to learn from his mistakes, while still being impressed by what he achieved given his specific time and context.

For Malinowski (1922: 11), scientific fieldwork had three aims: to describe the customs and traditions, the institutions, the structure, the skeleton of the tribe; to give this flesh and blood by describing how daily life was actually carried out, 'the imponderabilia of actual life'; to record typical ways of thinking and feeling associated with the institutions and culture. In the language of sociological theory that has since been developed we could say that Malinowski already identified the relevance of structures, actions, and meanings, and intimated practice theory (see Chapter 1). As Paul Willis and Mats Trondman (2021) have more recently argued, good ethnographers should now (still) gather information on people's feelings, thoughts and experiences (pay attention to agency); on institutions, patterns, and norms (pay attention to structures); and on artefacts and their use (pay attention to cultural products). The methodology of ethnography says that all individuals are located in wider contexts (cultures, settings, histories, geographies), do things they cannot always talk about or may have never reflected on, are motivated by desires and wishes that are themselves shaped by their view of the world, and these views (in the context of their backgrounds, experiences, and communities) will shape what they do and how they live.

Malinowski, and others like him, also understood that some things would be seen rather than heard, hence the need for observation. And he proposed the idea of sharing conversations rather than only doing interviews with people, of talking with them about things as, or just after, they happened while it is fresh in their minds and they are excited about it. Contemporary ethnography uses both casual and impromptu conversations as well as in-depth interviews, and a key feature of ethnography even now is that talking and understanding take place as things occur and in the context of daily life. Ethnographers also tread carefully, learning when to listen, when to talk and ask questions, when to keep pressing for more information, and when to shut up (Madden 2010: 65). Contemporary ethnography has also learned to interpret people's stories and accounts, because people reconstruct events through memory, narrative, and sharing folk tales (Fetterman 2010; O'Reilly 2015; Lumsden 2019; see also Chapter 4).

Malinowski's concept of foreshadowed problems is his way of conceptualising what I have described in Chapter 2 as holding theory lightly, letting it act as inspiration rather than burden you with preconceived ideas. His was not a naive form of inductivism, that saw the mind as a blank slate, but he did argue that theory and actual research should be 'separated both in time and conditions of work' (Malinowski 1922: 9). Now we use theory to sensitise, but in an iterative way, discarding those that do not enlighten, adapting those that offer some insight, and developing new ones as research progresses (see Chapter 2). Contemporary ethnography also seeks theoretical rather than (only) empirical generalisations (O'Reilly 2009; Candea and Yarrow 2023).

Malinowski's approach was *holistic*: not selecting exotic and shocking things for special attention but also noting the trivial, daily, and banal. Ethnographers retain this attention to the ways in which small issues and seemingly unimportant pastimes are all interconnected in the internal dynamics of a society. 'Ethnographic research is fundamentally a holistic project; we seek to understand shared practices, meanings, and social contexts, and the interrelations among them' (Boellstorff et al 2012: 67). But Malinowski's holism, as we can see when he describes the tribe as a body, also attempted to understand a whole 'tribe' or community, in a bounded *functionalist* way. We now understand functionalism's limits with respect to understanding wider forces, history and change.

Box 6.1: Interpretive, critical, public, applied, sensory, and visual ethnography: drug addiction and homelessness

Philippe Bourgois and Jeff Schonberg (2009), *Righteous Dopefiend*
This ethnographic study, through its numerous and graphic photographs, texts, quotations and field notes, gives the reader/viewer a vicarious experience of drug addiction and homelessness in the US today. It is based on extensive fieldwork conducted between 1994 and 2006, during which the authors 'became part of the daily lives of several dozen homeless heroin injectors who sought shelter in the dead-end alleyways, storage lots, vacant factories, broken-down cars, and overgrown highway embankments surrounding Edgewater Boulevard (not its real name), the main thoroughfare serving San Francisco's sprawling, semi-derelict, warehouse and shipyard district'. (Bourgois and Schonberg 2009: 4)

The analysis is threaded through the stories and accounts, and is interpretive, analytical, and critical. It invokes both agency and structural context, power and powerlessness, as illustrated in some final words:

At the turn of the 21st-century, most San Franciscans earned more money and lived in more expensive houses than the residents of almost any other metropolis in the world. The streets of their city, however, overflowed with people in visible physical distress who were incapable of paying for minimal shelter and food. The burden of lumpenization is even more extreme, painful and violent in non-industrialised, poor countries that are transitioning into neoliberalism … Anthropology in the early twenty-first century cannot physically, ethically or emotionally escape the hardship of the lives of its traditional research subjects' (Bourgois and Schonberg 2009: 320)

The authors call this critically applied public anthropology. One might also call it visual ethnography or sensory ethnography. It is certainly powerful and moving.

Where we are now: contemporary (adjectival) ethnographies

There have been many developments in ethnography (O'Reilly 2015). Some are in response to macro-level societal changes, such as the way global ethnography studies the relationship between globalisation and local community life (Burawoy et al 2000), and multi-sited ethnography adapts the methodology for a world that is increasingly interconnected (Hannerz 2003; Falzon 2009). Visual ethnography grew in response to the ongoing development of technologies for recording visual data (for example, Pink 2007). Digital and virtual ethnographies were designed to understand how the spread of digital technologies is leading to new forms of social living (for example, Hine 2000; Horst and Miller 2012). Sensory and design ethnography have responded to developing theoretical understandings of social life (Pink 2009; Pink et al 2022). Each considers in detail the implications of social change for contemporary ethnographic practice (Horst and Miller 2012), but 'do not abruptly challenge the core principles of traditional ethnography that guide practical and methodical choices' (O'Reilly 2015: 5).

FOR YOUR TOOLKIT
Contemporary approaches to ethnography contemplate the implications of social and technological change for contemporary ethnographic practice.

Nevertheless, these approaches do take ethnography forward and address criticisms and problems with the traditional approach. For Michael Burawoy (2000: 1), global ethnography challenges the functionalist holism of traditional approaches and (re)locates societies within the broader contexts of history, colonialism, and power. It also investigates the relationship between local and global power and knowledge, examining the lived experience of globalisation, how global forces are felt, experienced, mobilised, or resisted (Tsing 2005). Global ethnography also examines cultures of colonialism and colonial legacies (Crang and Cook 2007; O'Reilly 2015).

For Sarah Pink (2007: 24), while the goal is always a close 'understanding of the worlds that other people live in', visual technologies provided a critique of the 'visual realism' of earlier ethnographies and the unquestioned assumption that the 'camera never lies' (even as ethnographers sometimes reconstructed events as part of their writing up; O'Reilly 2012a). Many contemporary creative and participatory approaches first emerged alongside the development of visual ethnography (Box 6.1).

For Dhiraj Murthy (2008: 838), ethnography still tells social stories; they are just understood, mediated and communicated through slightly altered means.

For Tom Boellstorff (2008), virtual cultures should still be examined through participation in that virtual culture on its own terms, and the ethnographer should still be there in person, 'even when that embodiment is in the form of an avatar' (Boellstorff et al 2012: 1). For Hine (2000), virtual worlds are full of cultural activity and interaction that can be studied as sites of interest or as a facet of people's daily lived experiences.

Applying ethnography

Ethnography (along with other qualitative research methods) is increasingly being used in applied settings to help build an evidence base for actions, policies and interventions, especially in settings such as health, medicine, policing, social work and education (O'Reilly 2012a), or the private sector (Ladner 2014). As Lauren Cubellis and colleagues (2021) note, ethnography has an immense value in terms of understanding how norms and rules play out in practice; it is therefore useful for yielding insights that are more likely to work than understandings based on more positivist approaches (see also Hughes et al 2022), or that ignore the implicit and unstated, habitual and practical knowledge. Crucially, ethnography goes beyond what individuals say to what they actually do, including thinking about things that are difficult to talk about or difficult to express. Ethnography is thus useful for understanding the interrelationship of behaviour and context, over time.

> **FOR YOUR TOOLKIT**
> Ethnography has immense value in terms of understanding how norms and rules play out in practice; it is therefore useful for yielding insights that are more likely to work than approaches that ignore the implicit and unstated, the habitual and practical.

There have been numerous attempts to distinguish ethnography in applied fields from anthropological and sociological ethnography, leading to yet more adjectival ethnographies such as educational ethnography, organisational ethnography and medical ethnography. Other adjectives have been developed to conceptualise the difficulties of achieving the lone traveller, long-term immersion that traditional ethnographies led us to expect. For example, there have been 'insider' ethnographies (undertaken by those who are familiar with a culture or group), 'ethnography at home' (no long-distance travel involved) and autoethnography (acknowledges that we can also learn from our own experiences) (O'Reilly 2009; Denzin 2013). There are also diverse suggestions for adapting ethnography, such as focused ethnography (Knoblauch 2005; Pelto 2013; Wall 2015; Rashid et al 2019), 'hanging out' (Nair 2021), and even evaluative, short-term *and* multi-sited ethnography (Tevington et al 2023). There are also activist ethnographies, engaged and committed ethnographies (for example, Stuesse 2016), and militant ethnographies (Scheper-Hughes 2004).

Implicit in the rise of all these adjectival ethnographies is that there is some sort of pure ethnography that researchers are amending in order to do ethnography with a difference. But as Ulf Hannerz (2003: 202) argued:

> the hegemony of the (traditional) model seems remarkable since it is fairly clear that a great many anthropologists, especially those no longer in the first phase of their careers, have long, but perhaps a bit more discreetly, been engaging in a greater variety of spatial and temporal practices as they have gone about their research.

We do not need to use these adjectives to put up barriers between ourselves and others, but we can use them to think creatively and imaginatively about ethnography: 'the wonders of our holism means that the most insightful work we do is that which does not limit our scholarly boundaries' (Shah 2017: 52).

FOR YOUR TOOLKIT

To define something as ethnographic involves respecting its enduring principles and logic rather than being constrained by a traditional approach.

Ten enduring key principles

Ethnography is informed by an ethnographic sensibility not by a set time in the field or given methods. There is no official set of regulations by which ethnographic research can be judged as worthy or correct (other than individual reviewers, readers and editors), but taking all the aforementioned into account, and drawing on decades of experience using and teaching ethnography, I have identified ten enduring key principles for ethnography: be iterative-inductive; participate and observe; remember the context; share conversations; be flexible, creative and responsive with methods; take time; build trust and rapport; analyse social change; be ethical; and engage in reflexive practice. I will address the logic behind each of these ten enduring principles in turn.

Principle one: be iterative-inductive

Principle one is based on the logic that researchers do not want to impose their view of the world onto their ways of seeing. It involves constantly iterating between being inductive and deductive, with an inductive approach retaining the upper hand (see Chapter 1). Ethnography is in a unique position to do this well: ethnographers dip their toes into the field, learn a little, adapt as they go, talk to different people, go to different places, ask different questions as they learn more, and become 'omnivorous' in 'building up a skein of material whose import is emergent and changing' (2001: 34). Ethnography is adaptive; it involves learning on the job in a process 'that allows for ... an expansive and continual process of refining reasonable explanations based on subsequent encounters in the field' (Cubellis et al 2021: 8).

> **FOR YOUR TOOLKIT**
>
> Ethnography is in a unique position to be iterative-inductive; it is specifically designed to learn as you go.

For Willis and Trondman (2021), a key tenet of ethnography is the focus on lived experiences before theory: to bring theory in later and gently. Nevertheless, ethnography needs a guiding theoretical problem or general area of interest to guide ethnographic practice. These are inspired by (perhaps lay) theoretical ideas about the world, and are not rigid or fixed, but should be adapted as research progresses. For Malinowski, preconceived ideas were pernicious, but foreshadowed problems help to focus the attention, as long as they can be amended as one learns more about the world. Willis and Trondman (2021) argue for leaving theories aside and listening first; this is not to pretend we have no theories, nor to deny them, but to not let them close our eyes, shut our minds, or prevent us from being open to new insights. Ethnography needs to have a flexible design (Box 6.4; see also Chapter 1) as a way of ensuring that we can incorporate what we learn as we go along.

Principle two: participate and observe

Principle two is based on the understanding that people enact, practise, or perform social structures (including norms and policies) through their agency, in interaction (O'Reilly 2012b; Cubellis et al 2021; Willis and Trondman 2021; Hughes et al 2022), that people cannot always explain what they are doing, and that some things are not easily, or permitted to be, talked about. In this section, I cover participant observation as practical knowledge, learning a linguistic and cultural language, issues of access, making selections, the role of key events, the role of observations, data creation and collection, and writing reflexive field notes.

Participant observation is about feeling your way, doing, being, living, and sharing. It can make us uncomfortable, awkward and strange, but this is also its strength:

> True, anatomical knowledge is not usually a precondition for 'correct' walking. But when the ground beneath our feet is always shaking, we need a crutch. As social scientists we are thrown off balance by our presence in the world we study, by absorption in the society we observe, by dwelling alongside those we make 'other'. (Burawoy 1998: 4)

Being there when things happen will enable people to talk more easily because they are excited and engaged; they will reveal disagreements and ambivalences, complex negotiations, and solutions (Fetterman 2010). You can also learn yourself, through participation, experiencing things you can reflect on or talk about later with participants, enabling practical knowledge (Rock 2001).

> **FOR YOUR TOOLKIT**
>
> Participant observation is the sine qua non of ethnography and involves learning through being there, sharing, doing, observing actions, and practical knowledge.

Participant observation is an archetypal oxymoron. Participating requires the time and effort to gain access, build rapport, fit in, while also initiating conversations, and addressing research questions. It is involved and messy (Adler and Adler 2007; Williksen 2009). Observation attempts to be more detached and distanced, to impose order. But participation and observation have a dialectical relationship to each other in the practice of ethnography, with the two elements working together to produce novel insights (O'Reilly 2012a). Participant observation is a potentially revolutionary praxis. As Alpa Shah (2017: 45) contends:

> [I]t forces us to question our theoretical presuppositions about the world, produce knowledge that is new, was confined to the margins, or was silenced. It is argued that participant observation is not merely a method of anthropology but is a form of production of knowledge through being and action; it is praxis, the process by which theory is dialectically produced and realized in action.

For Malinowski, learning the language of the group was crucial, but we now realise this also involves learning about how people think, the cultural language, and how that shapes the way the group sees the world. Some called this being socialised into the culture, and that was useful in thinking about how we all learn to be members of any given culture (O'Reilly 2012a, 2012b), but we now recognise this understanding is complicated, and that we must use reflexive practice.

Something that is discussed less in methods textbooks these days but remains relevant is the issue of access, or getting people to agree to take part in the research. In ethnography this, like ethical dilemmas and sampling, is ongoing and access must be negotiated for different groups, different people, and even different topics (O'Reilly 2009). It is crucial to consider the attributes of the setting or group, which you will learn more about as you go along. In turn, your own attributes will shape how you are seen and spoken to. Ethnographic accounts are full of stories of ethnographers having to tread carefully, making mistakes, and learning from them as they tread lightly on the path to rich insights (for example, Williksen 2009).

The process of gaining access itself provides insights into what the participants want you to see and what they do not, and how they understand your own role. Stumbling, making mistakes, taking time, and renegotiating access can be insightful as long as you engage healthily in reflexive practice (Whyte 1993; see also Chapter 3). Think carefully about how to explain what you are doing, how to word it, how to explain it, and how to ensure people have fully understood and are on board. Think carefully about any gatekeepers or key participants you might use to enable you to gain access (O'Reilly 2012a).

FOR YOUR TOOLKIT
Ethnography embraces a sophisticated approach to ongoing sampling (Chapter 2).

Making selections for participant observation follows the same logic as discussed in Chapter 2, except there is more opportunity in ethnography for a sophisticated approach to *ongoing sampling*. Ethnographers also need to think and plan carefully for how and when to include busy and key participants, people of high status, or people who are difficult to access (O'Reilly 2012a; Nair 2021). Often this is because we are interviewing them in their capacity as the *role* they represent rather than as fully-fledged members of the community (Chapter 4). During my research in Spain, I was not able to fully engage in participant observation with the chief of police, the British consulate, or the woman who ran the foreign residents' department, for example, but I wanted to include them, so I used interviews for these people (O'Reilly 2000, 2020a). Of course, participant observation can involve busy, high-status people, and we can spend hours chatting casually or doing things with them, but when it comes to interviewing them in their role suddenly the dynamics change (Mbohou and Tomkinson 2022).

> *As an aside,* do more in participant observation than you have to. This is the best way to demonstrate that you are a caring person and that you are interested in the people and their lives and not just yourself and your research (Hayes 2018). Make a cup of coffee, play with the children, take the dogs for a walk, learn to dance (Morosanu 2016). In any research project the extent and nature of your participation can move along a continuum from non-participating observer to non-observing participant; your task is to engage with any roles reflexively (Whyte 1993; O'Reilly 2012a).

It is also worth thinking about the role of key events in ethnography and making sure to include time in your planning to attend these, because (as rituals have been viewed in anthropology, for example, in Malinowski's 1922 analysis of the Kula Ring) they can often be revealing of wider structures, can challenge normative assumptions, and highlight diverse aspects of community life that had been overlooked (see O'Reilly 2009).

Observation is the more detached and analytical part of the dialectic of participant observation and involves keeping and creating extensive records. I have an extensive section on making field notes in *Ethnographic Methods* (O'Reilly 2012a); see also Emerson et al (2011). In short, the point of field notes is to eventually have recorded any information that you think may be relevant to your research. Field notes and other recording methods are also a way to think and to sort out one's ideas.

Robert Emerson, Rachel Fretz and Linda Shaw (2011) make a useful distinction between mental notes or head notes (noticing something), scratch notes or jottings (quickly making a note of it), and full notes (making as thorough a record as possible, including your thoughts and reflections). Write frequently, regularly, and systematically. If in doubt, write it down, as soon and as much as you can. Do not rely on your memory to come back to something later: draw, sketch, map, chart, list, note, and think all the time to enable 'the dialectical relationship between intimacy and estrangement' that is at the heart of participant observation (Shah 2017: 51). Do not avoid it and do not be passive about it. Do not forget to also *collect* data to put into your field note diary or record. You may wish to take photographs, collect posters, draw maps, or sketch out the layout of the room; you might collect leaflets, and of course you might also wish to collect existing statistics as well as perhaps design your own surveys (see Chapter 2 for a note on previously existing and external data).

> Ethnography is about observing the use of, and relationships to, objects, artefacts and found resources and the conjunctions of discourses and being 'surprised' about their new articulations, not in textual forms themselves but as they are worked upon, used, shaken and stirred for purpose in living ways through practices in concrete contexts on the profane grounds of history. (Willis and Trondman 2021: 158)

Field notes are made reflexively; they are your observations, reflections and thoughts as you engage with the world. They are not a pure and accurate record of everything that you witnessed in the field (that would be impossible). From the start, you decide what to write down and what to ignore, and this will be somewhat directed by your research questions. Try to have an open mind and to reflect on things that surprise and puzzle you and write those down as well. Although in practice, it is quite difficult to separate analytical thoughts from pure observation, it might be useful to have an intellectual diary and a personal diary that you keep distinct from field notes.

Principle three: remember the context

Principle three is based on the logic that people's actions and choices are shaped by the context in which they grew up and now live, in the form of, among other things, culture, community, environment, landscape, smells and sounds, geography and history (O'Reilly 2012b; Benson and O'Reilly 2018). George Marcus (2012: xiv) warns that as ethnography becomes more and more popular so it runs the risk of dilution: 'that is, for the data derived from subjects to lack a rich, critically developed context for interpretation'. A crucial element of ethnography is that it is research in context; this is one of its defining characteristics. Do research in context by being there and doing things with people, flexibly, virtually or through travel (Box 6.3), but also analyse wider conditions. Learn what you can from prior research, from key informants, from what can be gathered via the internet and so on. Locate the study in what is already known and, importantly, provide what you need to locate the study in wider contexts.

We now appreciate that a functionalist view of 'a society' problematically views it as a discrete and coherent entity. Contemporary ethnographies may be mobile, historical, transnational, virtual; they include analyses of geography, and other notions of location, power and wider forces. They can be about other meanings of place or location, such as social or political movements, occupational or class groups; or themed, such as exploring landscape, the state, violence, or corruption. However, the holistic view we inherited from functionalism means we also continue to recognise the interconnectedness of elements within and beyond societies. We continually ask what is influencing and shaping that which is taking place, internally and externally (Box 6.1).

FOR YOUR TOOLKIT

Ethnography is built on an understanding that people's actions and choices are shaped by past and present contexts (cultures, settings, histories, geographies). Unlike other methods, ethnographic data collection or generation is *always* conducted within the context of people's daily lives.

Principle four: share conversations

Principle four is based on the reasoning that people explain their lives through stories and the spoken (or written) word, so it is important to talk with them and to listen (Chapter 4). Fieldwork is like having a long conversation with someone you are fascinated with (Rubin and Rubin 2011). A passive approach is usually best to begin with, where questioning and/or just listening take place within everyday conversations (perhaps as opportunistic interviews; O'Reilly 2012a; see also Chapter 4). Formal interviews rarely tap into daily life as lived in the context of wider conditions, the habits people share, the things they do without reflecting on them, automatic responses, and repetitive gestures. In these cases, conversations work best (Box 6.2). Ask questions opportunistically and sensitively, and always remember there are some things that are better learned from simply listening than asking directly. Whatever you do, remember to write it down as soon as you can.

Semi-structured interviews are also a powerful tool for your toolkit (see Chapter 4). It can be useful to set time aside to give people the opportunity to reflect at length and in detail, to talk to you slowly and carefully, to consider and reflect, and even change their minds. Ethnographic interviews tend to take place with people you have already shared time and built relationships with, and will likely see again (Heyl 2001). Trust and rapport have already been built or there is opportunity to build them at other times. Ethnographic interviews are undertaken in diverse settings, often led by the participant; you may make several return visits or come back to the person via social media, online communities or email (Box 6.3). It may be better to think of these kinds of interviews as guided conversations. They rarely happen in just one short window of opportunity (see Heyl 2001; O'Reilly 2012a). Ethnographic interviews are also valuable in helping to build relationships because you have given time and voice to participants who can then reflect and come back to you later.

FOR YOUR TOOLKIT

Ethnographic interviews are undertaken in diverse settings, often led by the participant. They rarely happen in just one short window of opportunity.

Ethnographic interviews should always be context specific, either because they take place in the context of people's daily lives, or because your participant shows you around their house or neighbourhood virtually, or because you have been there yourself or somewhere similar and can relate to the context. Ethnographic interviews may combine many approaches (including online, sharing photos, going for a walk), use life story interviews, and retrospection, imaginative interviews and so on (Chapters 4 and 5). Finally, ethnographers do not usually distinguish individual and group conversations. They just talk with whoever happens to be available and is happy to talk, in whatever group size naturally occurs.

Box 6.2: Flexible ethnography in private spaces: domestic energy consumption

An Ethnography of Household Energy Demand in the UK, Roxana Morosanu (2016)
The challenge of this ethnographic study was to understand the habits and rituals of daily life within households and their role in energy consumption, as well as how such practices could be altered in favour of ethically informed, transformative actions. How do you do ethnography in people's homes? How do you learn about their mundane tasks, interactions, and understandings as they go about their busy lives? Morosanu addressed these challenges by using collaborative interviews, participant observation and creative methods. First, she conducted semi-structured interviews in people's homes, while other family members spontaneously chipped in, and while other members of her team were sometimes in other rooms doing videos with family members or installing energy-use monitoring equipment.

In other words, interviews were relaxed, fluid, somewhat spontaneous, and collaborative. She then returned to the families on many occasions, joining them for meals, or spending the evening with them. She developed a Tactile Time Collage exercise as a fun interaction, and what we might call focusing exercise (focusing discussions on a topic). Here the family made collages together that represented their use of and feelings about digital devices. She asked them to make short video clips of themselves or their environment during the evenings and especially as they used digital media. She later did life-story interviews with all the family members in which they reflected back on their uses of media as children. This served to get to know her participants better (built rapport) and also helped locate present experiences in the timeline of the past. Finally, she developed her Five Cups of Tea method as a way of focusing more closely on the emergent theme of mothering, and to locate her understandings in the context of the whole family but also during private time. I discuss these creative methods in more detail in Chapter 7. These exercises or tasks were part of an ongoing interaction with her participants; while they were designed to yield insights, they were also part and parcel of getting to know each other, and sharing an ongoing conversation around the subject as well as things that were not obviously relevant.

Principle five: be flexible, creative and responsive with methods

Principle five understands that people cannot always express their thoughts or explain their actions; there are taboos and unspoken conducts, practices shaped by the senses or the emotions, habits and rituals (Box 6.2). Do not rely on the spoken word or on observations; use flexible and creative methods by creating (using arts-based methods), doing things (with participants), mediating (doing research using technology), combining (thinking about how methods complement each other), and collaborating (including your participants in design, implementation, and dissemination; see Box 6.4; also Chapter 7). Learn from sensory, embodied and design approaches to ethnography how to tune into the senses and emotions (including your own): to talk about them, sense them, and reflect on their role (Box 6.1; see also Lubit and Gidley 2021; Pink et al 2022).

Principle six: take time

Principle six is based on the understanding that social life is rich, complex and full of contradictions; that it unravels through agency, and that time enables a focus on process and change (Stones et al 2019; Willis and Trondman 2021). Iterating and learning as we go also take time. Serendipity also takes time: that delight of finding the unexpected and having the sagacity (and time) to know what to make of it (Rivoal and Salazar 2013). Or taking time to dwell reflexively and positively on adversity (Giabiconi 2013). Comparing anthropological methods with journalism, Nancy Scheper-Hughes (2004: 42) argues: 'Anthropology follows a much slower tempo and the anthropologist is more intimate, and more personally engaged with, and responsible to, the people and the communities being studied.'

For Malinowski (1922), we needed time for the familiar to become strange and the strange, familiar, to become a 'normal' part of the setting, in order to engage, participate, and to develop our ideas. We need time to build relationships, to share, to build trust and rapport. Ethnography is not a snapshot understanding of a situation – people have often spent from a few months to several years doing ethnography. It also allows time for the observer to make sense of what has been understood in the context of their own lives, linking to reflexive practice.

FOR YOUR TOOLKIT

Time is a quality not a quantity. Ethnographers spend enough time to focus on process and change, to address the research puzzle in a sensitive way, to pursue serendipity, to build rapport, to reflect on mistakes, to observe different contexts, to give participants the opportunity to change their minds and to elaborate, to learn the language and/or the culture, to be reflexive.

Principle seven: build trust and rapport

Principle seven is informed by the reasoning that people take time to trust and to open up to researchers, and that building rapport will help with shared understandings of a situation. Ethnographers take time to build trust and rapport in order that participants share insights into their worlds freely and happily, in different contexts and under different conditions. This is important in all qualitative research; in ethnography, when you are hanging around in people's lives and perhaps making a nuisance of yourself, it is even more important. It can be challenging if you are already a member of a society or group, or if you are known, or if you have a known status, perhaps as a nurse or teacher. Be very clear in these cases about what is happening with the material and that your research is inductive (Chapter 3). Be open with participants by sharing your ongoing analysis with them; convince them that your goals are important and that you hope to do something valuable, or be honest about the limitations of your goals. Doc was content for William Foote Whyte (1993: 293) to merely be writing about his world: 'I think you can change things that way. Mostly that is the way things are changed, by writing about them.' Also, as suggested earlier (and in Chapter 3), consider giving participants your time beyond the boundaries of the project by simply being helpful or caring, by listening when it is not immediately relevant, by doing things that might not obviously help you pursue your own goals. This is good ethical research practice.

FOR YOUR TOOLKIT

Ethnographers take time to build trust and rapport in order that participants share insights into their worlds freely and happily, in different contexts and under different conditions.

Principle eight: analyse social change

Principle eight is based on the understanding (often implicit in ethnographies) that people change things through their actions as well as being shaped by wider structures, and so ethnography tends to pay attention to time, change, and to the unravelling of processes of social life (see O'Reilly 2012a; Willis and Trondman 2021). As Tim Hallett (2019: 2) says, ethnography is about lived experiences that 'illustrate the nature and consequences of social structures'. What I have called the *practice turn* in ethnography (O'Reilly 2015) is far more widespread than is acknowledged and uses different terminology, including strong structuration (Stones 2005; Greenhalgh et al 2014; Hughes et al 2022), practice stories (O'Reilly 2012b), practice theory (Schatzki 2005; Postill 2010; Shove et al 2012); and structured phenomenology (Stones et al 2019; and see Chapter 1). Ethnography tends to be non-reductive: we are looking for the long and complex answer, not the quick and dirty one. Consider using longitudinal or returning methods (O'Reilly 2012c). Overtly analyse change and processes (Hughes et al 2022). Give people time to develop their and your ideas (Hayes 2018). Take account of changing times. Use gerunds in your analyses (see Chapter 8). Tell practice stories:

> Practice stories pay attention to people's feelings and emotions, their experiences and their free choices, but also to the wider constraints and opportunities within which they act. More than that, practice stories take account of how these different features of social life interact, and thereby how structures (for example, social classes) get produced or reproduced. Practice means studying the interaction of structure and agency, so how policies are interpreted, how colonial attitudes are adopted and resisted, what structures are in place as a result of colonialism that make it hard to resist, and so on (for example). Ethnographic methodology has the fundamental principles and flexibility of approach to enable researchers to pursue, theoretically and empirically, this holy grail of social science. (O'Reilly 2015:11; and see Benson and O'Reilly 2018)

FOR YOUR TOOLKIT

Ethnography is longitudinal by nature, paying attention to time, change, and to the unravelling of processes of social life.

Principle nine: be ethical

Using participatory and ethnographic methods raises ethical challenges that need careful, thorough and ongoing consideration. I recommend consulting guidelines that are specifically designed for ethnographers (Chapter 3). Being ethical is a *practice*, informed by principles, that, because ethnography is unpredictable, requires you to be responsive and malleable (Russell and Barley 2020). Be ethical by adhering to the moral principles that guide you through your organisation or discipline or funding body, as well as your own personal moral guide. Do your best to protect the rights of anyone involved in the research process while accepting that at times this can prove an extremely difficult balancing act, necessitating on-the-spot calculations and choices. And be kind, to yourself and to others, through being considerate, thoughtful and generous in spirit.

Being ethical is also a methodological principle: unethical research is unlikely to yield meaningful insights. But ethnography lends itself well to ethical practice. Participating in people's meaning worlds enables better understanding of them as people with whole lives, rather than as subjects or informants. Listening, hearing, sharing and doing things with people can be kinder, and more responsive to the needs of the participants, than less flexible methods; creative and flexible approaches are sensitive and adaptive to participants' worlds and lives. Taking time and learning as you go means you do not impose your own understandings of the world on them.

FOR YOUR TOOLKIT
Ethnography, being participatory, is gentle, slow, responsive, flexible, and sensitive, and thus lends itself well to good ethical and reflexive practice.

Principle ten: engage in reflexive practice

Principle ten is based on the logic of interpretivism. Ethnography has always been active and exhausting, engaging and immersive (for example, Adler and Adler 2007; Williksen 2009). We will always affect each other through such interactions, in our constant negotiation of the (social) world's contingencies as they confront us and as we decide how we might act. Reflexive practice continually considers and negotiates the relationship between researcher and researched, and as with ethical practice, ethnography offers its own special concerns and opportunities. Its flexible, negotiated and immersive nature means we can be careful, responsive and considerate. In Chapter 3, I described reflexive practice as a version of reflexivity that is collaborative, responsible, iterative, engaged, agile, and creative. This is also a good definition of ethnography: good ethnography and good reflexive practice go hand in hand.

Amending ethnography

One difficulty students of ethnography face is in determining whether what they are doing 'counts as ethnography'. Those working in more science-based fields (such as health and medicine), in policy, or for external clients are often confronted with positivist understandings of social science and find it difficult to explain their work in the context of sets of assumptions that do not fit their own epistemology. Those new to ethnography also often confront normative and intransigent ideas about the nature of a 'real' or 'proper' ethnography. Conventional ethnographies (at least according to the accounts of its main protagonists) involved massive personal investment with ethnographers moving long distances to live among 'strange' peoples for a long period of time, examining every aspect of life of the group they were studying, often at great cost to their own personal lives (O'Reilly 2012a). Contemporary ethnographies, alternatively, are much more fluid: they trace networks, move beyond boundaries, are creative with techniques, and may be shorter term, with people the ethnographer already knows.

I encourage you to be inspired by ethnographic methodology and methods, rather than worry about whether what you are doing can be called an 'ethnography'. As Boellstorff et al (2012: 4) argue: 'The successful deployment of ethnographic methods in virtual worlds is, for us, a ringing endorsement of their enduring power to illuminate novel dimensions of human experience.' You could do shorter-term ethnography (Pink and Morgan 2013), dipping in and out of settings, doing return visits, such as with self-employed nurses working at different sites (Wall 2015). You could spread your ethnography across locations, with foreign correspondents across the globe, for example (Hannerz 2003); or focus on aspects of a society, group or culture, rather than participate and observe entire lives, for example when understanding domestic energy use (Morosanu 2016). You can be more focused with respect to your research questions if a lot of research has been done on this field or topic in the past (see Knoblauch 2005). Methods look different in ethnography that is *applied* to a specific purpose, goal or outcome (Pelto 2013).

You can enhance your ethnography using creative methods: gaining insights into people's lives through life history interviews (Morosanu 2016); longitudinal interviews; using email and social media (Benson and O'Reilly 2020a); or walking or doing things with them, for example when understanding the sense of belonging of forced migrants (O'Neill 2011). You can try 'go-along' interviews that invite changes of direction, nuance and complexity, for example in research on health, wellbeing and place (Thompson and Reynolds 2019). You could try observational shadowing, such as with prisoners (Jewkes and Laws 2021). You can use participant observation to build rapport and to inform better interviews, with elite groups for example (Nair 2021). I could go on. I would rather you decide what you can do having read about all the exciting potential methods in this book (and others), and then decide what is important based on the key principles: 'ethnography is an art of the possible, and it may be better to have some of it than none at all' (Hannerz 2003: 213). Doing or undertaking a fully immersive ethnography is one possibility; also put ethnographic methods and an ethnographic approach into your toolkit.

FOR YOUR TOOLKIT

Ethnographic approaches are flexible, imaginative and responsive to participants in their attempts to understand what is important to you, the researcher, and to themselves.

Even in short-term ethnography you can use participation for *some* of its strengths: visit several times, participate in similar contexts, do other things with people that are not only about data collection to learn about the context, and build trust and rapport. In some ethnographies, the extent to which you can participate may be limited, but it is still important to consider its role in your research: 'ethnography is concerned with culture, shared practices and beliefs, and how the social context shapes, and is shaped, by individuals' (Rashid et al 2019: 1). Participant observation involves doing, talking, listening, seeing, and hearing to tap into shared practices and beliefs. It enables you to ask questions spontaneously, to understand the context because you are there, as you talk and listen with people, and to experience things for yourself. You therefore tune into aspects of a life that you may have otherwise overlooked. My research in Malaysia was ethnographically informed but did not involve extensive periods of participant observation. I used email conversations, online interviews, telephone interviews, and I analysed internet forums.

> However, goals, desires, and habits are often both intuitive and creative and are not easily accessed through interviews. The study also benefited, therefore, from periods of participant observation. To achieve more of a feel for the lives of the migrants, and to take the opportunity to ask questions in context, to observe behaviours, and to experience the lifestyle to some extent, Karen spent four weeks in Penang attending events and talking to people in public places and private homes. (Benson and O'Reilly 2018: 4)

In many contemporary situations, such as ethnography in organisations, educational settings, nursing and so on, researchers might struggle to engage in full immersion and to adopt a local role. In these cases, you are unlikely to be immersing yourself fully into the whole life of the individuals and societies you are interested in, but you can still be there, hang out, share, and care. Whatever you do, try to avoid representing the system or authority; consider taking on a few shorter, insider roles. You can ask your participants to take you there vicariously or virtually (through history, stories and the internet).

Box 6.3: Mobile and multi-sited ethnography: news correspondents

Ulf Hannerz (2003) interviewed 70 news correspondents, many of whom knew each other, who shared conditions of work and experiences (a culture), who shared expectations and demands (structure), but who were rarely together in one place or on the same continent. Hannerz tried to understand the relevant context of being a foreign news correspondent – travelling, and bringing places to each other through writing – but only examined segmented aspects of their lives. He travelled himself and spent time with the correspondents where and when he could, joining aspects of their work and social lives, but not their home lives and not in one place.

One of the advantages of long-term immersion is that you can use the time to collect lots of data in the shape of statistics, posters, charts, previously existing data, and data you generate yourself. In a short-term or targeted ethnography, you can still do this but do it quickly and intentionally. Do not forget to also analyse the context in terms of policies, procedures, rules, norms, practices, labour markets, housing markets and so on. Be prepared to generate your own data via statistics, life stories, observations, interview data, drawings, videos and field notes. In addition to interviews and periods of participant observation with geographically dispersed nurses, Sarah Wall (2015) 'also analyzed relevant documents such as legislation, application forms, nursing practice standards, guidelines for entrepreneurial practice, position statements, and participants' websites'. If your ethnography is shorter or more part time than you may have wished, you can still be sure to write good field notes, collect rich data, read and think as you go along, create data overtly with participants (Knoblauch 2005), and learn about the setting and context before you participate, as in Patricia Tevington and colleagues' (2023) study of the training curriculum for adult leaders in Boy Scouts of America. They call their approach fast-paced, with short, intensive and immersive fieldwork experiences, and say:

> [E]ven though researchers were in a new place with new participants, they were not going in 'blind' at each site. Rather, they knew the general timeframes, the staff hierarchy, and the customs of the trainings and overall Scouter culture. Thus, when they arrived at a camp during a Wood Badge training, researchers could usually identify what training module the troop was engaged in based on sight alone and would therefore place themselves into appropriate seating arrangements for the observation. Likewise, they also knew which volunteer staff positions were most likely to serve as their guides in the field. (Tevington et al 2023: 10)

In the end, I would always prefer an ethnographer to describe what they did, what access they got, and what value it added to the research, rather than rely on generic labels that seem only to excuse what they did *not* do.

Evaluating ethnography

However you approach your ethnography, whatever methods you use – whether it is fully immersive, rich and extensive, or short term, limited and focused, be it visual or sensory (Box 6.1), virtual or blended (Bluteau 2021) – be guided and evaluate it by its principles not by any false idea of how it should be. The checklist has been designed to fit with the ten principles detailed earlier, so refer back to those as you ask yourself these questions. Did you:

- take time to iterate, to tread lightly with your theories, to learn as you went along?
- learn through being there about things that are hard to express?
- give your participants the opportunity to reveal disagreements and ambivalences, complex negotiations and solutions?
- learn through your own experience?
- make thorough and iterative-inductive field notes?
- analyse artefacts?
- learn the spoken and/or cultural language of the group?
- allow for ongoing sampling?
- learn from any key participants or key events?
- keep good records of your observations, feelings, analyses, and reflections?
- collect data to help understand the role of artefacts?
- take context into account, however you understand it or define its relevance?
- provide context for interpretation in your writing?
- select interviewing, and talking and listening methods appropriately?
- give participants the opportunity to direct the research in some way, to consider and reflect, to change their minds and come back to you later?
- find ways for participants to express or reflect on taboos, norms, habits, and rituals?
- spend enough time to focus on process and change, to address your research puzzle in a sensitive way, to pursue serendipitous moments, to build rapport, to make mistakes and reflect on them, to observe different contexts, to give participants the opportunity to change their minds and to elaborate, to learn the language and/or the culture, to be reflexive?
- establish trust and rapport?
- employ an ethnographic approach (being participatory, gentle, slow, responsive, flexible, and sensitive) as part of ethical practice?
- understand and engage in reflexive practice?

Use this list to explain to readers, with relevant examples, how you approached ethnography, what you did well, and how you addressed its key principles. This is not an exhaustive list – feel free to add to it as you read more, do more, and learn more.

Box 6.4: Flexible design informed by ethnography: Brexit and British People Abroad

From 2017 to 2019 the project team, led by Michaela Benson, tracked the Brexit negotiations and what these meant for the political rights, social and financial entitlements, identity, citizenship and belongings of Britons living in the EU-27. The project used testimonials from a citizens' panel, life story interviews, email conversations, a survey, participant observation, visual methods, and video-call interviews. Work was presented using podcasts, reports, articles, a timeline, myth busters, evidence to select committees, and infographics.

What made this ethnographic? It was iterative-inductive, used participant observation, located insights in context, used interviews and conversations, was flexible and responsive, took its time and paid attention to time, built trust and rapport with participants, analysed social change, and engaged in ethical and reflexive practice.

Ethnographic analysis and insights

Ethnographic analysis follows the model in Chapter 8: it is iterative-inductive, with the goal to produce or construct explanations that are meaningful, intelligible to participants, and adequate. Ethnographic analysis begins with puzzled thoughts, nagging questions, and the occasional flashes of insight that arise as the result of what Paul Rock (2001: 35) calls 'the interplay between a receptive and curious mind and a world explored over time and with diligence'. One advantage of ethnographic analysis is that you can talk with your participants about the ideas and thoughts you are having, the insights that are emerging and what they think of them. Try to keep your key questions in mind as you proceed, but also be happy to revise them as you learn more from your participants and their world.

Interpretations may draw on insights from other studies, but carefully and sensitively. It may involve analysis of wider structures – rules, norms and institutional arrangements – of which your participants are not aware (Chapter 9). Ethnographic analysis can move forward from observations and descriptions to emergent theoretical explanations (Candea and Yarrow 2023).

Ethnographers can work together with participants towards interventions, as with Sarah Pink and colleagues' (2022) work in design ethnography that works critically with partners, devising slow burn ways to intervene together, and sometimes 'intervening up' by shifting perspectives, narratives, and processes. Ethnographers can recognise the transformative potential of art, narrativity and storytelling (O'Neill 2011). Loukia-Maria Fratsea and Apostolos Papadopoulos (2021), in their analysis of the spatial mobility trajectories of Romanian migrants in Greece, advise we pay attention to outcomes shaped by agency, as do Willis and Trondman (2021: 158):

Do not miss the multiple opportunities for new ethnic, gender, sexual and class meanings as ordinary possibilities for social agents to intervene in the symbolic orders of their own social universes even at the very bottom of social space and with a variety of affects and outcomes.

Cubellis et al (2021: 2) argue that the 'oscillation between theory and practice has helped address the well-known divergence between what policy and protocol look like on paper and what happens in the actual practice of daily life'. While for Shah (2017: 45), 'engaging in participant observation is a profoundly political act, one that can enable us to challenge hegemonic conceptions of the world, challenge authority, and better act in the world'.

FOR YOUR TOOLKIT

Ethnography can be a profoundly political act; it can work with participants towards interventions or address the well-known divergence between policy and practice; it can recognise the transformative power of agency; or at least alter how people see things.

Finally, consider this quote from James Arthur Baldwin, who (like Doc in Whyte 1993) believes you can at least begin to change the world by writing about it:

> You write in order to change the world, knowing perfectly well you probably can't but also knowing that … the world changes according to the way people see it, and if you alter, even by a millimeter, the way … people look at reality, then you can change it. (James Arthur Baldwin, cited in the opening pages of Denzin 2013: v)

Speaking of ethnography

'They told me their lives are always full and exciting, but I had days when I felt bored and lonely. I spoke to them about that and they admitted they sometimes feel the same. Some then went on to tell me how much they miss their grandkids.'

'The heat, the noise, the smells can be really oppressive. I don't think I'd have appreciated that if I hadn't been there myself.'

'He couldn't explain why he felt so much trepidation as he walked onto the ward, but once I'd walked with him a few times he found he could start to share that feeling through pointing to things he could see and feel around him.'

'I'm sure they weren't always truthful with me about the extent to which they were doing unhealthy things, but with time and once they could see I wasn't judging them, they were able to be more open, to themselves and to me.'

'I couldn't spare a year learning to be a nurse myself, but going to the ward and the café, walking to work with them, and chatting to them as they did their jobs, helped me understand their daily lives and the many tasks they do that aren't listed in their job description.'

Taking things further

For **extensive accounts** of what constitutes ethnography I recommend Gobo (2008), Madden (2010), O'Reilly (2012a), Willis and Trondman (2000, 2021). Other **specialist approaches** include evocative auto-ethnography (Armitage 2022), digital ethnography and blended methods (Bluteau 2021), activist and engaged, visual, filmic, public, critical, reflexive, and participatory ethnography (Palmas 2021). The online journal *Entanglements* is often visual, sensory, engaged, reflective, or reflexive, and employs **diverse styles of writing** such as art and poetry. Emerson et al (2011) is excellent for its extensive treatment of writing, recording and analysing **field notes**, as well as the nature of ethnography. See Condon et al (2019) for a discussion about **participatory research** using community members and community partners in the design of their work, issues about advocacy and third sector workers, trust, rapport, and understanding the language and meanings of a group. See Small (2009) for a useful and complex discussion of **representativeness** in ethnography. For a full and updated perspective on **ethics** in ethnography see Russell and Barley (2020). Doc's story in William Foote Whyte's (1993) *Street Corner Society* is a classic example of an ethnographic gatekeeper, and the whole appendix is a great read, including a discussion of **participatory action research**. See Heyl (2001) and O'Reilly (2012a) for an extended discussion of ethnographic **interviews**. Cubellis et al (2021), is a useful resource for understanding the **foundations** and **principles** of ethnography. It covers tacit knowledge and learning from asides; the logic of abductive reasoning; theory, analysis and oscillation; the role of serendipity; and reflexivity. It discusses defining a research question, how analysis proceeds, the role of time, how issues are interlinked, and even how norms, rules and wider contexts shape daily life. It even raises the concepts of focused ethnographies and how qualitative work can have impact.

Listen to the related episode for this chapter on
Qualitative Research Methods for Everyone podcast:

7

Being creative

What this chapter is about

The hegemony of a specific (positivist) view of science and of certain qualitative methods that have come to be accepted as valid (especially interviews) has often excluded or denied a more creative approach, to the detriment of good, interpretivist social science. The goal of this chapter is to help you navigate the complexities of research by having a strong toolkit that is used with an open mind, imaginatively and critically. Being creative with methods is a process (hence the gerund version of the verb); it involves doing things differently, thinking outside the box in your efforts to be responsive, agile, ethical, engaged, and collaborative.

Being creative must be done critically, with a constant eye to how it helps you address research questions, how what you are doing is meaningful, as well as ethical. Do not get so excited or inspired that you set out to use methods because you like the sound of them; it should always be the research problem and the participants that come first as you avoid the 'unbridled missionary zeal' of some methodologists (Crow 2022: 1). Being creative with methods is not just fun (although it often is fun); it enables you to do the important things I emphasise in this book. Creative methods honour the inextricably linked nature of the process of understanding, and therefore this chapter does not stand alone within this book, it forms part of its overall argument.

> **FOR YOUR TOOLKIT**
> Being creative (imaginative, inventive, inspired or visionary) in qualitative research honours the inextricably linked, iterative-inductive nature of the process of understanding.

Having discussed the interpretive, iterative, flexible, ethical, and transformative nature of creative methods, I go on to introduce five novel interlacing ways of thinking about how to be creative with methods: creating, doing, mediating, combining, and collaborating. In the process, we shall see how conventional approaches to data collection (or generation) have been adapted, developed, altered, reimagined, and recreated. My goal is to inspire you, to open your minds and your imaginations to learn from others and to be brave enough to be creative and imaginative yourself with regard to the possibilities for your own research and participants.

Being creative and the logic of qualitative research

The term 'creative methods' has been used to mean all sorts of approaches to being creative or doing things differently that have been developed ever since people started doing qualitative research. Bronislaw Malinowski (1922: 8), in the Trobriand Islands in the early 1900s, took photographs, made charts, and shared in 'games and amusements'. William Foote Whyte (1993), in 1940s Chicago, went bowling, shared meals, played cards, and mapped group (gang) structures. As Helen Kara (2020: 11) says, '[T]he development of research techniques, whether quantitative or qualitative, has involved enormous creativity', and she gives the fascinating example of how 'crochet thinking' has been incorporated into geometry and architecture. So, there is a tradition of being creative with data collection and generation. The fundamental principles of qualitative research, as spelled out in previous chapters, include interpretivism, an iterative-inductive process, flexible and responsive practices, being ethical and reflexive, and an aspiration to be transformative. I discuss how creative approaches support allegiance to each of these fundamental principles.

Interpretivism and being creative

In Chapter 1, I clarified that all qualitative research is informed by the interpretivist paradigm. Interpretivism, in its basic meaning, is 'to interpret' or 'to make sense'. We aim to understand and make sense of other people's worlds, first for ourselves and then for others. This is an ongoing act of interpretation. Phenomenology is a version of interpretivism. A 'descriptive phenomenology' is focused on describing lived and embodied experiences as natural phenomena with no need for interpretation. An 'interpretive phenomenology' attempts to understand the idiosyncratic and mutual patterns of meaning behind lived experiences. A structured phenomenology then pays close attention to how these inner lives are deeply interwoven with relevant structural contexts.

Doing things differently, such as creating something together with participants, can assist a *descriptive phenomenology* by helping them express themselves. These methods respect the fact that people cannot always put their lived and embodied experiences into words – maybe what they are doing is too practical or intuitive, or what they want to talk about is taboo, or too normative or sensitive. Maybe the words for their feelings and experiences, and how they understand them, don't even exist. Maybe the insights are just too nuanced for words (Mannay 2010). Being creative yields depth and quality (Benson 2020; O'Reilly 2020b).

Doing things differently (or more creatively) can assist *interpretive and structured phenomenology* by working with participants on the patterns and themes as they emerge, or as you create them together, addressing the problem as you go (which is also flexible and collaborative). Doing things with people also enables us to locate understandings within their lifeworld context, using narrative, life stories, participating, and sharing experiences and practices. Remember that many conventional methods take people out of their everyday contexts and expect everyone to be able to discuss abstract ideas and to recontextualise them. Creative methods work with the double hermeneutic process introduced in Chapter 1.

FOR YOUR TOOLKIT

Being creative with methods can support descriptive phenomenology by helping people express themselves, an interpretive phenomenology by working with participants to identify patterns, and structured phenomenology by locating understandings in the lifeworld.

Some participants, because of their age, experience, culture or medical conditions, are not able to express themselves using the words, categories and concepts we are familiar with (Dowlen 2019; Bloom et al 2020; Fleetwood-Smith 2020; Parsons et al 2021). Creating artwork, drawing, collaborating, going for a walk together so that the pressure is taken off the situation, letting them talk to you by email or over the phone, might be easier ways to think, reflect, express, and share (Box 7.7). As Laura Lundy (2007) said, giving people a voice is often not enough; too much emphasis has been placed on knowledge through the spoken or written word (Lewis-Dagnell et al 2023).

An iterative-inductive process

An iterative-inductive process recognises that researchers have preconceived ideas and theories about how the world works – they will have read the literature and studied the field a little, they will have had personal experiences – but that they should hold these ideas lightly and test out (in as open-minded a way as possible) where and when they might be helpful in clarifying emerging insights. They should be open to being wrong and tune in to things that surprise them and thus challenge their preconceptions. They should be open to discarding, changing, and developing new theories and concepts (Box 7.3). They should constantly iterate between being inductive and deductive, with an inductive approach retaining the upper hand.

Being creative with methods facilitates learning as we go because we are less likely to impose our way of looking at the world. Creative approaches tend to generate new insights, perhaps even new to the participants themselves (Box 7.8). There is plenty of scope for surprises to arise and be taken into account (serendipity: Chapter 6), and they enable reflexive practice (Chapter 3), which in turn ensures good-quality sense making.

Flexible and responsive practices

Qualitative research proceeds in a flexible and responsive manner so that we can learn as we go from our participants and from our own experiences. Even with more conventional approaches such as interviews and focus groups we use flexible, non-standardised methods, such as discussion guides, that are adapted for our participants and for ourselves as we learn and understand more. We collaborate by involving people as participants in research (rather than as subjects, informants or respondents), enabling us to work together towards meaningful interpretations, even if only by ensuring we listen, hear and adapt. Elsewhere in this book I have described qualitative research as agile, dynamic, and live. Qualitative research is essentially creative.

> **FOR YOUR TOOLKIT**
> Qualitative research is essentially creative, flexible and responsive: putting a spotlight on *being creative* merely encourages us to embrace these principles.

Creative methods are specifically designed to be even more flexible and to respond even better to participants' needs and abilities than conventional methods (Markham 2013). Collaborating, for example, leads to better research because people have the chance to direct *your* research towards *their* experiences and understandings. It enables learning as you go and shared sense making, rethinking, and developing ideas together (Boxes 7.8 and 7.9). This is in tune with other arguments in this book that argue qualitative researchers need to be comfortable with uncertainty, and acknowledging uncertainty of outcome requires flexibility towards both methods and analysis:

> By acknowledging uncertainty as a fundamental starting point in our research and interventions, the unknown, unknowable and the possible become counterpoints to the predictive, quantitative modes of seeking to understand and act on futures that characterise industry, policy and government agendas ... The design ethnographic research we discuss in this book consistently complicates the certainties that reside in the visions and imaginaries represented by the predictive or quantified visions of futures advanced by consultancies and futurists, as well as the utopian and dystopian versions of futures that inhabit popular media. (Pink et al 2022: 17–18)

Being ethical and reflexive

Being ethical and being reflexive are ongoing practices that should shape and inform your work in an enduring process from inception, through design and implementation, all the way through the various interactions that constitute research, to conclusions, dissemination and beyond. Reflexive practice involves continually considering the relationship between the researcher and those researched. Reflexivity in practice is adaptive to our surroundings, our communities, our experiences, and our perceptions.

Being creative is fundamentally ethical for at the very least making space to include groups that have been excluded from research because of difficulties gaining ethical clearance to study with them (Campbell et al 2023); or difficulties of gaining funding for such unpredictable research (Lewis-Dagnell et al 2023). Being creative keeps you in tune with participants' needs and with your own preconceptions; it involves closeness, collaboration, and ongoing positioning and adaptation (Box 7.5). Doing things with people and participating in creative activities with them supports a reflexive approach by learning through experience, using all your senses. They enable us to navigate our methods as well as our sample (Chapter 2), and thereby to engage in reflexive practice (Chapter 3). Creative methods often focus on wellbeing, empowerment, social justice, and care.

Collaborating is ethical because it gives people a voice and agency, and because you do what feels comfortable for them, responding to their needs. You might even help them a bit beyond what is necessary for the research, as when in our research project, Brexit and British People Abroad (Benson and O'Reilly 2020a), we gathered as much information as we could about all the changing rules and regulations so that we could advise participants or at least know where to direct them for reliable advice. Mediated methods give people time to reflect and to think, can fit into people's daily schedules better (Crow 2022), and empower them to come back to you later, as with ongoing interviews (see Chapters 5 and 6). Being creative means fitting the research into participants' lives: for example, using digital media, meeting them online, recognising they feel different on different days (allowing them to come back to you another time), or if they are busy or easily tired accepting a few short conversations as opposed to one long and exhausting one.

> **FOR YOUR TOOLKIT**
> Being creative is a fundamentally ethical and reflexive practice. It is less likely than other methods to impose researchers' preconceptions.

Being transformative

I confidently argue, in Chapters 1 and 2, that all of us who do research hope that somewhere along the line having a better understanding of people's practices (our insights into what shapes participants' worlds and how they respond) will lead to making the world, or a tiny part of it, a better place. Qualitative research often aims to be transformative. Perhaps we can develop policies or interventions that lead to better outcomes, in which case we need to understand processes and pathways to outcomes. Maybe we wish to intervene actively, or just to be evocative: creative methods yield richness and complexity with which to achieve both better. Some researchers aspire to shape or inform better futures (O'Neill 2011; Pink et al 2022). Philippe Bourgois and Jeff Schonberg (2009: 297–8) call for a 'good-enough applied anthropology, rooted in critical theory and aimed at redressing the "useless suffering" that is imposed politically and institutionally on the socially vulnerable'. However we view our impact, near or far-flung, planned or serendipitous, we all hope to have one.

Creative approaches can be transformative in transforming yourself, the participants and the wider world (Kara 2020: 45–59). Collaborating can involve working together on useful and meaningful interventions. Being creative is a means of ensuring excluded voices have been heard (Lundy 2007). Creative and imaginative approaches help you locate things in context, to observe the passing of time and processes as they unravel (Benson and O'Reilly 2018, 2020a). You can notice what people do not just what they say, gaining embodied and sensory insights. Being creative can inform an understanding of the social world as made up of individuals, social structures and processes, and their interaction over time (O'Reilly 2012b). They give people the opportunity to talk about their lives, to tell their own stories in their own way (O'Neill 2011, 2018).

Five inspirational ways to be creative

I propose five inspirational ways to conceptualise being creative with methods. These ways (heuristics) are inspired by Kara's (2020: 5) typology of creative methods: arts-based, embodied, technological, multi-modal, and transformative. But there are subtle differences between my list and Kara's, the main one is that I view being transformative as an outcome of research (though of course it can happen simultaneously) and have discussed it in the context of the fundamental principles of qualitative research. I also use gerund versions of verbs to focus on the ongoing and emergent nature of creative approaches (Pink et al 2022). As Kara says, approaches clearly overlap in practice, with each other and with the more conventional approaches discussed in previous chapters, and so my five ways are a lens not a box (see Benson and O'Reilly 2015), a heuristic tool for thinking with, not a container for mutually exclusive allocations. My main goal at this point is to enthuse you to do things differently, as appropriate, by:

- Creating
- Doing (with)
- Mediating
- Combining
- Collaborating

In Chapter 1, I introduced a distinction between data as writing, found data, and creative production. I repeat this here because it will be useful for thinking in more detail about creating. 'Data as writing' usually refers to visual data produced, perhaps collaboratively, to support your case when writing up or disseminating findings. While not exactly data collection it might overlap in practice as you make photographs or even restage events to illustrate what you learned. 'Found data' are data that existed prior to the research, and are analysed, probably interpretively, but maybe using discourse analysis or semiotics. 'Creative production' is where data are produced collaboratively to create meaning or insights or are used as prompts to encourage talk about meanings and feelings. Being creative fits perfectly with an iterative-inductive logic, enabling qualitative research to proceed in a flexible and responsive manner so that we can learn as we go from our participants and from our own experiences. Being creative also facilitates a reliance on diverse methods that involve listening, hearing, watching, thinking, co-creating, and reflecting.

FOR YOUR TOOLKIT

The conceptualisation of creative methods as *creating, doing, mediating, combining*, and *collaborating* is provided as a lens, to open your mind to possibilities.

Creating

Creating as a research practice involves working with research participants using arts-based (and other productive, constructive or design) methods, in the co-construction of insights. Creating means to bring something into existence; it includes making drawings, timelines, or web diagrams, taking and sharing photographs, asking your participants to write short letters or essays, using play dough or construction bricks to think with, making or using geographical maps, mind maps, or journey maps to think about mobility or one's life journey, video diaries as sensory approaches, graphic novels to concretise thoughts, and as many more techniques as the imagination permits.

The goal usually is to use these creative methods to help participants to think, feel, reflect and then to talk, or to express themselves in ways other than talking (Box 7.1). The researcher does not simply analyse what is produced but uses 'creating' and talking together with participants to generate insights relevant to the research aims (Box 7.2). Creating is responsive and flexible, and transformative (Kara 2020: 27).

FOR YOUR TOOLKIT

Creating means to bring something into existence. The goal is usually to help participants to think, feel, reflect and then to express themselves.

Dawn Mannay (2010, in Kara 2020: 26) was studying the experiences of mothers and daughters living on a UK social housing estate. She asked her participants to take photographs of places that were meaningful to them, to draw maps of their environments and to make collages that expressed how they felt about their natural and social worlds. The mothers and daughters were able to use these photographs, collages and maps to share their nuanced feelings about their homes and lives during interviews.

As part of our research on the effects of Brexit for British people living in the EU-27, we asked participants to send photographs or postcards that expressed how they felt about where they lived. We received images of a choir, an underground station, a tranquil beach scene, and a beautiful garden, each accompanied by heartfelt stories about life in Germany, the Netherlands, Spain, and France. The photographs and accompanying stories yielded a richness, depth and life quality that interviews alone would not have. They especially helped us understand the incredible ambivalence that accompanied the Brexit negotiations and yielded subtle insights into meanings of home (Benson 2020; O'Reilly 2020a; also see Benson and O'Reilly 2018).

Box 7.1: Learning through creating: photo elicitation

Graham Crow (2022) has been researching how academics experience and manage the transition to retirement and has used photo elicitation (Pauwels 2019) – a technique where images are used during an interview to elicit a response – as well as 'imagined futures essays', in which participants are free to recount their own hopes, dreams and desires. Crow (2022: 14) celebrates the capacity of such techniques 'to reveal aspects of time and purpose that would otherwise have remained opaque' and the vivid nature of the responses that emerged as a result of touching and sharing images and diaries.

Robyn Dowlen's (2019) study of the experiences of those living with dementia used videos for observation and elicitation, and participants' diaries as a way of reflecting on music-making activities, because talking would be difficult and because 'living in the moment' became an important research focus. Rebecka Fleetwood-Smith (2020) used creative methods involving 'multisensory encounters' in her work on the lives of people living with dementia in a care home as a better way to understand everyday lived experience. Sarah Parsons and colleagues (2021) used digital stories created with adults who know a child living with autism, video clips representing actions and behaviours the adults wished to share, and children's wearable cameras to capture the child's perspective of the world. Ashley Bloom and colleagues (2020) used a toolkit of methods that their diverse group of children with special educational needs could choose from, including letting them select emotional cue cards to illustrate what they liked and did not like.

Jessica Ringrose, Kaitlyn Regehr and Betsy Milne (2021) used participatory drawing, walking and talking, relational maps, and other arts-based methods to explore young people's use of social media platforms and consumption of images (see also Ringrose, Regehr and Whitehead 2021).

Box 7.2: Learning through creating: a tactile time collage

Understanding the everyday temporalities of energy use in the home requires creative methods. Roxana Morosanu (2016) developed the Tactile Time Collage exercise as a fun interaction and focusing exercise. This was a 'form of focus group that took place in the participants' domestic settings, and it asked family members to make series of collages together that showed the ways in which they spend time at home around various digital devices' (p 64). Morosanu provided the materials and placed the picture of the device in the centre of a large sheet of card; and family members added photos, coloured notes and images, to represent the times of day a device was used, to talk about it. They then added tactile material samples to show and discuss how they felt about this period of time. The activity gave participants the opportunity to reflect on family routines and to talk to each other about how different times of day felt to them: 'By linking the intangible experience of time with the sense of touch, my research questions about time were transformed' (p 64).

Doing (with)

Doing things with participants is usually an embodied, and often sensory, approach (see Pink et al 2022), though researchers do not always include an analysis of its embodied or sensory nature. It includes sharing experiences and practices with participants, perhaps as they go about their daily lives, joining in or going along, or perhaps more actively designing a practical method like filling in a fictitious form together, or testing a prototype. As discussed in Chapter 6, ethnography essentially involves doing things (participating) with participants, and in it you will find lots of examples of being creative or imaginative with methods; but there are even more purposeful ways of generating insights through doing things with others.

FOR YOUR TOOLKIT

Doing things with others can be passive (going along to or sharing in existing activities), or proactive (asking participants to direct a walk, workshopping), or can involve becoming a full member of a community.

Participating in activities with others can include going for a walk together, shopping, or even becoming a firefighter (Desmond 2006) or an exotic dancer

(Barton 2007). Matthew Desmond learned through his own body what it was like to become seasoned to the hazards faced regularly by fire crews. Bernadette Barton experienced how to separate her dancer persona from her 'authentic' self. Participating has been also conceptualised as a go–along method (Kusenbach 2003) or as field walking (Ingold and Vergunst 2008).

Doing things with participants can at the very least be used as a form of access, if not a way to learn more about the experience itself. It gives the researcher a sense of context and a feel for a way of life; it shows commitment and care; and it gives participants time and distance during which to reflect, and to think practically as well as literally. But doing things with participants can also be more proactive than just going along. Transect walks, for example, ask participants to *direct* a walk through a neighbourhood in a way that is meaningful to them (Pelto 2013). The purpose is to walk, talk, see, feel, hear, and to share the experience they direct. An extreme example of 'doing' is autoethnography, in which, in both evocative and analytical approaches, researchers learn from their own life experiences (see Goode 2019).

Box 7.3: Learning through doing: mixed martial arts

Dale Spencer (2014) converted his hobby of combat arts into an ethnographic study of mixed martial arts: he trained and fought, as well as taking notes and interviewing other participants. Through doing martial arts (with others), Spencer learned about the lived experience and back-stage world of mixed martial arts, coming to understand it as a sensory world of smells, sounds and pain that leaves its mark on bodies. His research and interview questions were shaped by his experiences and these interviews in their turn shaped his interview guide and his research focus on everyday mundane violence.

Doing things with others can include creating with them. Maggie O'Neill (2011, 2018) has spent over twenty years employing participatory methods, such as walking and talking and making art together with forced migrants and has celebrated the transformative potential of combining collaboration, art, narrative, and storytelling. She calls for 'a radical democratic imaginary in arts-based research' (2011: 13) that gives space for analysis and critique, as well as understanding and insight.

Workshopping is also a type of *doing* with others. In *Design Ethnography*, Pink and colleagues describe working with participants on a 'routine map' that visualises how people travel to work, and how 'this is entangled in a diverse range of routines for picking up children, doing social calls, running errands, etc.' (2022: 167). The point of workshopping is not just to produce or create but to open up possibilities for future creativity and collaboration.

Mediating

The term 'mediating' encourages us to think about doing research using (online) technology such as video-conferencing, email, social media apps, internet forums, using film and sound, and so on. Mediating draws on the many emerging technologies for doing research while also acknowledging that how new technologies are used and what it means for people is a constant source of fascination for understanding the social world as it changes and adapts. However, we should avoid fetishising new mediating technologies: while much of everyday life is mediated, it is not more mediated than previously, just differently (Horst and Miller 2012).

FOR YOUR TOOLKIT

Mediating is a way of being creative with methods through (online) technology while also respecting the role of technology in people's daily lives.

Christine Hine (2000) drew a useful distinction between ethnography *of* the internet and ethnography *through* the internet and, although we now understand these are merging through practice, the distinction is useful and not only for ethnography. The internet and mediating technology can be treated *sui generis* as a social fact, as a structure created, used, recreated, and affecting the lives of human agents (O'Reilly 2009). Studying 'the internet' or technology use could involve studying virtual worlds and networked environments as fascinating social phenomena (see Boellstorff 2008), or you could incorporate a focus on technology as an aspect of people's lives that shapes the social worlds they inhabit (see Miller 2011). You might also be interested in ownership and production as well as uses and impacts of technology. All of these require the use of mediating methods.

Hine's notion of studying *through* the internet is about methods of research. For example, you can do email interviews, use online open-ended surveys, or communicate via forums and networks. These approaches have the advantage of being low cost and anonymous, with a global reach and easy use of snowballing techniques (see Chapter 2). On the other hand, anonymity can be problematic in some cases. There can be a low response rate because participants find it easier to ignore virtual communications, and because of online fatigue; you need to be aware of time pressures and time zones. Interviews via video platforms can be short or long, one-off or repeated, casual or more formal. You can build rapport by meeting with participants more than once (even virtually); they can show you around their homes carrying their laptops or phones, share a coffee, introduce you to the dog or the family. Virtual interviews can be recorded and transcribed easily, and written conversations such as through email and WhatsApp are transcribed instantly. You can do focus groups online using the same techniques as in Chapter 5, or you can do asynchronous (Finch et al

2014) focus groups, where participants are not all together at the same time. Transferring methods online takes a lot of managing and I advise reading more about it before you start, thinking about context, platforms, ownership, how cultural rules shape interaction, and what consent means in these circumstances. But it has a lot of exciting potential.

People now accept that offline and online worlds merge in our lives. If this is what you want to understand, then you will need to use a variety of methods (Box 7.6; see also O'Reilly 2009). Alternatively, you can use this insight to creatively adapt conventional methods, by doing a qualitative interview face to face first, then having a further discussion online (using video-conferencing, or even the phone) and then continue the conversation over email or WhatsApp, as it suits the participant (see Chapter 6). Policy and applied researchers are now commonly using online, video, or otherwise mediated interviews since the COVID-19 pandemic (Keen et al 2022).

When I was doing online (combined with face-to-face) research in Malaysia (Benson and O'Reilly 2018; Stones et al 2019) and in Spain (O'Reilly 2020a), we would often share a virtual coffee together, and I might be shown their view via the computer, walked around the house via the laptop or smartphone, and introduced to pets who popped up on screen. Participants then sent further stories through email, photographs and films, and messages via WhatsApp or Facebook when they had some news or new thoughts. I also did some interviews over the phone: not all technologies are online (Boxes 7.4 and 7.5). As a caveat, when mediating, do be careful to make yourself and participants aware of who else is listening since it might affect the interaction, ethically or behaviourally.

Box 7.4: Learning through mediating: noise transformation

Mediating is not only achieved through the internet. Sarah Pink, Melisa Duque and Shanti Sumartojo worked with sound artists and engineers to develop and understand how 'waste' noise (such as traffic noise) could be transformed into melodic sounds. The team set up noise cancellation and noise transformation spaces under canopies in a park and then walked through them with participants, recording them visually and orally and using the sounds (or lack of) to 'probe participants to articulate their immersed embodied and emplaced sensory impressions and their shifting feelings' (Pink et al 2022: 132). It enabled them to explore emotions that could not be accessed through everyday life.

When we wanted to understand the experiences of British people of colour living in Europe during the Brexit process (Benson and Lewis 2019), we did interviews online rather than visit separate places, and Europe featured as a diverse yet unitary context. When we learned that we needed to include Ireland in the research (Benson and O'Reilly 2020b), we did a few online interviews but also went there and spent time with people, learning more about the specific context of Ireland. Our 'Picking for Britain' research (O'Reilly and Scott 2023a, 2023b) with farmers and workers was conducted online entirely, but members of our team had spent time on farms and alongside farmers and workers in prior research and I had done farm work in the past as a young woman. All these experiences informed, shaped and *mediated* the interviews and our interpretations.

In Panama and Malaysia, we included online ethnography as just another field site, as in both countries there was a vibrant virtual community with prominent forums and blogs written and created by the migrants. 'It quickly became clear that the (virtual) community forum was a significant hub for the migrant community, through which information and requests specific to this community were communicated and circulated' (Benson and O'Reilly 2018: 8) These virtual spaces became additional, complementary sites for our ethnography.

Box 7.5: Learning through mediating: filming evening times

For Morosanu's (2016) Evening Times method, participants were asked to film short video clips during evenings and weekends, thinking about their uses of digital media. The videos were shared with each other and with Morosanu, and led to fascinating reflections and insights about family time, routines, and energy use. They captured 'the spontaneity of domestic life', intimate interactions, private perspectives, emotions, and collective habits (2016: 65–6), and gave participants the opportunity to reflect on these among themselves. The dropping off and picking up of cameras, and the meetings to discuss the videos also meant Roxana and her participants got to know each other better.

Combining

Combining is self-explanatory; it involves using and thinking about how methods complement each other, what purposes each serves, and how they address aims and objectives. Many of the examples described earlier combine methods, and ethnographers almost always do so. All the projects in *Design Ethnography* (Pink et al 2022) combine techniques, including combining participating and experimenting, workshops and discussions, walking and talking, videoing and sharing experiences. A study, in partnership with the City of Melbourne, wanted to understand how a major refurbishment of the much-loved Queen Victoria Market would be received. The 'research design meant making research materials by a range of means, which emerged as the project proceeded' (Pink et al 2022: 50). First, the ethnographers needed to know how people felt about the existing market. This involved a lot of 'doing'. They spent time at the market, day and night, filming their own impressions, and auto-ethnographically (see Chapter 6) built their own sense of community with the market through their immersions. They did in-situ interviews with stall holders and go-along interviews with regular shoppers and visitors. They ambled, browsed, shopped, and talked, coming slowly, inductively and reflexively to understand the market's 'intangible heritage' (Pink et al 2022: 51).

FOR YOUR TOOLKIT

Being creative through combining involves thinking about how methods complement each other, what purposes each serves, and how they address aims and objectives.

Annette Markham's concept of *remix* inspires researchers to mix it up, in terms of both method and activity (2013; also Kara 2020: 35). Think, she says, beyond field notes to doodles and diagrams, maps and notes; play with ideas; borrow techniques from other disciplines; move and be moved; and constantly interrogate (the literature, yourself, power, context). The British Heart Foundation undertakes a lot of research with children living with heart disease. Researchers might take them to the zoo for fun, then to a small classroom for discussion, to play, draw, create, relax, stick stickers on leaflets to identify what works and what doesn't, speak in funny voices to think about how adults talk to them about illness and treatment, watch videos, and more. It is important with children to break things up into small chunks of activity so they don't get bored, distracted, or overwhelmed, and can find ways to communicate their perspectives.

Box 7.6: Learning through combining: a blended approach to online and offline lives

Joshua Bluteau (2021), for his study of tailoring in London, has developed what he calls a blended approach that combines mediating and doing (participating). In this case, the mediating aspect involved having an online presence on Instagram, sharing photographs of himself almost every day for two years. The participating aspect involved extensive fieldwork with bespoke tailors, wearing the clothes, becoming a client, and attending fashion shows. The Instagram element of his study, he contends, was not so much digital ethnography as immersive cohabitation: 'a blended method, which considered these two fieldsites as part of the same field: a postdigital field' (Bluteau 2021: 280). The approach respects the online and offline aspects of tailors' lives, provides for better understanding of the nature of 'digitised lives', and 'the ease with which digital photos and images can be created, manipulated, and shared offer untold opportunities for research in the field of visual anthropology' (2021: 282).

Box 7.7: Learning through combining: play

Stephanie Lewis-Dagnell, Sarah Parsons and Hanna Kovshoff (2023) used various forms of play – a graffiti wall, talking mats, preference cards, and a mosaic approach – in their research designed to enable children with complex needs to have a voice about their education. These all involved selecting images and items, sharing them, displaying and recognising emotions visually, stickers (such as smiley faces), storyboards and photo elicitation.

Caroline Knowles' (2014, 2015) work is inherently creative and combines working with photographers and artists, mapping spaces, following traces, and walking for her ethnographic studies of globalisation and inequality (travel the Flip-Flop Trail yourself: www.flipfloptrail.com). Many researchers who are creative combine their methods with an ethnographic approach (Chapter 6; see also O'Reilly 2012a), to get to know the participants a little, to become familiar with the context, for the participants to be comfortable with them, and perhaps even to do more than would be expected or is strictly necessary for the research – to be helpful, supportive and collaborative.

Box 7.8: Learning through combining: eating, filming, talking, and sharing

Morosanu (2016) used multiple methods and approaches. She visited her participants' homes to share meals or light refreshments, met them in other places for coffees or walks; some joined her as she learnt Morris dancing. One key activity was to film them as they did things that used energy in the home, which led to some great reflections, considerations, and discussions, such as when she was filming Cynthia doing the laundry. This led to a rich and detailed conversation about managing work and time, and even the pairing of socks (p 111). The experience, among others, led Morosanu to use and adapt the concept of the Mother-Multiple, which was designed to draw attention to kinship-situated caring activities regardless of age, gender, and child-bearing. It means that when someone takes on a role in the household, they take on that role and its responsibilities 'not from the standpoint of an individual, but through accounting for a set of relationships' (Morosanu 2016: 113).

Of course, researchers might also combine quantitative and qualitative approaches. Kara's (2020) term multi-modal is useful in thinking about this and what the implications are. My advice here is to be sure what role each approach is playing in the overall research. We tend to avoid the term 'triangulation' where qualitative research is involved because it has come to mean cross-checking, or confirming the truth. This has its uses but be careful not to assume that one response a participant gives has more meaning or weight than another – responses vary by context. It is better that we think in terms of dimensions of a phenomenon and complexity of issue when combining.

Collaborating

Collaborating is a way of thinking creatively about methods that includes the participants in the development of the research, with regard to design and implementation, in learning as we go, and sometimes in dissemination too. All interpretivist qualitative research is now at least somewhat participatory and collaborative (this is why we use the term 'participants', not 'subjects' or 'informants'), but collaboration and participation can take shape anywhere along a continuum from learning with participants as we go along (being iterative-inductive), to activist or militant research. With any collaborating it is essential to be clear to yourself, the participants, and readers of your work the extent and nature of collaboration. Similarly, as you proceed, navigate, through discussions and transparency, who has what role and pay ongoing attention to power and resources. Although these activities overlap in practice, I distinguish five collaborating heuristics: *learning with participants, co-production research, participatory action research, activist research,* and *decolonising methods.*

Learning with participants. Collaborating is about learning with participants, asking them to think about the questions you ask, adding more questions or taking the research in different directions, talking to them about developing analyses, working with you through creating, mediating, and doing, and broadly ensuring participants are freely taking part and have some agency in the process. Roxana Morosanu's (2016) diverse methods of research all lend themselves to enabling participants to collaborate more openly, freely, overtly and creatively (Box 7.10).

FOR YOUR TOOLKIT

Collaborating occurs along a continuum from simply learning with participants to activist or militant research. Five collaborating heuristics are: *learning with participants, co-production research, participatory action research, activist research,* and *decolonising methods.*

Co-production research is a more overt and proactive form of collaboration. It might involve participants in the design of the project, in undertaking interviews themselves, and in co-producing interventions and reports (Box 7.9). Community groups, third sector organisations and businesses may be involved in design and dissemination or have an advisory role (Renold et al 2023). Co-production is always creative in its understanding of research participation and practice.

Participatory action research has become a loosely used term to mean participatory research that works towards action or transformation. For Kara (2020: 46), 'Participatory research, also known as participatory action research, focuses on communities or groups and emphasises the full involvement of participants at every stage of the research process.' Maggie O'Neill (2011, 2018) uses the term alternately with participatory arts, invoking participants as co-researchers, learning through collective walks, and in other democratic ways of doing research. Participatory research is also designed to disrupt the researcher-researched relationship and facilitate participant 'voice' through narrative

(Aldridge 2015). In practice, the extent of involvement varies from project to project, but there is some agreement that the research should empower or benefit those involved in it (Bhana 2006, cited in Kara 2020: 46).

Box 7.9: Learning through collaborating: children's voices in design and implementation

Research by Renold et al (2023) for the National Society for the Prevention of Cruelty to Children in the UK, when exploring how young people learn about relationships, sex and sexuality, used a range of participatory and creative methods. It was co-produced with a young people's advisory group, which 'was composed of 10 young people (ages 15–17) from a range of socio-economic, cultural backgrounds and locales, who met (virtually) every month to inform the research methods and contribute to the process of analysis and to co-construct the creative outputs' (Renold et al 2023: 6).

The Young Voices programme in Plymouth, UK, 'involved young people in the design of campaigns to promote healthy relationships and prevent peer-on-peer sexual harm'. Claire White and Kandy Sisya's (2023) evaluation of the programme used focus groups and interviews with the staff and students who were involved in the learning and design process. Collaborating is thus written into both the initial project and its evaluation.

Maggie O'Neill's work is collaborative (and combining) through participatory action research, employing ethnographic, arts–based and biographical methods, working with community groups and artists, and informed by social justice, in areas such as forced migration and sex work (O'Neill 2011, 2018; FitzGerald et al 2020). Yolande Strengers, Melisa Duque and Sarah Pink collaborated with other colleagues, with aged care providers, and with seniors to understand how older Australians engage with smart home technologies. The participants were given the exciting opportunity to try out the technologies and the ethnographers learned through doing things with them: 'For us, this was a chance to learn alongside the seniors about how they would learn, live and improvise with smart home technologies, including digital voice assistance, robotic vacuum cleaners, smart lights, and smart kettles' (Pink et al 2022: 83).

Activist research might work with activists as collaborators or advisers (Shah 2017), or be more overtly activist in terms of focusing on the creative process of transformation (Bartlett 2015). Activist research can involve insider research with activist groups (Stuesse 2016); it can be militant and engaged (Scheper–Hughes 2004), and visual, filmic, public, critical, reflexive, and participatory (Palmas 2021). Angela Stuesse (2016) calls herself an activist anthropologist and her study of Latin American migrants working in chicken processing was undertaken in collaboration with a workers' centre, and focuses on mobilisation processes. Alpa Shah (2017: 56) warns 'there is a real tension between the democratic commitment to the truth in a holistic sense demanded by participant observation and the commitments of partisanship expected of the activist'. She is referring to ethnography and participant observation, but the warning is relevant for us all.

Activist research overlaps with critical approaches and with *decolonising methods*. The plea to decolonise research has a long history, perhaps beginning with the publications of Edward Said's (2021 [1978]) *Orientalism*, and Talal Asad's (1973) critique of coloniality in anthropology. Kathy Dodworth (2021) also traces it through the insider/outsider distinction (see O'Reilly 2009), that was 'precipitated by the increase of researchers from groups previously excluded from the chauvinist academy' (Dodworth 2021: 168), including 'minorities' and women. The debate then threads through feminist epistemologies and methodologies (for example, Sandra Harding 1986), through to recent activist and feminist work. Decolonising calls for the excluded to be put back in, and for a structural readjustment of the 'biases and limitations of the 98 percent Anglo white composition of the [sociological] profession' (Moore 1973: 66, cited in Dodworth 2021: 168).

FOR YOUR TOOLKIT

Decolonising calls for the excluded to be put (back) into social research, and for a structural readjustment of its biases and limitations (Dodworth 2021). Responses are diverse, collaborative, and imaginative.

The debate continues with little resolution but lots of creativity, imagination or thinking outside the box. I wish I could do it more justice here; it warrants a whole chapter at least and I do not feel qualified. Kara (2020) includes several related discussions in her book, for example about feminist research, transformative research, indigenous research, and queer research. Hilde Jakobsen (2012) has a wonderful discussion about her efforts to decentre herself in her research exploring women's experience of violence in Tanzania. In their book, *Decolonizing Ethnography*, Carolina Bejarano et al (2019: back cover)

> show how social science can function as a vehicle for activism and as a tool for marginalized people to theorize their lives. Tacking between personal narratives, ethnographic field notes, an original bilingual play about workers' rights, and examinations of anthropology as a discipline … they offer a guide for those wishing to expand the potential of ethnography to serve as a means for social transformation and decolonization.

Box 7.10: Learning through collaborating: self-interviewing over Five Cups of Tea

Morosanu (2016) developed the Five Cups of Tea method because she had come to see the role of mothering and its individual and cultural meanings as a crucial context for understanding domestic energy use and family life. She saw stopping for a cup of tea as an opportunity for the mothers in the study to take a little time out, to reflect, and to think about their own lives. So, on five separate occasions she set just two questions for them to think about, and she asked them to video their thoughts. The questions explored what the woman was doing before she stopped for the cup of tea, how she felt about this time out and the drink itself, and some further questions about their personal motivations and wishes. The exercise 'created a situation of self-interviewing that was flexible and non-intrusive' (p 67). It is important to note that Morosanu had already built relationships with her participants by this time, so their self-reflections in this exercise were as much about continuing a conversation with her as they were conversations with themselves (or self-reflections).

Final thoughts

With any attempts to be imaginative or creative, give a thought to how technology (be it paint, the internet, or getting on a bus) will be accessed, received, and experienced by the participants. Have a back–up plan for when things go wrong or don't work as you had envisaged. Test things out with colleagues and friends first, or with key participants. As Graham Crow (2022) and others have noted, when using creative methods it may be that you will need to hire, borrow or learn from other people who have different skills from yours, such as an artist, film maker, designer, or photographer.

Put creative methods in your toolkit but be aware of how each benefits your research. Communicate, collaborate, be flexible, let the fundamental principles guide you. Keep remembering what is important: detailed subjective understandings; lived experience; insider perspectives: a grounded sense of a community member's perspective; hearing people's recollections and interpretations of events; generating a variety of responses; giving a voice.

Speaking of being creative

'I think it would be fun to try out different methods such as drawing and maps, but I need to know why they might help. I don't think the surgeons I'm interviewing will appreciate it.'

'They couldn't find the words to tell me how they felt but we shared some photographs and talked about them and lots of stuff came out. I loved the way they would touch the photos, stop and think, and tell me stories.'

'Interviews weren't working, they felt so oppressive, so I sat with them while they made their quilt and we talked about all sorts of things. I began to understand things in a whole different way.'

'He agreed to talk to me for half an hour via Zoom, but in the end we chatted for almost two hours and he even picked up his laptop and showed me around the farm.'

'We are going to meet online again next week, because we've decided it would be better if they learn how to do the interviews themselves and I just watch. After all, they understand this life better than I ever can.'

Taking things further

I recommend Helen Kara's (2020) book *Creative Research Methods* for its depth, insight and inspiration. Mason (2018) also has a chapter titled **Being Creative with Methods**, that I discovered after this was written, and is very good. The hegemony of certain (White, Western) approaches has also involved a lack of recognition of **indigenous** methods and practices, and Kara (2020) cites relevant literature to correct this imbalance. For recent reflections and tips on the use of **internet-based** qualitative research methods, see Archibald et al (2019), Irani (2018), Lobe et al (2020) and Wilkerson et al (2014). Lewis-Dagnell et al (2023) provide a great review of 14 papers published since 2003 about facilitating the voices of **children with complex needs**, with lots of useful references. For an in-depth consideration of **ethics, reflexivity, research design, dissemination and creative method**, see Campbell et al (2023). For more on **co-production and participatory methods** see the UK Research and Innovation's web resource on co-production. *Creativity in Research* (Ulibarri et al 2019) is a fabulous book to help you put creativity at the heart of all aspects of your research, using mindfulness, tuning into your emotions, learning to tolerate ambiguity, and prototyping (among other techniques).

Listen to the related episode for this chapter on
Qualitative Research Methods for Everyone podcast:

8

Analysing and interpreting

What this chapter is about

Interpretivist social science works to understand other people's experiences and feelings, and the meanings behind them, to help them to clarify and express them, to make sense of these for ourselves in the context of our own lives and experiences, and finally to interpret or make sense of them for others so that our readers can make sense of them in the context of their own experiences. I thus begin here by reminding readers of the logic of interpretive analysis and the importance of remembering your research goals.

Researchers working in specific identifiable traditions (such as discourse and narrative analysis) can eschew more generic approaches such as thematic analysis as not relevant for their purposes. However, I agree with Virginia Braun and Victoria Clarke (2022) that the logic is similar no matter the tradition, and to illustrate this I review the analytical process of authors working in five different traditions. This highlights consistency in approach and shows how what I term *interpretive analysis* is informed by a shared logic and heuristics.

> **FOR YOUR TOOLKIT**
> Qualitative analysis is not a separate step in a linear process but incorporated as a spiral that moves forward and closes down while curling back on itself as qualitative research proceeds.

I then describe nine heuristics for achieving interpretive analysis while also being constantly mindful of the logic behind, and oscillating process of, interpretivism. The heuristics are: learning as you go; inductive immersion (becoming very familiar with all your data); annotating (adding notes); coding (making sure your notes can be found again and you can sort them into groups; sensitising (checking to see if a theory or concept helps); seeking coherence (sorting and clarifying); memoing (making longer notes that make sense of your codes); iterating (always remembering to look back and forth from time to time); and being reflexive.

> **FOR YOUR TOOLKIT**
> Heuristics are models that provide short-cut ways for thinking practically about analysis and its complex and interlocking nature.

I end with some tips to help you be iterative-inductive, a discussion of data management, and finally an example of qualitative analysis in action.

Interpretive analysis: the logic

Interpretive analysis as sense making begins as soon as data collection (or generation) begins. Qualitative research is iterative-inductive, constantly iterating between being inductive (open-minded, bottom-up, learning from the field) and deductive (testing out existing and new theories and concepts to see if they help clarify understandings), with an inductive approach retaining the upper hand. It employs a spiral logic of understanding that moves forward and closes down while curling back on itself as it goes. This enables the voices of the participants to be heard and the insights we learn to be incorporated into our research, learning as we go.

The first heuristic, then, is to learn as you go: analysis should not be left until you have collected all your data. Nevertheless, all researchers must confront the mass of data at some point (maybe returning at several points) to make some sense of some parts or all of it for a specific audience or reader. This involves looking for patterns, organising, reducing, and illuminating interconnections. This is challenging work that requires overt interpretations; it involves your input and will not emerge as if by magic no matter how objective you think you are being.

Always keep your goals in mind. When you designed your project, you should have made an argument for why qualitative methods would help you address your concerns or interests; now analysis needs to make sense of your data with these concerns in mind. Usually, the goal is to enrich our understanding of how things came to be, how they are, how people experience something, whether a new product or service is useful. What are the needs and choices of women with cerebral palsy, and what shapes these choices? (Box 8.1). How do people talk about vaccines when pregnant? (Box 8.2). How did farmers and workers experience COVID-19? (Box 8.3). The analysis should start here, with these questions in mind. Your goal may also have been to understand people in sensitive or complex situations, hard-to-reach groups, taboo topics and so on, and so the analysis must make sure to hear these voices.

> **FOR YOUR TOOLKIT**
> Qualitative analysis is interpretive, it will not emerge as if by magic no matter how 'objective' you try to be. Keep your research concerns in mind as you proceed, even if these have been adapted slightly as part of the iterative-inductive process.

Remember your philosophical position (Chapter 1). If you are drawing on phenomenology, you will be listening to, and findings ways to represent, the voices of the participants. If you are (also) influenced by a hermeneutic understanding you may wish to consider the wider context of culture and socialisation and make attempts to understand your participants' worlds in the context of your world as well as the worlds you are writing for. It may be that you are also interested in what people do, as well as what they say, or even what they don't say or do. You may want to draw conclusions from what people say about what they might do in future, making predictions, in order that you can propose how things might be changed to try to achieve desired outcomes.

Box 8.1: Linking research questions and analysis: women with cerebral palsy

'RIghts and CHoices for women with cerebral palsy (RICH study)' (Shah and Jones 2023) is a qualitative study to understand what works in the provision of maternity care for such women. The main research question was 'What shapes the experiences and choices in relation to pregnancy, childbirth and the postnatal period for women with cerebral palsy (CP) in the UK?' Sonali Shah and her colleagues aimed to 'Understand needs and choices of women with CP' to 'identify shared and divergent views … capture best practice … [and] understand experiences of health care professionals' leading eventually to some 'key themes and recommendations' (2023 np). In their analyses, they would be expected to ask of their data: what shapes experiences and choices? What are the needs and choices of women? How do these views diverge? What are the main themes? What is best practice? And so on.

The ultimate goal of qualitative analysis is to reduce the mass of information – spread across transcripts, notes and visual and creative data – into something meaningful, communicable and coherent. We want to achieve useful understandings, to use theories and concepts lightly, sensitively, and carefully, to benefit from preconceived ideas and our own knowledge, to shine a light onto things, but never to *impose* external ideas in a deterministic way. But during analysis, in all its phases, remember we also aim to be empathetic, reflexive, iterative, inductive, ethical, and kind.

FOR YOUR TOOLKIT
Remember the goal of qualitative research is to produce something meaningful, communicable, coherent, and useful.

As an aside, I do not use the term 'thematic analysis' in this chapter. This is not to deny the phenomenal achievement of Braun and Clarke (2022) in describing in rich and exhaustive detail the nature and process of what I call interpretive analysis. I draw extensively on their work, learning from them, sharing useful insights, and making comparisons; they have unwittingly contributed a great deal to the chapter. But thematic analysis when taken literally means analysing and looking for things. A theme can be a meaning, understanding, insight, norm, psychological strategy, or almost anything you are interested in (a recent word search generated 35 synonyms for 'themes'). I avoid the term thematic analysis because looking for or generating themes or things is a step within interpretive analysis not an end in itself.

FOR YOUR TOOLKIT

Thematic analysis is a step within interpretive analysis not an end in itself.

Five traditions and their common approach

In this section, I closely examine the analytical process of researchers working within the context of five different theoretical traditions and begin to identify heuristics they share in common. Different approaches or traditions are theoretically informed ways to think about how to make sense of data, related to understandings about how the world works (theories informed by epistemologies shaped by ontologies). They shape the sense making or the higher-level analysis (see Chapter 9) that will be used in final outputs. As the chapter proceeds, I also draw from other authors who have written about qualitative analysis as well as from my own experiences of using, teaching, and writing qualitative (usually ethnographic) research for over 30 years. I hope to give readers confidence that (1) although we are all using slightly different language, there is a great deal we all share in common, and (2) it is better to be guided by heuristics than to follow steps.

In their book *Five Ways of Doing Qualitative Analysis* (Wertz et al 2011: 6), the authors employ discourse analysis, narrative theory, grounded theory, phenomenological analysis and intuitive inquiry to analyse two texts: an interview transcript and a moving personal account. The texts come from Teresa, who wrote her own story and was interviewed on the topic of human resilience in the face of trauma or misfortune, as part of a graduate class exercise about qualitative research. Teresa is a pseudonym, although she had offered her real name. When aged 19 and while training to be an opera singer, Teresa developed cancer of the thyroid to the extent that it threatened her voice and career. 'As the cancer spread to her brain she entered into a struggle for her life and lost much of what was of value to her. In a courageous effort to live as fully as possible, she profoundly altered and expanded her life' (Wertz et al 2011: 6). I scrutinised these five different traditions and how they approached qualitative analysis and found some fundamental commonalities.

FOR YOUR TOOLKIT

The different approaches I have reviewed all employ versions of what I term learning as you go, inductive immersion, annotating, coding, sensitising, seeking coherence, memoing, iterating, and some also employ reflexive practice.

Discourse analysis

Linda McMullen, using discourse analysis, first read the accounts in an undirected way, making no notes. I assume this is because she wanted to be open-minded, to not shape the stories immediately but to listen and to hear them first. I identify this, later, as the heuristic of *inductive immersion*. One week later, McMullen read the accounts again, this time making notes in the margins. Here she is combining closeness and distance: the notes give her the opportunity to step back from the data and think about what is coming out from her close reading. This then is more iterative-inductive, to and fro, and I refer to it as the heuristic of *learning as you go*. The notes she made were paraphrases, key words, and descriptions (McMullen 2011: 209). I identify this as the heuristic of *annotating* or adding notes. It requires also summarising those notes using some sort of shorthand, so that what has been noted can be found again later using a search term. This is best done by what I am calling *coding* or adding short labels. McMullen did not impose her theoretical framework or insights but tested after several readings to see if they helped with the sense making: later readings of the texts were more directed, drawing on analytic concepts from discourse analysis. This I identify as the heuristic of *sensitising* or testing to see if a theory or concept helps. McMullen says she stepped back from analysis and thought about how concepts such as resilience, coping, and recovery were framing the discourse because of the way the original project was set up. Here she is *iterating*, balancing an inductive approach with her own insights, and *seeking coherence* for her higher-level sense making.

Eventually, McMullen's higher-level sense making informed by discourse analysis understood the text in terms of a Western cultural discourse of 'resilience as exceptionality' (2011: 214), requiring her to refer to literature in that field.

Narrative analysis

Ruthellen Josselson conducted a narrative analysis of Teresa's story. Again, my goal is to examine the analytical process Josselson took that led to her higher-level sense making, rather than expand on the concept of narrative analysis itself. Josselson (2011: 228) says: 'There is mercifully no dogma or orthodoxy yet about how to conduct narrative research.' Rather, it is a way of thinking, a way of asking questions, of interrogating the voices, in context. Nevertheless, she first read the texts overall for a sense of structure and general themes (*inductive immersion*). Later, she read the texts multiple times, with the purpose of identifying different voices of the self, and further iterative readings seeking themes that cover contradictions (*learning as you go*) and reaching overall coherence (*seeking coherence*). I presume at this stage that Josselson also had to start making some notes (*annotating*) and maybe also did some *coding* so that she could come back and find what she wanted to sort into themes. In order not to impose her ideas onto the data, she slowly and gradually draws on the wider theoretical literature, using concepts from narrative theory, to 'remain sensitive to nuances of meaning' (Josselson 2011: 228); she is *sensitising*. It is important to note that Josselson also considered the interpretive context of the interview; this is a crucial aspect in which discourse analysis and narrative sense making differ.

Josselson's (2011: 230) higher-level sense making is that both of Teresa's 'tellings … can be read as narratives of transformation and integration'. She had a whole sense of self that was predicated on her being a singer, which was lost, along with her relationship with her coach, when she became ill. Teresa's narratives recount how she had to reinvent herself and find 'new ways of being with others and in the world' (2011: 231). The narrative analysis is taken to a higher level still when Josselson says 'I have also read this narrative as a romance in which resilience inheres in the journey of struggle rather than the outcome' (2011: 237–8).

Grounded theory

Kathy Charmaz attempts to analyse Teresa's accounts using grounded theory. Grounded theories tend to be substantive, developed to address given problems in specific situations; although they can also be generalised to broader situations. Grounded theory is more commonly used in medical, educational and criminological settings, than in academic settings where researchers identify with specific academic disciplines. It is crucial to be aware that there are objectivist (or positivist) and constructivist approaches, and these can exist at quite an extreme distance from each other (Taghipour 2014). Kathy Charmaz is a self-claimed constructivist grounded theorist. The advantage of grounded theory for my purposes here is that it identifies clear steps in its analysis; indeed, this is exactly why grounded theory was first developed by Barney Glaser and Anselm Strauss (1967). Grounded theory can be used as a methodology: it is a grounded theory of interpretive analysis. A disadvantage is the expectation that each researcher might develop a new theory to address the specific problem at hand.

Charmaz (2011) outlines the steps she would take, which begin at the design stage of the research process. Grounded theory begins with research questions and opening interview questions then, as the researchers start to collect (or create) data, they begin open *coding*. 'Codes *arise from* the researcher's interaction with the data; they are not preconceived and *applied to* the data, as occurs in quantitative research,' Charmaz argues (2011: 165, emphasis in original). Grounded theory develops by trying to be as open-minded as possible when collecting data, but also tuning in to the insights the researchers learn as they go along, redesigning the research questions and even the sample as they proceed so that they can ensure that they have asked the right things of the right people in order to have the confidence to talk about what they wish to talk about in the final high-level analysis or in the grounded theory they develop (see the heuristic of *iterating*). Charmaz also uses memos and talks of raising codes to categories. To put it another way, she suggests that we continually *annotate* and the heuristic of *memoing* is a really good way to formalise this, helping sort the data and *seeking coherence* as we proceed.

Charmaz also uses the concepts of 'theoretical sampling' and 'directed data collection', by which she means that the sampling proceeds during the project in order to shape and confirm the developing theory. These techniques are specific to grounded theory, but they are also used to a greater or lesser extent, depending on the project design, in all qualitative research. Certainly, in ethnography, although we may not be developing a theory from the ground up, we are often developing a rich and complex understanding of the situation, group, or phenomenon through interaction with the field and with analysis as an ongoing process (*learning as you go*). Charmaz then describes writing more advanced memos, refining the developing categories, adopting these as theoretical concepts, sorting them, and then integrating them. These are all useful means to enhance *seeking coherence*. Her higher-level sense making, in this case a grounded theory, finally identifies a process that Teresa went through of: receiving bad news, telling news, experiencing a disruption of self, loss of self, facing loss, and regaining a valued sense of self.

Phenomenological psychology

Frederick Wertz (2011) uses phenomenological psychology to analyse Teresa's texts. First, he talks of doing an open reading that is holistic (*inductive immersion*), using a technique he calls 'evenly hovering attention' that he takes from Freud. He then suggests we should 'discriminate meaning units or segments' (Wertz 2011: 131) that he will attend to later for fruitful reflection (here I expect he would need to do some *annotating* and *coding*). For Wertz, psychological reflection overlaps with open reading, annotating and coding, and this reminds me that *being reflexive*, as an ongoing part of the analytical process is a useful heuristic. Eventually, for Wertz, it is important to develop a structural understanding and description (*seeking coherence*). Throughout, Wertz emphasises the importance of immersion, empathy, suspension of belief, explicating meanings, relating insights to the whole, and using received concepts as heuristics (*sensitising*) to guide descriptive reflection (Wertz 2011: 132). Wertz's final higher-level analysis is complex (and as I am not a psychologist I find the language difficult) but, crudely, Wertz argues that Teresa's stories help us understand the meaning of trauma and its role in a person's life.

Intuitive inquiry

Rosemarie Anderson uses intuitive inquiry to analyse Teresa's accounts. This is based on 'cycles of analysis and interpretation that pivot around the researcher's intuition' (Anderson 2011: 244). Anderson's process (2011: 251–54) emphasises: extensive engagement through reading, listening and viewing (*inductive immersion*); generating preliminary lenses from extant literature in a dialectic process (*sensitising*); a willingness to be influenced by the data; and settling on a final set of interpretive lenses (*seeking coherence*). She highlights parts of the text that interested her (*annotating* and *coding*), sorts meaning units into themes, reconfigures and reframes (*seeking coherence*). She argues that if she were to continue she would interview several dozen adults and analyse patterns, but as a tentative conclusion she suggests that Teresa's ability to recover, and to accept the need for surgery and treatment, was facilitated by her directing her anger at her cancer rather than at her body.

The spiral of heuristics in interpretive analysis

Remembering that analysis proceeds in a spiral not a line (is iterative-inductive), the following heuristics are ways to think about the overlapping steps that are employed by researchers from diverse traditions. With any of these heuristics, try not to get hung up on semantics; it is the process that matters not how we label it. Heuristics are models that provide short-cut ways of thinking practically about something that is more complex and interlocking in practice. The nine heuristics are:

- Learning as you go
- Inductive immersion (becoming very familiar with all your data)
- Annotating (adding notes)
- Coding (making sure your notes can be found again and you can sort them into groups)
- Sensitising (checking to see if a theory or concept helps)
- Seeking coherence (sorting and clarifying)
- Memoing (making longer notes that make sense of your codes)
- Iterating (always remembering to look back and forth from time to time)
- Being reflexive

Learning as you go

When you developed your discussion guide based on insights from participants (see Chapters 4 and 5), or asked a different question in a different way in an interview, or decided there were other people you needed to talk to, different things you needed to ask, new techniques you wanted to use (in ethnography or when being creative), or wider structures you became aware of, in each of these cases you were learning, thinking, and analysing, or being iterative-inductive (Chapter 1), and working towards reflexive interpreting (Chapter 3). Robert Emerson, Rachel Fretz and Linda Shaw (2011: 198) talk of remaining 'open to the varied and sometimes unexpected possibilities, processes and issues that become apparent as one immerses oneself in the written data'.

The heuristic of learning as you go emphasises the recursive and ongoing nature of interpretive analysis and asks that you do it consciously and overtly: take notes, write memos, add notes or codes as you *generate* data. I am not suggesting you draw conclusions so soon, but that you label things you might want to find later, identify potential themes, work through developing thoughts, start coding, annotating and memoing straight away. This, in turn, enables you to hear better, think more, and to engage with the field as you learn from it.

> **FOR YOUR TOOLKIT**
> Analysis begins with listening, thinking and learning as you go. Do it consciously and overtly by annotating, coding, and memo writing.

Inductive immersion

Inductive immersion is like swimming in the data, being intimately familiar with it at the beginning of the research, and as you go along. Always begin any analysis session by looking, listening, hearing, and thinking (again). The purpose of this heuristic is to ensure you approach the data with an open mind. It does not involve systematic coding from the very beginning of the research, but it does mean constantly being attentive and starting to think, and starting to make notes that draw attention to observations, to pull out what you have begun to think might be important. Inductive immersion enables you to consider all dimensions of the data, including any you may have overlooked in a rush to analyse, and to see the whole as well as its parts. Tread lightly but thoroughly.

> **FOR YOUR TOOLKIT**
> Inductive immersion means being familiar with your data as you go along and at the start of any new analysis session.

Do this as you collect data, but do it again when you decide to become more focused on a specific output or summary. Stay close to your data by every now and then having another relaxed read or look at the whole transcript, an entire section of notes, or a set of images. Braun and Clarke (2022: 43) call this data familiarisation and suggest you think of it as 'settling in to the cinema to avidly enjoy the latest, much awaited release in your favourite movie series'.

In the Picking for Britain and Global Labour in Rural Societies projects (Box 8.4), one of the things that came out during inductive immersion was an implicit acceptance that current farming and market conditions compel farmers to use short-term, precarious, temporary migrant labour. This was difficult to code because although it was pervasive it was also in what was *not* said and in assumptions *behind* comments. Analysis of this involved making notes and memoing – asking what evidence or quotes we had to back up this overall feeling, and how it differed for farmers and workers. It eventually led to an analysis of symbolic bordering (O'Reilly and Scott 2023a). It is worth noting that neither systematic open coding nor even line by line coding would have revealed this insight because the words were not there.

Annotating

Annotating simply means making notes: it is the act of noting what comes to mind, be it in writing, drawing, sketching, or making a map. Annotating draws attention to what you started to think might be important; it objectifies ideas, making you see, question and develop insights. Annotating involves reflection, consideration and clarification. It is an active process that leads eventually to coding as you become more confident of your analytical directions. Annotating is more than simply highlighting passages (although that can also be useful); you need to make a note (annotate) to explain to yourself why you thought a passage was worth highlighting. Annotating is a heuristic to aid interpreting.

FOR YOUR TOOLKIT
Annotating is the act of making a note of ongoing interpretations.

Think within and across the data. Grounded theorists talk of making *constant comparisons* when doing analysis. By this, they mean that you should always be sense making, annotating and coding, both *within* a single piece of data and conceptually *across* the data at the same time (zooming in and zooming out). Constant comparisons are enabled by the fact that you have done proper inductive immersion, you are familiar with your data and with your participants' responses and your own observations.

Coding

Coding is the act of putting words or short phrases next to passages of text or visual data so that you can find them again and start to work on connections between elements, pathways, and processes. Heuristically speaking, coding is not analysis but a technique to facilitate and record analysis. I distinguish open coding, analytical coding, and structural coding, as heuristics, but you can conceptualise this in any way that works for you. Coding summarises meaning, but it is an active process in as much as identifying and labelling also makes you look closely and analytically and see what is coming to light. As Mai Skjøtt Linneberg and Steffen Korsgaard (2019: 7) suggest, because coding involves looking minutely at data, it also enables you to 'acquire deep, comprehensive and thorough insights'.

FOR YOUR TOOLKIT
Coding is the act of putting words or short phrases next to passages of text or visual data so that you can find them again. It is a technique to facilitate analysis.

Coding should not mean mindlessly or systematically sticking labels on things:

In some ways, coding is similar to how the craftsmanship of the stroke, the mixing of colours and the preparation of a canvas are conducive to the artfulness of both abstract and figurative painting. As such, structuring your data and achieving an overview of it, carefully considering the relevance, meaning and importance of segments of data, and making the data accessible for subsequent data analysis are all likely to constitute good practice and to enable good analytical work in most of the approaches used in qualitative research. (Linneberg and Korsgaard 2019: 260)

Codes need notes (*annotating*), and coding overlaps with *inductive immersion* and involves asking questions of the data, such as what is this about, what is going on here? Annotating and coding are techniques for 'hearing the data' (Rubin and Rubin 2011) and for identifying and labelling analytic insights. I describe open, analytical and structural coding but you can develop your own heuristics; for example, reflexive coding could mean adding a code so that you can find a specific reflexive note again, task coding could identify things you want to go back and do or check.

Open coding

Open coding begins to identify what is interesting and what might be relevant. Here the main focus is the 'data', the participants responses, and actions, the things you have observed. Open coding assists your analysis and opens avenues of enquiry; it is the beginning of your sense making. At first, try to move quickly and keep codes simple and precise: 'speed and spontaneity ... can spark your thinking and spawn a fresh view' (Charmaz 2014: 118). You will have plenty of time to elaborate later, to annotate, to sort and to write memos. Start coding in an open-minded way (but with the research question in mind) and simply jot down anything of interest. Delve into what is not immediately apparent; listen to the data, hear the arguments (the insider perspectives).

This is also sometimes called inductive or descriptive coding (Bingham 2023), or initial coding (Charmaz 2014). I use 'open' as a reminder that the code and notes should be open to further revision: be prepared to change, rethink, sort, rewrite and to do it all again, differently. Code 'without regard for how and whether ideas and categories will ultimately be used, whether other relevant observations have been made, or how they will fit together' (Emerson et al 2011: 175). Open coding leads to more analysis, and perhaps in the earlier stages of a project, to more data collection.

Remember that you are *constructing* codes (Charmaz 2014: 116). As with annotating, this is an active process and simply highlighting text is not adequate. You need to *make* a note or a code label or add a word or two so that you can find the segment of data again. 'A code label should reduce the mess of the data and summarise the meaning you're identifying in the data extract' (Braun and Clarke 2022: 60).

The extent to which you can open code before moving swiftly on to analytical coding depends on the nature and quality of the data. Field notes should already be somewhat coded and annotated, as should visual and creative data, because it should always be clear why you created and collected material. Braun and Clarke (2022: 63) have some great examples of codes while simultaneously illustrating how open and analytical codes are difficult to distinguish. Open codes tend to be more descriptive: our early ones in the Picking for Britain project (Box 8.4) included 'dentist', 'family', and 'buses' (which eventually we came to see as aspects of people's daily lives that must be fitted around work time).

Coding is an iterative process in its attempt to always remain somewhat inductive, to hear the data, while also working to narrow down the analyses to focus on a few themes, a process, a narrative account or whatever higher-level sense making you will develop (Chapter 9). And remember that it is easy to get stuck on one track, but you may want to code for different things (themes) at different times.

To give one example, when open coding the transcripts from the Picking for Britain (PfB) and Global Labour in Rural Societies (Glarus) projects (Box 8.4), we began to notice a constant reference to time, such as in the following quotes (O'Reilly and Scott 2023b, emphasis added):

> We're flexible because of course weather conditions change the crops so much, so that's when we need flexibility of our labour, so we tell our employees at two o'clock today what *time* we'd like them to work tomorrow or whether they're on day off. Now that doesn't necessarily suit someone who's, you know, got rent to pay, got a mortgage, needs to have that stability of work. It does suit someone who's living cheaply onsite, who has made the decision to come to, to make money really. (Paul, HR manager, large farm, Glarus project)

> The first few days did feel really, really long. They felt endless really because it was so early and getting used to getting back into that and you're on your feet for a very, very long *time* as well. (Diane, worker, PfB project)

> Strictly speaking you would really struggle to make a real career out of such a thing as seasonal work. The seasonal pickers that I worked with over the summer knew very well that they were here for X amount of *time* ... I deem myself to be a young professional. I am thinking about career and opportunity and all of these things and I don't know that you can find that in that particular area of work. (Neil, worker, PfB project)

I will return to the topic of time in analysis later.

> ### FOR YOUR TOOLKIT
> Open coding focuses on the data with an open mind. Analytical coding goes back to the data to see how and where open codes work. Structural coding helps you shape the analysis. They are heuristic devices not discrete steps.

Analytical coding

Analytical coding facilitates sense making; it is more focused, analytical, selective, and conceptual than open coding. Here, the stronger analytic directions that have come from open codes and inductive immersion are taken back to the data for a more fine-grained or focused inspection (Emerson et al 2011). In the Picking for Britain project (Box 8.4), for example, we took 'family' back to the data to see what it was made up of, and ended up distinguishing between family sizes and generations, as well as local and migrant families.

Analytical coding tries to determine the adequacy of analytical insights for larger segments of data, but also breaks them down, reconsiders and revises them. It is your opportunity to focus on and refine emerging (or co-created) insights. All coding is iterative, not linear and so open coding and analytical coding overlap in practice, while moving in the direction from open to analytical to structured. Analytical coding is comparative because it thinks across and within data, and it overlaps with annotating by refining, defining, and unpacking codes (and starting to write more).

Other authors allude to this heuristic using words such as 'focused coding' (Emerson et al 2011; Charmaz 2014) and 'selective coding' (Strauss and Corbin 1998). Andrea Bingham (2023) and Linneberg and Korsgaard (2019) distinguish inductive and deductive coding, though in practice such a distinction is hard to make. This is also one of the few instances where I differ quite profoundly from Braun and Clarke (2022). I find their six phases of analysis, that include going from coding to generating initial themes in one step, does not adequately represent the recursive nature of iterative-inductive analysis. For an example, take a look at how Roxana Morosanu (2016; Chapter 7) developed the analytical concept of the Mother-Multiple.

Box 8.2: Linking research questions and analysis: pregnancy and COVID-19

In the qualitative study 'Pregnant women's perceptions and the acceptance of vaccinations during the COVID-19 pandemic' the main questions and aims are: 'How do pregnant women perceive and feel about vaccinations as a result of the COVID-19 pandemic … to identify barriers and facilitators to uptake of vaccinations … provide health professionals with improved understanding of pregnant women's vaccination decisions, and how COVID-19 has affected perceptions' (Parsons et al nd).

In their analysis, then, Jo Parsons and colleagues would need to draw out the perceptions that have been uncovered. They would need to discuss what women say about how they feel about vaccinations and how they believe Covid has affected their perceptions. They would then need to sort these into barriers and incentives for different types of women and circumstances (note that it is unlikely the participants worded their answers as barriers and incentives, so the researchers would need to employ higher-level analysis (Chapter 9). Similarly, learning how participants feel is one thing, but drawing conclusions from this about vaccination decisions is a further step in the analysis, since we cannot always assume what people say is the same as what they will do.

In the Picking for Britain and Glarus projects (Box 8.4) we soon started to notice that the concept of time was complex and not always used with the word itself. We returned to the transcripts, using time as an analytical code for large and varied segments of data and it became increasingly complex. Our next cycle of open coding involved looking closely at where we had coded 'time' and to open code those sections (while always remaining familiar with the rest of the data through *inductive immersion* and *constant comparisons*). This led us to see time in terms of seasons and seasonal work, daily (home) life and other commitments, temporary work and future plans (different for migrants than locals), energy limits, the time demands of the farm, the weather and the crops, but also things like how harvest work fits with family time and people's life-spans and careers, and finally how farm work is often spoken about in a historical context.

Structural coding

Heuristically speaking, structural coding involves identifying passages of text or other data in accordance with the way you are structuring or organising the analysis. It includes identifying and labelling relationships and interconnections, or drawing on other variables such as gender, class, income, pregnant women and healthcare professionals (Box 8.2), farmers and workers (Box 8.3), local and migrant workers (Box 8.4). In other words, code anything you may want to find again for other reasons than the sense making you have done so far but that helps you structure and shape your analysis. Structural coding enables the complexity and diversity of responses to be recognised, and will require the assistance of memoing, diagramming, mapping and other ways to conceptualise structure.

FOR YOUR TOOLKIT

Coding is iterative and designed to facilitate sense making. Do *not* systematically code label everything in order as you read or see it. You will code different sections in different ways at different times. Some text will have several codes, some will have none because (having used inductive immersion) you decided it was not relevant to your analysis at this time.

Structural coding can be used to help identify what Braun and Clarke (2022) call central organising concepts, and to relate themes to sub themes. You may also develop categories, or higher order concepts (Strauss and Corbin 1998: 113). Axial coding is used by Anselm Strauss and Juliet Corbin (1998: 117) to formalise the linking of categories into a framework, and to specify the properties and dimensions of a category. Axial coding is a tool you can use, along with mind maps, and other more creative structuring techniques as well as any of the higher-level organising principles in Chapter 9.

Box 8.3: Linking research questions and analysis: seasonal labour

Feeding the Nation: Seasonal Migrant Workers and Food Security during COVID-19 Pandemic aimed '(1) to provide information in real time on worker recruitment and retention in order to support evidence-based rapid interventions and mitigate risks for UK the food supply; (2) to provide information to limit contagion on farms; (3) to document the experiences of seasonal workers and farmers; (4) to inform decisions on the post-Brexit immigration system in light of possible future pandemics; (5) conceptually, to contribute to theories about the high demand for migrant labour in periods of high unemployment and (6) and to debates on the contributions of low skilled migrants as key workers' (Barbulescu nd).

Clearly, not all of these are addressed through qualitative methods of data collection, so it is important to clarify how objectives will be met. When it comes to their qualitative analysis, Roxana Barbulescu and colleagues will be asking: what are the diverse experiences of seasonal workers and farmers? How can we now understand recruitment from the perspective of farmers and migrant workers? They will be sensitive to theories about migrant labour and low-skilled work.

Sensitising

Sensitising is being constantly sensitive to what external ideas and literature might aid sense making and carefully bringing in theories, concepts and frameworks to see where they help illuminate the data (Chapter 2). I am talking here about ideas that come with conceptual baggage or that require references to wider literature, as well as theoretical frameworks that you adopt or even develop to inform a theoretical explanation. During analysis, literature is consulted iteratively, in an ongoing process of immersing, annotating, coding, reading, sensitising, memoing, and seeking coherence, until explanations become gradually more refined and more useful. But other imported ideas, such as preformed problems, typologies, classification systems, and common-sense concepts should also be used consciously, explicitly and reflexively to aid analysis not to be imposed on it.

> **FOR YOUR TOOLKIT**
> Sensitising involves being sensitive to what external ideas (theories, frameworks, concepts) might illuminate meaning making.

Bingham (2023) uses the concept of deductive coding as a strategy for applying theory and explaining findings in the context of an inductive-deductive process. Sensitising yourself to wider literature and to other externally sourced ideas may involve theory testing, development or refinement, in analytical cycles (Linneberg and Korsgaard 2019). Indeed, as Emerson et al (2011: 198) have clarified: 'it is misleading to dichotomize data and theory as two separate and distinct entities, as data are never pure but, rather, are imbued with or instructed by concepts in the first place'.

Continuing to analyse the data from the Picking for Britain and Glarus projects (Box 8.4) we stepped back to think and read, *sensitising* ourselves to wider literature while seeking coherence, and discovered Hartmut Rosa's (2015) work on acceleration. Rosa distinguishes daily time (which is cyclical, repetitive, here and now), longer time (which recognises agents have one eye on future time in the context of their personal biographies), and past times (a perspective that often looks nostalgically on times gone by). This informed an article on harvest work, migration, and the structured phenomenology of time that uses time as a lens for understanding our participants' perspectives (O'Reilly and Scott 2023b). Interestingly, this lens of time also provided a *structure* and *coherence* for other themes we had identified through open coding, such as pressure to get fruit picked, the weather, the UK benefits system, the fact that migrants suspend family life, the difficulty of local workers to adapt to the needs of the farm, and so on. Our broader argument, or higher-level analysis (Chapter 9), is that this conceptualisation of harvest work highlights how solutions cannot be found because time is used as an excuse for the status quo.

Seeking coherence

Now we need to move on to sorting, clarifying, and seeking coherence, which I cover in extensive detail in Chapter 9. Seeking coherence involves moving away from the data towards more abstraction, analysis, reduction, and synthesis. Start to step back and examine the codes and see how they fit together, compare codes in one piece of data with other pieces (as you collect data where possible), then take them back to the data in a more focused way, simultaneously with analytic coding. This will be facilitated by memoing.

> **FOR YOUR TOOLKIT**
> Seeking coherence, sorting and clarifying involves moving away from the data towards abstraction, analysis, reduction, and synthesis.

Memoing

> Memos are creatively developed little documents based on intuition, hunches and serendipitous occurrences. (Saldaña 2015, in Linneberg and Korsgaard 2019: 18)

Memoing is writing, sketching, recording, or mapping, using whatever tools you wish to help draw connections between elements and elaborate what they might mean. A good way to think about them is as working your ideas out on paper, and facilitating structural coding. Braun and Clarke (2022) use the notion of visual mapping of a central organising concept, or of a candidate theme, or for theme generating. While annotating involves creatively jotting down rambling thoughts, memos are more analytical, giving shape and meaning to notes, yet are still creative. They provide an opportunity to develop ideas into bigger concepts such as themes, sub themes, overarching themes, processes, or other organising principles (Chapter 9). Analytical memos are the pivotal intermediate step between coding, seeking coherence, the development of higher-level analysis, and writing. They mark the beginning of theorising or conscious interpretation as opposed to pure description or summarising of topics (see Braun and Clarke 2022: 77). As a practical tool, analytical memoing enables the ongoing task of sorting and seeking coherence and as such may direct further data collection, coding, annotating or immersion. Memoing, as with annotating and coding, is writing for yourself not (yet) for anyone else, but you are doing it with readers or consumers in mind (Emerson et al 2011).

Memoing is work in progress. When memoing, try not to structure too much at first, be creative and imaginative, moving between ideas, data, coding, to and fro, in an iterative development of analysis leading to more advanced memos (Strauss and Corbin 1998). Use mind maps, sketches, diagrams, long pieces of writing, as well as systematically developed arguments and schema. Remember to include data as examples (quotes, stories, images) so that you avoid abstracting away from the data and your examples are always intimately linked to your argument. Start at the inductive immersion phase (Braun and Clarke 2022 talk of making familiarisation doodles) or when annotating and open coding. Remember, qualitative analysis is not a linear process.

FOR YOUR TOOLKIT

Memoing is the act of writing, sketching, recording, or mapping, to help draw connections between elements and elaborate what they might mean.

Iterating

Heuristically, iterating is checking you have not jumped to conclusions, that you have heard the data by going back through the loops of the spiral, engaging in inductive immersion, annotating, coding, memoing, and sensitising before rushing to seek coherence. Qualitative research is iterative-inductive, constantly iterating between being inductive (open–minded, bottom-up, learning from the field) and deductive (testing out existing and new theories and concepts to see if they help clarify understandings), with an inductive approach retaining the upper hand. The process that Braun and Clarke (2022) describe is an adventure, messy and organic. It is important that your codes do not too quickly become a strait-jacket: try not to be constrained by what you develop, as David Silverman (2009) warns.

> **FOR YOUR TOOLKIT**
> Iterating is going back and forth through the spiral of heuristics to ensure you have not jumped to conclusions.

Being reflexive

This heuristic reminds us that qualitative analysis engages reflexive interpreting or sense making. Being reflexive can involve acknowledging any presuppositions you might have (for example in first defining your research problem), identifying any expectations, being clear about the literature you have read and how it shapes your research, clarifying any theories you favour, or your philosophical leanings, as well as thinking about who you are and how your own background and experiences shape the research as it proceeds (see Chapter 3). *Reflexive annotating* and *coding* could track, reflect on, and consider personal motivations, experiences, and emotions, and how they are impacting the analysis as you proceed. *Reflexive memoing* could involve articulating your thoughts, reflecting on them and acting to allow them to shape interactions (between you, participants, data, literature, and concepts). Interpreting data always involves considering the emotions and assumptions of all involved. Reflexive interpreting (Chapter 3; Benson and O'Reilly 2020b) acknowledges the reflexivity and positionality of the human individuals and groups with whom we undertake research, and therefore views social life itself as a (constantly shifting) reflexive process of negotiating and accommodating.

Tips to help you be iterative-inductive

I have described the aforementioned as heuristics rather than as phases or steps because I want to avoid readers taking them too literally or trying to rigidly distinguish one from another (conceptually or practically). Because rigidity with techniques can curtail the imagination, I outline here a number of techniques specifically designed to help you deal with biases and preconceptions and to add even further richness and complexity. I cover teamwork, looking for in vivo codes, using gerunds, line-by-line coding, waving the red flag, and playing, but be creative and design your own (maybe even using artificial intelligence, as long as you remember the logic of interpretive analysis).

Teamwork

Teamwork is productive for facilitating imagination, creativity, and reflexive practice. Share your thoughts, annotations and open codes, and discuss and reconsider them together. Work on memos together and iterate while giving space for different perspectives, challenging and bouncing ideas off each other. If you are not working in a team, share short passages of text with a colleague, ask them to code it using open codes, and then discuss it with them, to complement the more inductive aspects of coding. I have found it refreshing, over the years, that this exercise tends to reassure students that they are all seeing similar issues and concepts albeit that different people focus on them in slightly different ways. Team insights supplement the overall picture with different dimensions rather than conflicting your own findings. Of course, this will depend on your and their philosophical perspectives: a discourse theorist, for example, may well focus on discourses that shape participants' responses and you, in turn, might decide that while these discourses do exist, they are not your focus for this particular project, and you are more interested in views and needs (Box 8.1).

FOR YOUR TOOLKIT
Teamwork facilitates imagination, creativity and reflexive practice.

Looking for in vivo codes

Strauss and Corbin (1998: 105) suggest we can reveal important insights about categories and concepts by taking and analysing 'the words of respondents themselves' that are *in vivo*, or living in the data. For Emerson et al (2011), this involves appreciating local meanings, classifications, and descriptions, and avoiding imposing our own understandings. Strauss and Corbin (1998) use the example of hearing about a nurse who was described as the 'tradition bearer' on a ward and how it made them think about rule enforcers more broadly as well as those who don't follow rules well. Tuning in to words or phrases that keep being repeated and/or that seem to have significance for the participants can be illuminating. It enables you to be inductive, to use serendipity wisely, or to come to see what had not been in plain sight. In my research in Malaysia (Benson and O'Reilly 2018), migrants often spoke to me of their 'maids'. This made me feel uncomfortable because it is a derogatory word that is rarely used now in British culture. It invokes class differences, exploitation, status and hierarchy, privilege, and lack of awareness of all of these. Having first noticed its use (and using reflexive practice to think about how I felt about it), I began to pay more attention to how and when the word was used and slowly became aware that several research participants themselves seemed uncomfortable with it too and were often using it reflexively, critically, or ironically. Following more discussion, I found they were happy, even relieved, to reflect on the word and what it meant for their position in Malaysian society. Note that in my case, this technique was used not just during analysis of transcripts but as part of ongoing analysis that was taking place as I did the research. The in vivo coding led me to ask more questions and share more conversations with participants.

Coding for actions

Another suggestion from Charmaz (2014: 116) is to code for actions rather than themes or topics. Try using the infinitive or gerund version of a word or phrase when coding. Turning words like 'freedom' into expressing feeling free, or experiencing freedom, added a sense of process to my analysis of life in Spain for British migrants (O'Reilly 2020b). Think of words like identity or nationalism and compare them with identifying, expressing, or denying a national identity. It changes the focus of your analysis from static features to what is going on, what is being done, or what is happening.

Line-by-line coding

Here we take one section of transcript or field notes and try to add a code or little note to every single line. The activity makes you slow down and look closely and is particularly useful for those who tend to rush to conclusions. Do not start with line-by-line coding, but a bit of close and systematic coding here and there 'prompts you to remain open to the data' (Charmaz 2014: 125). Please do not take line-by-line coding too literally: the length of a line in your data will depend on how you have formatted the page. And do *not* try to do it with all your notes or transcripts: use it for a section you have overlooked or that you think might be particularly dense or interesting. Always have the rest of your data loosely in mind (as a result of inductive immersion), so that you can do what grounded theorists call constant comparisons (zooming in and zooming out).

Waving the red flag

Strauss and Corbin (1998: 97) remind us that 'persons are the products of their cultures, the times in which they live, their genders, their experiences, and their training. The important thing is to recognise when either our own or the respondents' biases, assumptions, or beliefs are intruding into the analysis.' Waving the red flag involves being alert to phrases that close down conversation or analysis, phrases such as 'I would never do that' or 'we all say this is important' should cause you to stop and think. Similarly, a word that is used often (such as 'freedom', used liberally by the British on the Costa del Sol; O'Reilly 2000) without being explained should cause you to sit up and ask questions. Try

not to take what you see and hear at face value or think you have understood something without questioning it.

> **FOR YOUR TOOLKIT**
>
> Looking closely at *in vivo* codes means tuning in to repeated words or phrases or those with significance for the participants. Coding for *actions* contributes a sense of time, change and process to analysis. Line-by-line coding keeps you close to the data. *Waving the red flag* alerts you to phrases that challenge assumptions. *Playing* with data keeps you creative and imaginative.

Playing with data

Pat Thomson (2017) asks you to engage in play to ensure your analysis is creative and imaginative: 'Play that is designed to help you see new ways of connecting, new patterns, new groups, new associations, new commonalities, new aspects of context in your data. Get out of the rut of the anticipated. Get rid of the grip of the immediately obvious.'

She suggests a few techniques. *Random associations* involves taking your themes, at any stage, and looking to see if there are associations you've missed or that might become meaningful when you force links between them. *Scatter gun* is like making a randomly generated mind map; it forces you to think again, or to move away from fixed ideas. *Redactions* involves playing with words you notice, and words you don't. *Side by side* involves comparing and contrasting images (and see Strauss and Corbin 1998: 95). Charmaz (2014: 124–5) has further suggestions for techniques to help keep an open mind. Strauss and Corbin (1998: 94) suggest a 'flip-flop' technique, whereby concepts are turned upside down or inside out to think about them differently, and argue that words such as 'easy', 'always', or 'never' are questioned or challenged (perhaps during interviews or at least during analysis). You can make up your own exercises as long as you remember the point is to help you move away from oppressively searching for what you already thought was there and to prevent you reaching conclusions too easily, quickly, and superficially.

Data management

Interpretive analysis is an iterative process of making sense of all or parts of the data for a specific reader or user. Data will be moved from chronological order into themes, categories, stories, or theoretical areas. Managing your data and all the codes and notes therefore involves dividing, moving, and classifying, and is always both practical and epistemological (Mason 2018: 187). Do not feel you have to retain all your codes and notes: changing your mind is learning as you go and is a positive thing. But you will want to keep some of them, as well as some memos, and visual and creative data. Try to get everything in a format where you can analyse it easily: writing up notes from memory, noting why videos were used, recording observations. Think about how such things can be coded or how meaning can be made from them; and remember that data can be assigned to categories or codes but should also remain within the rest of the data so that you can easily recall the context. Categorise to meet your own demands, and be prepared to change: institutions, people, groups, themes, concepts all count as categories or classifications.

> ## FOR YOUR TOOLKIT
> Computer software and other tools facilitate analysis and data management; they do not *do* analysis.

Computer-assisted qualitative data analysis software (CAQDAS) facilitates a variety of analytic styles in qualitative work, and supports coding, searching, reporting, retrieving, images, and modelling, as well as video and variable type data. Spend some time learning about different types of software that are available to you. Get some help and consider using one that is supported by your institution or that you know colleagues use. You may need various other forms of organisation as well, such as a spreadsheet program, word processor documents, lists, charts, and mind maps. Computers, software and other tools, help you manage but not analyse the data: beware reifying your data and beware losing the context.

Box 8.4: For illustration: Picking for Britain and Global Labour in Rural Societies

The Picking for Britain project explored the experiences of UK-based harvest workers and employers post Brexit and during the COVID-19 pandemic. It consists of 20 in-depth interviews from different fruit and vegetable producing farms. We also talked with representatives from the Department for Environment, Food and Rural Affairs, the Association of Labour Providers and the Countryside and Communities Research Institute. The Global Labour in Rural Societies (Glarus) project was interested in migrant labour across European societies and how its increase transforms rural labour markets and communities. It has culminated in numerous publications (for example, Rye and O'Reilly 2021) and has led to rich insights into the precarious nature of harvest work and how this is reproduced, managed, justified, and masked (O'Reilly and Scott 2023a, 2023b).

Using the spiral of heuristics

FOR YOUR TOOLKIT

Another way to think about analysis is to explore, discover, identify, refine, repeat, sort, cohere, link, associate, disassociate, deconstruct, reconstruct, explore, discover, identify, refine, repeat.

As soon as you start to collect or create data, engage in *inductive immersion* so that you are always and constantly immersed in the responses. If you start to notice some things of interest (*learning as you go*) annotate them and identify them again using *open coding*. Store these notes and codes carefully but don't be afraid to change or scrap them later. As you learn more from your participants and the research field, continue to read, listen, observe, and hear (*inductive immersion*), to think and reflect and make notes about it all (*annotating* and *memoing*). As time goes on your insights will become more elaborate and complex; diversity and complexity of responses will muddy or confound those initial thoughts. You will need more memoing and to begin *structural coding*. Return to your open codes and think about them again, determine whether some are more useful as *analytical codes*. *Sensitise* yourself to what extant literature or concepts might help to clarify the insights that are emerging from this constant interaction (*seeking coherence*). Remember that 'Themes do not emerge from data but are actively produced by the researcher through their systematic engagement with, and all they bring to, the dataset' (Braun and Clarke 2022: 8). To ensure you don't jump to conclusions too soon, use some of the techniques to help you be iterative-inductive and reflexive.

Do all this lightly until you have finished data collection. When you get to that stage, start again with working through the spiral process of immersion, stepping back, distance and closeness, in and out, to and fro. Eventually you should feel confident to start to pull thoughts together for a paper, chapter, report, or other output.

For those of you working in policy and applied settings, this can all be done in a targeted way and more quickly than appears from the above. Sometimes a project is quite focused or targeted (see Chapter 6), designed to produce a short report or a single chapter. As long as you have pursued the heuristics and engaged in thorough interpretive analysis, been reflexive and iterating, you don't have to get lost for months in the middle of the spiral.

Speaking of analysis

'It hadn't occurred to me to ask harvest workers how they felt about the environment. After two or three of them had waxed lyrical about the view and the fresh air, I raised it myself in future interviews if it didn't come up naturally. It turned out to be a crucial aspect of my analysis.'

'Faced with all those transcripts and photos and the maps we'd drawn together I was a bit overwhelmed, then it dawned on me I had been trying to make sense of it all the time so I went back to look at earlier notes.'

'It's not as if I was just gathering data blindly, my research questions and goals had been guiding me. I wish I had made more notes as I went along.'

'After coming home, I felt a bit out of touch with it all. It was like a different world to me now. But I spent some time listening to all the recordings and it took me right back there.'

'I felt a bit like I was going round in circles, but using the heuristics eventually led me to develop some insights I felt were worth sharing.'

Taking things further

For **general introductions** to qualitative analysis, I recommend Braun and Clarke (2022), Linneberg and Korsgaard (2019), Saldaña (2015), and Emerson et al (2011). To learn more about analysing **visual and creative data**, see Kara (2020). Morosanu (2016: 63–9) also has a great discussion about design and analysis using **inventive methods**. See Wertz in Wertz et al (2011: 137) for more on **phenomenological approaches** and 'the many faces of phenomenology'. Grounded theorists use **theoretical sampling** in a way that is somewhat related to what I have described as learning as you go, but with more focus on overtly developing a theory from the ground up (see Charmaz 2014: 129–212).

Listen to the related episode for this chapter on
Qualitative Research Methods for Everyone podcast:

9

Communicating

What this chapter is about

This chapter moves on from analysis to thinking about how to pull qualitative insights together for specific audiences and reaching higher levels of analysis. Acknowledging the interpretive and organisational work that needs to be done to produce coherent presentations and writing, this chapter addresses the elements of structure of written pieces, the importance of knowing your audience, and specific challenges of writing and communicating *qualitative* findings. Writing up qualitative research is especially challenging because of the need to reduce the infinite complexity of the social world into something digestible while remaining faithful to the people we have spent time with. There are many available styles and little consensus as to how to write. Hopefully, this chapter will inspire you with its many fantastic examples of communicating well.

> **FOR YOUR TOOLKIT**
> We research so that we can learn; we communicate so that others can learn and build on that knowledge. Do not try to write up all your qualitative research in one go. You are not *writing up* you are *writing for* someone; you are communicating insights.

As an aside, while I mainly talk here about writing, it should be taken as given that the same arguments apply to visual, aural, and other ways of communicating and reporting.

Higher-level analysis: categorising, conceptualising and interpreting

Each fresh attempt at communication should begin with remembering why you chose to do qualitative research, what you wanted to know, and what you now want to communicate. The goal of qualitative research is to create insights that explain people's behaviour in the context of their life, experiences and culture, or to explain how policies and actions are practised. Sometimes, to suggest how things might be done differently in future. We need to organise themes into a coherent narrative – seeking a balance between 'displaying the subtlety and detail of the original material and its classification, explanation and interpretation' (White et al 2014: 372). If you have done iterative-inductive analysis, developing the discussion guide as you went along, listening to your participants and thinking about the insights they share, making notes or keeping memos, and starting to develop themes (as discussed in the previous chapter) then the good news is that you have already begun to work towards coherence and communication.

FOR YOUR TOOLKIT
Approach your outputs as building blocks that fit together across articles, papers, chapters, and creative outputs, to contribute to a coherent story throughout all your work.

There are many and various organising principles you could use for higher-level analysis. Narrative analysis, discourse analysis, grounded theory, phenomenological psychology, and intuitive inquiry (Wertz et al 2011), discussed at length in Chapter 8, each provide coherence for a set of insights or themes within a specific frame or perspective. But it is not essential to follow a given field with its own body of literature; there are many other approaches that do not have a named tradition. My advice is to start reading, looking and thinking about how material is organised in good communication and reporting. Having analysed numerous published works myself, and drawing on the chapter by Clarissa White and colleagues (2014), I present a few potential organising principles, but these are just *some* ways of organising material. There are many others you could choose from, or you can develop your own. They also can be used together in different parts of a presentation and for comprehensive, summary, developmental, or selective outputs. Here, then, is my selection that I will look at closely in turn: themes as organising concepts; themes with complexity and coherence; themes with interpretive analysis; describing a process (across time); a narrative arc; typologies ; character narratives; structuration and the integration of macro, meso and micro; developing a realist analysis; and using theory and concepts.

FOR YOUR TOOLKIT
Higher-level analysis is the categorising, conceptualising, and interpreting of material to enable the communication of interpretive analysis. It uses organising principles and concepts.

Themes as organising concepts

One straightforward, if somewhat uninspiring, way to organise findings is around a number of themes that 'emerged' from the study. For a piece of research for the Welsh Government, Jane Prince and colleagues (2014) wanted to understand attitudes to parenting and child discipline and to learn what help was available to parents. They present and illustrate five themes that emerged from their analysis:

- Expertise and expert knowledge
- Parent as the expert
- Positive parenting
- Formal structures and legislation
- Respect

In a subsequent section, their findings are discussed in relation to research aims, followed by the implications of the research in the next section. The report is easy to read and typical of its style and assumed audience. It could be improved by being more coherent, with the order in which themes are presented, and the terminology used for them, pursued consistently throughout the report, but it is clear and concise. It could also be more interpretive. As argued staunchly by Virginia Braun and Victoria Clarke (2022), themes do not *emerge* from qualitative data. To suggest they do is an objectivist approach that treats themes as things that merely have to be discovered, as latent or *real* objects, that exist independently of the researcher's interpretations or sense making, as in objectivist versions of grounded theory. Themes presented as topics, in no obvious order and not overtly linked to analysis, are better thought of as initial topic summaries that still require further development (Braun and Clarke 2022: 77; and see Chapter 8). But as always, forms of communication are shaped by perceptions of audience expectations.

Another common, and simple, technique is to organise findings around barriers and incentives (Hippolyte-Blake et al 2022). This is normally used when it was an initial goal of the research and written into the design. Interpretations of qualitative data should really be more interpretive and complex to make full use of the quality of the data and to respect the time and commitment granted by your participants. Nevertheless, identifying themes, barriers and incentives as organising principles can be a useful starting point and can be adequate for some audiences.

FOR YOUR TOOLKIT

Identifying themes, barriers and incentives as organising principles can be a useful starting point in higher-level analysis.

As an aside, some readers of this book will be writing for audiences who believe that to say themes, data or insights are 'generated' or 'co-created' suggests that they are made up. Rather than adapt your writing for those audiences it might be advisable to find a shortcut way to explain to them what you mean by these terms or how themes emerged as part of iterative-inductive analysis (see Chapter 1).

Themes with complexity and coherence

Themes can be portrayed in detail with complexity and richness, as part of an overtly interpretive analysis. Liz Spencer and Ray Pahl (2006) introduce the themes of simplicity and complexity in friendships, and then identify simple friendships (including associates, useful contacts, neighbourly or favour friends, or fun friends) and complex friendships (including helpmates, comforters or rocks, confidants, and soulmates). In *The British on the Costa del Sol* (O'Reilly 2000), I identified themes that often *emerged* as a surprise to me, but it was me who drew attention to and named them as I came to better understand life in Spain for British migrants. The themes of freedom, language, the contrast of 'bad' Britain versus 'good' Spain, the informal economy and volunteering, were complex themes that embraced a great deal of diversity and complexity and which cohere around the concepts of settlement and home-making.

> **FOR YOUR TOOLKIT**
>
> Themes can be portrayed in detail with complexity and richness, as part of an overtly interpretive and analytical analysis.

Themes with interpretive analysis

Much later, as I was working on a book about migration and social theory (O'Reilly 2012b), I was able to develop a more sophisticated theoretical interpretation of the relationship between the themes I had identified and my research question about integration. I then proposed a more coherent and longitudinal analysis about how the marginalisation of British people living in Spain consolidates over time, related to: (1) the way they interpreted freedom of movement to mean they didn't always have to register or to work formally (or pay taxes); and (2) the way they worked to make Spain a good place to live (compared with 'bad' Britain) by creating a sense of community among themselves and engaging in informal and volunteer work.

In *Gringolandia*, Matthew Hayes (2018) develops themes of geoarbitrage (or the offshoring of retirement), imaginings (how American migrants imagined their lives in Ecuador), 'whiteness' (and their self-perception in relation to others), and heritage (and their involvement in the preservation of heritage sites). These thematic areas are each part of an overall higher-level analysis of how the migration trend is informed by cultural imaginaries, and how it exacerbates rural inequalities and reproduces unequal relations of labour and space. Hayes's goal is both to understand his participants and their lives and loves, as well as to analyse their place in global inequalities.

In *Lifestyle Migration and Colonial Traces in Malaysia and Panama*, Michaela Benson and I (Benson and O'Reilly 2018) include themed personal stories that describe 'trailing spouses', resourceful volunteers, stories of self-realisation and adventure, stories of friendship, and of finding a new home. These are themes many of the participants in that study could relate to but that are also wrapped up in an interpretive analysis of the global inequalities of power that facilitate and shape lifestyle migration to the Global South and East. They are interpretive themes.

Describing a process (across time)

A further potential higher-level organising principle is to describe a process. Processes link themes as they relate and interplay over time, and are useful ways to draw attention to time, change, adaptations, and how practices take shape. They can also be transferable, with sufficient contextual information, to similar situations (see Chapter 2).

The way I interpreted British settlement in Spain also describes a process through which British migrants come to be marginalised. Ewa Morawska's (1996) description of the ethnicisation of Jews in the US at the turn of the 20th century also describes a process whereby their ethnicity takes shape through the interplay, over time, of their cultural and habitual practices in the context of their new environment.

FOR YOUR TOOLKIT
Processes link themes as they relate and interplay, drawing attention to how practices take shape, adapt and change over time.

Grounded theory approaches, because they aim to understand substantive and problem-focused events, often end up describing processes. In the previous chapter, we saw how Kathy Charmaz analysed Teresa's painful story of throat cancer by drawing attention to the process of receiving the bad news, telling people about the news, experiencing a disruption of self, loss of self, facing the loss, and eventually gaining a valued sense of self (Charmaz 2011: 186–9).

A narrative arc

Paul Statham (2019) has undertaken extensive qualitative research on Thai-Western marriages (Thai women married to Western men), and much of his work has been overtly critical, drawing attention to the inherent inequalities of the relationships. A critical analysis is itself a form of higher-level analysis (Chapter 1) – it is not essential to use only one form of analysis at a time – but one paper takes a different turn by using phenomenological analysis to give the women a voice in expressing their own perspectives on 'the radical life-course transformations of women who partner older Westerners' (Statham 2019: 1562).

In a great example of how research can be analysed and presented in different ways for different purposes, Statham organises this paper around the concept of a 'narrative arc' and describes how, as time passes within such marriages, almost every aspect of the women's lives transform as they gradually become less subservient and acquire increasing levels of independence. Factors that affect this growing empowerment include: increasing access to individual formal rights (through marriage) leading to relative financial independence and security; differential ageing and a shifting balance of physical dependency; changing obligations to natal family members; and how these all shape their wellbeing. These 'factors' are yet another form of higher-level analysis, another way of organising the data to make a specific argument.

> **FOR YOUR TOOLKIT**
> A narrative arc is a higher-level organising principle that analyses personal narratives across time.

Typologies as organising concepts

Patton (2002: 457) describes typologies as 'classification systems made up of categories that divide some aspect of the world into distinct parts'. The categories and elements should help to clarify what is learned about the social world in relation to the research question. Simple typologies are one-dimensional as with social class, ethnic group and so on. Complex typologies are multi-dimensional as with an intersectional approach, or when we categorise groups within groups (Spencer et al 2014). An Jacobs, Katrien Dreessen and Jo Pierson (2008), for example, identify mobile phone users as *pluggers* (who use the phone to plug time gaps), *social fillers* (who use the phone to fill social gaps), and *long viewers* (who watch films and so on).

> *As an aside,* I recommend identifying types of behaviour (plugging, social filling, and long viewing) rather than types of people as it is often the case that people would relate to more than one type of behaviour (and none of us likes being put into boxes). Typologies are ways of thinking about forms of behaviour and are not usually designed to homogenise discrete categories: they provide a lens onto our findings rather than boxes for capturing things (see Benson and O'Reilly 2015).

Typologies can aid theoretical interpretation, or sense making, by using what I call *meaningful units*. When I first started to do research with British people living in Spain (O'Reilly 2000), I assumed it would be easy to distinguish tourists and migrants. The world tourism organisation at that time defined a tourist as anyone who stayed more than one night but less than a year! With contemporary fluid forms of mobility this was meaningless and given that I wanted to understand how people felt about where they lived, their sense of belonging and what home meant to them, it was crucial to recognise that people were living different lengths of time in different places. I thus developed an *emic* typology of full residents, seasonal visitors, returning residents, and peripatetic migrants, to capture a differing orientation to, and time spent in, one or other country. Of course, there were people who did not quite fit the typology, or who moved from one category to another during the time I was doing my research. But the typology helped me to conceptualise attitudes to belonging and home in the context of their lives; it was not an attempt to fit people permanently and discretely into immutable categories (O'Reilly 2000; and see Benson and O'Reilly 2015).

FOR YOUR TOOLKIT

Typologies can aid theoretical interpretation by using *meaningful units*. They can be simple or complex, and can distinguish discrete, or discursive and overlapping, groupings.

Kathy Charmaz (2014: 109–10) uses a typology to illustrate how ways of experiencing illness can be conceptualised into *meaningful units* that understand how living with physical impairment shapes daily lives: illnesses like diabetes that demand daily monitoring; illnesses that are episodic; illnesses that progress rapidly; and illnesses that mean changing one's daily life (for example, avoiding the sun). Each of these has its own relationship to time and to work/life balance. Again, not every illness is included: this is a way to think about illness not a classification of all illnesses.

Typologies, classifications and categorisations can be more discursive, and the categories not discrete, while nevertheless indicating diversity and variability. In our study of lifestyle migration in Malaysia and Panama, we acknowledged that our sample included: people who have lived in a destination from a few months to over 40 years; people experiencing a short stay before returning home (perhaps new to migration); people having a short residence before moving elsewhere, in a long migration trajectory; those who have moved permanently to a new forever home; men and women, from ages 20 to 95 years; retired, working, students, self-employed; voluntary workers; and trailing spouses (Benson and O'Reilly 2018: 145). The acknowledgement of diversity in such a discursive way allowed us to return to it as necessary to draw attention to insights that were relevant for all participants (for example, all were privileged migrants on a global scale) and others that pertained only to some types (only some struggled financially in absolute terms).

Visual representations can be useful as a way of organising and presenting higher-level representations, including typologies. Figure 9.1 uses a table to present the complex typology of British migration to Spain that I introduced earlier. I did not enjoy fitting this into a table because I could think of so many individuals who did not fit the typology, and if I were to revisit this work, I would refer to behaviours rather than individuals: that is, residing fully, returning, visiting seasonally, and peripatetic visiting. On the other hand, the typology and table serve to draw visual attention to a point Michaela Benson and I have tried to emphasise over and over again, that not all British people in Europe are retired (Benson and O'Reilly 2020a).

Figure 9.1: Visual of higher-level analysis using a typology

Type/ category/ persona	Dimensions included in the typology		
	Home orientation	Work situation	Time spent in Spain
Full residents	Spain	Mostly retired or working informally	Most or all of the year
Returning residents	Spain and UK	Mostly retired	Return to UK during summer months
Seasonal visitors	UK and Spain	Mostly retired. Some seasonal work	Spend several months in Spain in winter
Peripatetic visitors	UK and Spain	Mostly working, online and/or temporary work	Move backwards and forwards between both countries

Character narratives

Character narratives are a neat way to interpret, classify and explain. Lydia Hayes characterises perceptions of homecare work by referring to a Cheap Nurse (which communicates how workers are undervalued), being Two-a-penny (that narrates some of the poor conditions of homecare work), Mother Superior (which tells the women's stories of care and competence); and Choosy Suzy (that examines the neoliberal discourse of freedom of choice that shapes homecare workers' agency). These character narratives draw attention to the institutionalised humiliation workers suffer and to how their labour is judged as inferior (to nursing for example), while simultaneously giving voice and agency to the workers themselves. Hayes says:

> In this book, I create word pictures (which I call character narratives) as points of departure from which to explore how hierarchies of class and gender structure the everyday experiences of homecare workers. To see the world through the eyes of homecare workers means viewing homes as workplaces, seeing physical dependency and

mental impairment as a source of employment, and understanding acts of caring as paid work. (Hayes 2017: 1)

The characters are imaginary devices, not meant to represent individuals but a way to draw attention to aspects of working life and how these relate to legal concepts.

> **FOR YOUR TOOLKIT**
>
> Character narratives, as with all higher-level analysis organising principles, are used to conceptualise and articulate what is important for the analyst to convey.

Macro-, meso- and micro-interaction

A higher-level analysis might distinguish macro-, meso- and micro-level frameworks, drawing on a (micro) phenomenological approach to explore how people think and feel and their experiences, and a (macro-) structural approach to analyse legal frameworks and rules and so on. The meso level is employed in different ways in different publications but usually refers to intermediaries, gate keepers, key players, communities, and so on, or to the interaction in practice between the two other levels (see Chapter 1).

Practice or structuration accounts are narrative accounts (or holistic and temporal explanations) of the interaction of the macro-structural and the agentic phenomenological in the practice, or living out, of daily life. They employ structuration theory (Giddens 1984), or strong structuration theory (Stones 2005), practice theory (Schatzki 2005; Shove et al 2012), or *practice stories* in my own work (O'Reilly 2012b). It is worth distinguishing the following aspects:

- Wider global and historical structural shifts that shape actions (O'Reilly 2012b: 23–5).
- The more approximate or immediately relevant structures that may be somewhat malleable by agents (O'Reilly 2012b: 23–5; and see Morawska 2009).
- Habitus and internal structures – the typical ways of thinking and being of the various agents involved (O'Reilly 2012b: 26–8; and see Bourdieu 1984).
- Conjunctly specific internal structures – the ways in which people learn to adapt habitus in daily life (O'Reilly 2012b: 26–8; and see Stones 2005).
- Communities of practice (O'Reilly 2012b: 26–8; and see Lave and Wenger 1991).
- Practices and outcomes, which recognise that social life is lived and practised on a daily basis in the context of social structures, and is shaped by taken-for-granted ways of doing and being (O'Reilly 2012b: 28–32; 2017a).

FOR YOUR TOOLKIT

Practice or structuration accounts are holistic and temporal explanations (higher-level analyses) of the interaction of the macro-structural and the agentic phenomenological in the practice of (meso-level) daily life.

Versions of this approach have been used as higher-level analyses of qualitative research in the work of, among others: Benson and O'Reilly (2018: 2–4) in an analysis of lifestyle migrants' lives in the context of a colonial past and neoliberal present; Greenhalgh et al (2013) in a study of what matters to older people with assisted living needs; Hughes et al (2022) in a study of how and why efforts to integrate health and social care in England have failed to produce desired outcomes; and O'Reilly and Rye (2021) in an integrated analysis of harvest work and migrant labour across the EU and US. As such, higher-level analyses employing structuration or practice theory lend themselves well to holistic understandings that address the gap between theory and practice in policy and applied work.

Developing a realist analysis

A realist analysis is another version of a higher-level analysis. A word of warning here that people use the word 'realism' in diverse ways (as discussed in Chapter 1), whereas I am referring specifically to the work of Michael Fell, Katy Roelich and Lucie Middlemiss (2022) in their research in the energy sector in support of fairer climate action, and others who apply a similar logic. In these renderings, realist analyses are higher-level analyses that move beyond themes and other types of insight to the next level, to present clearly and succinctly an understanding of *what works for whom under what circumstances in answer to a specific set of questions.* This can also lead to developing or evaluating an intervention.

Realist analyses can be deductive, by applying earlier literature and looking for specific mechanisms in context, or inductive, by grounding understandings in the emergent analysis (Fell et al 2022). In qualitative research it should follow the iterative-inductive model I describe in this book. Realist evaluations can also be transferable by looking across different contexts and revealing them in more detail.

> Based on thinking about how mechanisms lead to outcomes in different contexts, they provide a powerful way of translating between sectors and contexts an understanding of how activities lead to outcomes, and how these might be different for various groups. They also provide a means to synthesise evidence from across disciplinary domains. When used effectively, realist approaches can help justify decisive action without waiting years for dedicated trialling – years we can no longer afford to waste. (Fell et al 2022: 918)

> **FOR YOUR TOOLKIT**
> Realist analyses are higher-level analyses that work to present clearly and succinctly an understanding of *what works for whom under what circumstances in answer to a specific set of questions*.

Using theories and concepts to frame an argument

It is common, especially in academic work, to use theory and concepts to frame and explicate arguments (Box 9.1). Theories are accounts of how the world works; concepts are ideas to help us think about how the world works. In Chapter 2, I noted that theory has various roles in qualitative research. Initially it informs sensitising concepts (Charmaz 2014), foreshadowed problems (Malinowski 1922), or guiding theoretical problems (O'Reilly 2012a); later it will be applied, amended, tested, in an abductive or iterative cycle (Chapter 8). The final chapter of *The British on the Costa del Sol* (O'Reilly 2000) offers some coherence through theory by arguing that the British residents in Spain, at that time, were living betwixt and between two cultures and two worlds, partly by choice and partly by circumstance, but ultimately maximising their advantage in an inherently marginal situation. A later theoretical argument suggested that British people living in Spain could be considered symbolic of Britain's relationship to the outside, and especially to Europe (O'Reilly 2002). I did not know then what the future held with respect to that relationship.

Matthew Hayes's book, *Gringolandia* (2018; Box 9.2), has an overall theoretical argument about how the reproduction of global inequalities is informed by colonial legacies. Each of his chapters also has its own theoretical argument, and he reviews and applies theories as required for his ongoing interpretations, on the concept of geoarbitrage, on social imaginaries, on whiteness and identity, and on understandings of lifestyle migration and gentrification.

Box 9.1: Using theory to frame arguments: lifestyle migration

Lifestyle Migration and Colonial Traces in Malaysia and Panama (Benson and O'Reilly 2018) is an academic book based on two ethnographic studies. We use theory to frame our argument in separate chapters, each with its own brief literature review on the topics of: narrative; home, belonging and migration; home-making and the reproduction of privilege; and therapeutic landscapes. We also have an overarching framework of practice theory and a general literature review locating understandings of privileged migration in theories of colonialism, neoliberalism, and tourism imaginaries.

Using analytical concepts to illuminate themes and insights is far more common than you might have realised and can be powerful. Concepts can be developed to clarify an elaborate theory, as with Davina Allen's (2018) translational mobilisation theory, which encapsulates the processes through which nurses and their work hold healthcare organisations together.

Concepts can be inductive – borrowed from the participants and developed for your own use – as with our concept of lifestyle migration (Benson and O'Reilly 2015), and Spencer and Pahl's (2006) use of 'fun friends' and 'soulmates'. Concepts can be borrowed from elsewhere and adapted to help interpret your data, as when Anna Åberg and colleagues (2005) elaborated the concepts of 'a hierarchy of preferences', 'balance', and 'adaptation' to illustrate how participants understood and achieved quality of life in older age. They also used the inductive (or in vivo) concept of 'taking it as it comes' from participants to draw attention to the process of using mental adaptation to help cope with physical changes. Roxana Morosanu (2016; Chapter 8) similarly developed the concepts of spontaneity, anticipation, and family time, drawing on insights from her participants. Concepts can also be borrowed, applied and adapted from extant literature as with Hartmut Rosa's conceptualisations of the structured phenomenology of time to understand harvest work (O'Reilly and Scott 2023b; see Chapter 8, this volume). Theories and concepts are organising principles that aid higher-level analysis.

> **FOR YOUR TOOLKIT**
>
> Put all of the organising principles I have suggested into your toolkit as potential ways to sort your data and reach higher levels of analysis. Find or create further organising principles for yourself.

To summarise higher-level analyses

Higher-level analysis or abstraction goes beyond descriptive themes to overtly categorise, conceptualise and interpret findings for a specific audience. It elaborates how themes/things fit together and their variability across populations, or types, and considers how insights address aspects of the research question. Higher-level analysis might describe a process or a narrative arc; it might develop a typology or employ character narratives, and/or visual representation. You may distinguish macro-, meso- and micro-levels of analysis or elaborate how these different levels of social life interact in practice. Of course, you may also develop or use theory and concepts to elaborate and illuminate insights. There are many other potential ways to organise your work – using a key event as a conceptual frame, to give one example (O'Reilly 2012a) – so use this chapter as a launching pad not a conclusion.

Outputs and audiences

There are many potential output products for qualitative research, each with their own conventions that do not necessarily have to be adhered to, but from which you can learn. First, it might help to identify what, of the following, you are aiming to present (adapted from White et al 2014: 370):

- Comprehensive results: the full overview (book, thesis, report)
- Summary findings: key findings (for a shorter report, a policy report)
- Developmental results: early indications, ideas for debate (interim reports, blogs)
- Selective findings: selected themes or theoretical areas, for specific audiences (presentations, posters)

Stop and ask: what is it important to convey? Who for? What style will I use? How much time have I got? How many words/how much space can I use? Do not try to write everything: you are not 'writing up' all your qualitative research (just as you would not try to write up all the results of a survey). You are always writing something, for someone, for a purpose, at a given time, with set goals.

> **FOR YOUR TOOLKIT**
> Acquire a critical knowledge of diverse styles of writing and communicating, and reflect critically on style, layout, language, and genre. Look within and beyond your own discipline, academia, and policy to acquire tools for your own communications toolkit.

Next, read avariciously and critically and become familiar with diverse styles. The world of communication is your oyster: consider social media, blogposts, media reports, long reports, short reports, bulleted reports, meeting notes, consultations, presentations, slides, chapters, articles, books, and theses. You could also write policy briefs, deliver a podcast, write poetry, design a graphic novel, present audio, video or word clouds, posters and other visual data.

Each medium and style offers its own gifts. A full report, a book, or a thesis provides scope for rich details, nuance and complexity across a range of themes and variability – but sadly, few people will ever read them in their entirety. A journal article is restricted in terms of word length, and you must be selective in terms of themes, variations, and arguments. Their readership is broad, but readers are likely to have certain expectations shaped by the journal itself. A social media post or a media article can present a few ideas, briefly and succinctly, but might reach an even broader audience (for example, O'Reilly 2018b).

Policy makers usually have little time to digest material and little inclination to read at great length the subtleties that you might wish to include in a qualitative report. Keep it brief, digestible, memorable and probably also visual. Cover aims and methods briefly and emphasise policy implications and take-home messages. In formal reports for funders, commissioners and colleagues there is more expectation that reports will be longer and detailed. You can give a more detailed description of aims, methods, findings and conclusions. But keep it memorable and digestible by including an executive summary, or some key takeaway points, and always remember that some people think visually and will remember things more if they are laid out well, perhaps with charts and/or images.

Clearly, for academic papers, you are more likely to cover aims, literature review, methodology and methods, findings and analysis (perhaps together) and a conclusion, or discussion. Academic papers are less likely to be visual in terms of using images – although there are journals and publishers that are better at using images than others – but try to think visually anyway, in terms of using clear headings, bullet points, charts, indented quotes, different fonts, and so on, so that your reader can follow the argument and take away some key messages. I hope I have achieved that in this book, so perhaps use this as something of a guide in terms of layout and visuality.

The various forms of communication can also stack or interlink. A short tweet can come from or feed into a longer blog post; a blog post can be developed into an article; an article can be unpicked backwards to make a blog post. That way you can take full advantage of all these available ways to communicate your research without (hopefully) exhausting yourself. Now let's think about the structure of a piece of writing, from abstract to conclusion and recommendations.

> *As an aside,* a tip for those who wish they could add more qualitative richness and depth to a report is to make this available somewhere else, in an appendix or in a link to a separate report designed for the general public, or even in an exhibition.

Structuring your communications

As argued earlier in the chapter, once you have chosen an output style make yourself familiar with what is expected in terms of structure, layout, sections, length, and so on. Plan the assembly carefully with an awareness of how much space you can allocate to each section. Spend more time on the title, keywords and abstract than you might have. These are important: for example, the title of Hayes's (2018) book *Gringolandia: Lifestyle Migration under Late Capitalism* invokes both the language of the Ecuadorian locals as they denigrate the North Americans living among them, and the critique of power and privilege that provides a thread through his work. The title of *The British on the Costa del Sol* was clear but limited to one community, whereas when Caroline Oliver (2008) called her book *Retirement Migration*, she instantly intimated a broader trend than the older migrants living near Nerja, in the Costa del Sol, where she did her ethnographic research.

Avoid writing with too much of a sense of discovery. Start with what journalists call your 'lede', or your main argument, and guide your reader to the conclusion using signposting, so they know what is coming and so that your conclusion merely makes that more transparent and lucid. If the clarity of the argument dawns on you as you reach the conclusion, you need to start again and thread that through. Drafting and redrafting in qualitative research and writing are themselves forms of analysis. Most outputs demand us to write in a linear way, but we travel several hoops and loops before we get to the point of presenting our mind maps, drawings, sketches, and memos in the form of logical progression.

FOR YOUR TOOLKIT

Drafting and redrafting in qualitative research and writing are part of the process of analysis.

Let's have a think in detail about the abstract, the executive summary, introduction and background, literature review, methodology and methods, findings and discussion, and conclusion.

The abstract

Writing an abstract should take more time and care than is normally given; searches are conducted on abstracts, and it may be the only thing people read before deciding whether to read the paper. Read abstracts critically, thinking about what constitutes a good one, and perhaps develop your own formula or template. It should be enticing, with a pull factor (Rivas 2018); it should not simply repeat what is in the paper's introduction; and it would not usually contain references (although an abstract that is *proposing* a paper might do so). You could copy out key sentences from the article, put them together, and rewrite them so they flow well. This ensures consistency of both language and sequence. Some journals have explicit guidelines or expectations, so watch out for this; and there is now lots of guidance available using a simple internet search.

FOR YOUR TOOLKIT

Plan the assembly carefully; spend more time on the title, keywords and abstract than you might have; start with your 'lede'.

The executive summary

Executive summaries can be particularly useful whether or not you include them in the published work. Give it a go: they are great for making you aware of your own key points. They work especially well for big and complex reports. Remember they may be the only thing people read, especially with qualitative reports for clients. They look good numbered or bulleted, but they don't have to be. I suggest writing the executive summary and then going back and checking that the points you are making are also clearly made, in similar language and the same order, in the article or report. Carol Rivas (2018) proposes writing down your key points from memory and then checking back that you have remembered what was key in the article. Another possibility is to take the key sentence from each paragraph or section. These all work well for checking consistency and coherence.

> **FOR YOUR TOOLKIT**
> Executive summaries are great for making you aware of your own key points and the order and language in which you've made them.

Introduction and background

This section, whether it is in the shape of an introduction, background, or a description of the field, contextualises the research and provides any background information the reader needs such as history, geography, or a policy review. This can be the most tedious section to write, especially in a thesis where it can be a long and detailed exposition of stuff you are already familiar (and perhaps bored) with. But it is often the most informative section for the reader. Sam Ladner (2014) suggests, in relation to ethnographic research, that you can use this section to be dramatic, to set the stage, and perhaps introduce some of your key players. Hayes (2018) does this well in *Gringolandia*, his ethnographic study of North Americans in Ecuador. His introductory chapter starts with stories of people he spent time with as rich and nuanced examples of his themes of transnational mobility, expatriation, lifestyle migration, successful ageing, and whiteness and privilege. He goes on to introduce theoretical treatises on global inequalities, power and privilege, whiteness and decolonial sociology. The chapter also takes us to the geography and the social and political history of Cuenca in Ecuador, the site of his ethnographic research.

> **FOR YOUR TOOLKIT**
> Use the introduction and background to set the scene. Use wider literature as scaffolding, to give shape and form to your arguments.

Literature review

In qualitative research the literature serves several functions. As a framework, it will probably need to explain what is already known in a field, and how, and what still needs to be known. When reviewing in advance of a project it serves to sensitise you to potential theories, concepts and understandings (Chapter 2). During analysis, literature is consulted iteratively, in an ongoing process of immersing, annotating, coding, reading, sensitising, memoing, and seeking coherence, until explanations become gradually more refined and useful

(Chapter 8). When writing, think of the literature review as scaffolding; it introduces and then moulds and shapes your argument as you develop it. There may, then, be a literature review that is a separate chapter that locates the work; literature might also be introduced in the introduction or background chapter to introduce readers to literature that will be applied later (as with Hayes 2018), and then it comes into use again in findings and discussion where it is applied to make sense or interpret data.

Methodology and methods section

The *methodological* approach is the understanding (ology) of how the research will be approached, the logic behind decisions about what methods to use. *Methods* are means through which data are collected or generated. When writing, use this section or chapter to explain to your reader how you understand your specific methodology. You may feel, for certain audiences, that you need to spend more time explaining the role and value of qualitative research and your methodology than you do for other audiences, using some of the language from Chapter 1. Then outline your methods.

> **FOR YOUR TOOLKIT**
> For certain audiences it might be helpful to spend some time explaining the role and value of qualitative research and how you understand methodology. Then be confident in your methods: give the reader specific details; outline the selection techniques; describe the heuristics that guided your analysis.

In most types of output, it is useful to include how long you spent doing your research, how many days, weeks, or hours doing fieldwork, how many people you interviewed for an average of how much time, where and when interviews were conducted, and anything else that would help clarify the extent and value of your research. This provides a sort of audit trail (White et al 2014). Hayes, as part of a longer discussion in the appendix to his book, summarises his approach as follows:

> In all, I spent thirty-nine weeks in Ecuador, with visits ranging from three weeks to three months. During this time, I conducted ethnographic research, participating in the social life of North Americans in Cuenca, and coupled this with semi-structured qualitative interviews ... In Cuenca, I conducted 83 semi-structured qualitative interviews with 108 separate individuals (55 men, 53 women, and 23 couples interviewed together). Of these interviews eleven were with Canadians. I interviewed 10 participants a second time. Interviews ranged in length from just under thirty minutes to longer than two hours, with most interviews lasting about an hour.

> The vast majority of participants are in their 60s (n=57); however, they ranged from twenty-nine to eighty years. (Hayes 2018: 215–6)

Outline your sampling or selection methods (see Chapter 2), especially now clarifying your final sample fitness. Remember also to describe the steps or heuristics that shaped your analysis in your own words, illustrating that you have understood and thought critically about this (see Chapter 8). Always think about your reader and what *you* think they need to know. In qualitative work, insights are deeply entangled with the research process itself and you may feel the need to explain this. In *The British on the Costa del Sol* (O'Reilly 2000), I incorporated a bit of methodology and methods in the introduction; Hayes, in *Gringolandia* (2018), has a methodology appendix that explicates several logical and practical decisions (following the celebrated tradition of William Foote Whyte 1993). Finally, demonstrate confidence in your methods:

> The tone of your methods discussion should be quietly authoritative. Make sure you do not sound apologetic for not having carried out a quantitative design. If you apologize for having only 10 interviewees or for an inability to generalize because your interviews were not picked at random, you come across as if you do not understand either the qualitative interview model or the quantitative one. (Rubin and Rubin 2011: 263)

> *As an aside,* if you do not feel confident about your methods and their value, then spend some time thinking about why not, do more research or do it better. If you do feel confident then there should be no need to apologise for anything you did not do.

Findings and discussion section

As Rivas (2018: 546) says in qualitative research 'interpretation and data reporting are often … intermingled', in other words we would not usually present results followed by a separate discussion. This is because by acknowledging our own role in the interpretation of the data we also acknowledge there is no such thing as pure description (Chapter 1; see also Braun and Clarke 2022). Various levels of sense making will be drawn on as the findings are discussed: the higher-level analyses outlined in this chapter do the job of both summarising and interpreting the findings in light of the research question.

To return to the Space to Care study (Chapter 1), in their first paper from the project, Jo Birch, Penny Curtis and Allison James (2007) present selective findings relevant to the built environment on the topics of: children's perspectives on outdoor space; window views and lighting; sound, smell and temperature; and age-related meanings of hospital spaces. They make sense of (interpret) these data as they go along, noting for example that children found some spaces too 'babyish' yet were less bothered by smell and temperature than adults might expect. In other words, their topics or themes both describe and simultaneously offer ways to understand the perspectives, feelings, and behaviours revealed in their findings. They conclude that children's perceptions matter, that they can and should be understood, and they go on to make a few design suggestions.

That said, you could present somewhat descriptive themes followed by a further section or chapter that uses higher-level analysis, provides a framework, or develops an intervention. Spend a bit of time thinking about how to organise the structure of your findings section/s. Think of building blocks that fit together across articles, papers and chapters and more creative outputs to contribute to a coherent story throughout all your work. Use any combination of the higher-level analyses models I have discussed or develop your own.

> **FOR YOUR TOOLKIT**
> In qualitative research interpretation and findings are intermingled because it is iterative-inductive – we learn as we go. However, it is possible to present somewhat descriptive themes followed by a further section or chapter that advances coherence.

The conclusion: bringing the research full circle

The conclusion of any piece of work should be relatively short and memorable and should not introduce any new material. It will usually be the last thing people read and what they remember most; it is what they take away with them. Try not to end on limitations, unless you have potential solutions. Focus on what you have achieved, remind the reader of the main things you have covered and the main messages you want the reader to take away. It is useful to return to your initial aims or research questions and to illustrate how you have addressed those. Pull out the implications of your findings for your research puzzle, and perhaps devise policy recommendations or implications for good practice, or even calls to action. If your work is more conceptual or theoretical, then summarise your main theoretical/conceptual points. In our paper on harvest work and time (O'Reilly and Scott 2023b; Box 8.4), we introduced the concept of time and said we would use it to analyse the lived experiences and structural framing of temporary farm work in the UK; in the conclusion, we reminded readers how we had done that, and argued that, as a result of these perceptions and behaviours related to time, other ways of organising harvest work are not even imagined.

> **FOR YOUR TOOLKIT**
> The conclusion is what readers take away with them. Try not to end on limitations; focus on what has been achieved.

Finally consider turning to the discussion about the value of qualitative research (Chapter 2) and emphasising the key points in your own conclusion. That is to say, tell your reader what the value of your work is.

Box 9.2: Illustrating, illuminating and complicating insights: North Americans in Ecuador

In *Gringolandia*, Matthew Hayes (2018) intersperses theoretically informed analyses with personal stories that serve to illustrate, illuminate and complicate his interpretations and insights. In chapter 1, he introduces Colin who has retired from North America to Cuenca in Ecuador because he can't afford to retire in North America despite being in his late sixties. He calls himself an economic migrant. Hayes's account of Colin's story is rich, sensitive and respectful of the complexity of a lived life and of a story told. But his story also sets the reader up for the theoretical argument that follows. Hayes says, for example, that calling himself an economic migrant is an exaggeration that also makes some sense. In the discussion that follows Colin's story, Hayes shows how apparent economic motivations are wrapped up with other cultural ideas about successful ageing, active ageing, and a class-based fear of falling (or failing?). All of these insights and concepts are followed up with references to further reading. Colin's story is an elegant way to both understand someone's perspective and to analyse it critically.

Hayes (2018) also uses Diana's story to illustrate several themes. Diana (a 60-year-old retiree from Eastern Canada) had been keen to escape the cold winters of Canada. She sought an affordable location, had moved to Ecuador knowing very little about it, wanted somewhere she could feel safe and secure, but also wanted an adventure. Hayes (2018: 3) says: 'Diana's experience of transnational mobility is typical of the experience of many of the North Americans living in Cuenca with whom I spoke.' Hayes's work reminds us what we learn from the narrative approach to qualitative research – that any story whether told by our participants or by ourselves is an account that has been chosen and told with a specific angle and for a specific purpose. Hayes also blends his own narrative with shorter and longer stories, quotes, and field notes. For example, he uses the words of Melanie (age 55, from Wisconsin) to illustrate a common discourse around the perception that women who migrate alone are more adventurous. Melanie said: 'I think the kind of single women that come here are more adventurous, and they are risktakers too. And they're very brave. And they're willing to try new things. Meet new people. Have new adventures. Travel … The single women community, here, we are always out and about. Always. We don't sit at home at all' (Hayes 2018: 48).

Illustrating richness and nuance

We are often told that 'good qualitative reports are rich and nuanced' (Rubin and Rubin 2011: 265). A research narrative is rich and nuanced if it presents not just the main themes, but also variability, context and detail, illustrated with clear examples. It should convey complexity without losing readability, giving contrasts and contradictions. The 'how, when, for whom, under what circumstances' questions should be addressed. It should include enough context to make findings understandable while respecting the diversity of the population. It involves re-presentation (White et al 2014: 368).

> **FOR YOUR TOOLKIT**
> Richness and nuance in your communicating can be achieved through rich description, illustrative cases, quotations, diagrams and pictures, and field notes.

Rich description

One way to ensure analyses are nuanced is through rich description. In their higher-level analysis of friendship, Spencer and Pahl (2006) develop a typology of friendship types. Such a typology runs the risk of losing the richness, complexity and contextual framing of the data if it is not subtle. To get around this they display and illustrate the range of responses that fit under each of the separate headings in the typology. In this example they go into further detail and complexity about what they term simple friendships:

> In simple friendships, friends play well-defined and somewhat circumscribed roles. The friends may be *associates* who share a common activity, *useful contacts* who exchange information and advice, *neighbourly* or *favour friends* who help each other out, or *fun friends* who socialize together. Of course, other friendships also involve fun and favours, but the key feature of simple friendships is that the relationship is based on one main form of interaction.
>
> Associates are friends who share a particular interest or activity, for example, golf, tennis, bridge, darts, model boats, meeting in a particular context such as the workplace or pub, or belonging to a particular organization such as club or church. These relationships are 'tightly framed', and the friends do not usually meet outside the shared activity or context. (Spencer and Pahl 2006: 60–1)

Hayes also illustrates similarity (patterns) and difference (nuance) within the telling of his participants' stories. Earlier (Box 9.2) we met Diana who, Hayes said, was typical of many North Americans. On the next page, he says 'not all lifestyle migrants to Cuenca are like Diana. Many refer to themselves as "economic refugees". They express the same cultural ideals as Diana, but are also clear that what enables them to live out the ideals of an active adventurous retirement is the lower cost of living' (Hayes 2018: 4). In other words, most lifestyle migrants in Cuenca are not poor, but some are (rich, nuanced).

Illustrative cases

Illustrative cases are also useful for demonstrating richness, complexity, nuance and (especially) context. As discussed in Chapter 2, it is important to distinguish the case study as something we are studying and trying to learn from, and an illustrative case that is used to illuminate and clarify an argument we are making. Jane Kerr and colleagues' typology of gambling types (which I have argued should be about types of gambling rather than types of person) uses the case of Maureen to illustrate peripheral gambling.

> Maureen and her husband play the National Lottery each week. She finds it boring but they have always played the same numbers and so feel they cannot stop in case their numbers come up and they miss out on winning a lot of money. Maureen also enjoys going to the Grand National but more for the social aspect than for the gambling. She does not really understand how to place a bet so gets someone else to do this for her after she has chosen her horse. She enjoys the day out regardless of whether she wins any money. Maureen does not consider playing the National Lottery and the occasional day out at the Grand National to be gambling. The amount she spends on these activities is minimal and has no adverse impact on her finances. (adapted from Kerr et al 2009, in White et al 2014: 392)

Of course, an illustrative case can be much more elaborate and can use an entire village or community to illustrate a case of something, with serious caveats about not extrapolating in a simplistic way from the whole to its parts (Crow 2020). Anna Lowenhaupt Tsing's (2005) fabulous study in the rainforests of Indonesia, for example, illustrates some of the ways in which the forces of globalisation violently reshape the landscape and local communities.

This takes us to thinking a bit more about how best to use quotes, diagrams, and field notes in our work.

Quotations

Quotations are widely used in qualitative writing. Please ensure that quotations are not disembodied – that is, that they don't float on the page as if they don't apply to any particular human being. Include some stories or some background information or at least add in the question that was asked. David Fetterman (2010) reminds us quotes should convey mood, laughter and so on. They can also be written in a way that is true to the speaker. There may need to be some translation (from another language or making meaning), and think about colloquialisms. As a rule, keep your quotations as close to what was originally said as possible, and if you need to translate or enable some sense making on behalf of the reader, then consider including the original as well.

FOR YOUR TOOLKIT

Quotations are widely used in qualitative writing as evidence of the richness of the data. Diagrams and pictures can show connections and illustrate arguments. Field notes can illustrate stories, details, and complexities for a coherent and complex analysis.

Diagrams and images

You can use diagrams and pictures to show connections between elements of a higher-level analysis, to incorporate the original complexity and diversity in your writing. Quotations are often indented, which serves to visually highlight them. Spencer and Pahl (2006) illustrate their concept of personal communities using concentric rings with the friendship types added in terms of distance from the participant in the centre. They also list and associate friendship types using charts, and pepper the text with rich quotes. In our book about lifestyle migration in Malaysia and Panama (Benson and O'Reilly 2018: 207), I use a photograph (Figure 9.2) to illustrate my argument that, while places like Penang can feel like home to lifestyle migrants because of their colonial pasts and welcoming presents, at the same time the residential segregation of gated communities serves to physically exclude others, making them feel out of place

Figure 9.2: Promotional poster marking the boundaries of a gated community in Penang

Photo © Karen O'Reilly

and unwelcome. The photo shows a long poster advertising a welcoming and luxurious new development; the poster itself is also a barrier bordering the development and the broken pathway that runs alongside it.

Field notes

In ethnography and participant observation, field notes can be used to illustrate the stories, details, and complexities behind the more coherent analysis. Field notes are also faithful to the fact that qualitative research is iterative-inductive; they can show your 'working out' or your developing thoughts, as well as your own emotions. They can emulate mood as well as conditions under which insights were gleaned. In this example, I illustrate how, despite the fact most of the British people in Spain emphasised the positive qualities of their lives, spending time with them also allowed them to reveal more nuanced perspectives.

> Later on that morning, Joan and Beryl sat chatting over a cup of coffee. I heard Beryl say that she is much less bored here now that she has something to do with herself. She said that she used to get very bored and lonely, and people never really understand because they don't think you should. Joan seemed relieved to hear her say these things and started to tell how lonely and bored she gets, that she misses her family and how she feels she must not admit this to anyone. They said that people do not talk about things like that here, they do not admit that they are lonely. When they realised I was listening to them, they felt uncomfortable and laughed. (field notes, June 1994; O'Reilly 2000: 83)

However you decide to organise your work for dissemination or publication, remember the power of the human story. Throughout the theoretically dense critical analyses in his book, for example, Hayes (2018) ensures that his research participants take central place. You used qualitative research because you wanted to understand human lives so ensure these are not lost in your writing.

Having a sense of style

Taking my lead from Steven Pinker (2015) I'd like to end by thinking about a few style issues that are especially relevant for those writing up qualitative research: avoiding the tendency to quantify; acknowledging the agency of participants; and thinking about how your work looks and reads.

Avoid the temptation to quantify

There is a tendency (temptation?), especially in policy research, and research addressing the needs of clients who don't understand the value and contribution of qualitative research, to reduce findings to numerical summaries. Qualitative research is not designed to study prevalence, instead it aims to be more widely applicable through its elaboration of broadly meaningful insights, themes, and typologies, through being evocative, enabling the transferring of the findings to similar contexts, or using theories and concepts (Chapter 2). It is disingenuous to use percentages when you have small samples and when these samples have not been selected to be numerically representative. Furthermore, you lose sight of the significance of what you are trying to impart. When there are numbers, these tend to be emphasised and therefore heard more clearly than the actual insights that you wanted your readers to remember. *If* Lydia Hayes (2017) had said the following, you would find yourself more concerned with the quantities than the useful and insightful concepts she has elaborated:

> Twenty participants told me they felt they were treated like a cheap nurse, ten thought clients saw them as cheap and easily replaceable (two-a-penny), three told me the people they cared for saw them as a kind of mother (mother superior), and six had to spend a lot of time thinking about whether they could afford to have me or their medication (choosy Suzy).

Try reading it out loud to see where you place the emphasis. Fortunately, Hayes didn't say this. She used stories and character narratives that unveiled qualitative insights and understandings.

The best way to deal with the tendency to quantify is to be sure to emphasise your insights, first, in answer to your research questions (White et al 2014). When I talked of the British living in Spain as full residents, seasonal visitors, returning residents, and peripatetic migrants, it wasn't necessary to know how many participants were in each category because it was patterns of mobility I was elucidating, not numbers of people. These were *meaningful units*, not numerical ones.

You do not have to avoid quantities altogether. You may hear or see the same sort of thing repeatedly: British people in Spain *often* told me things like 'people are happier here because they are mixing with holidaymakers all the time, no one ever wants to go home'. I added nuance to that by remembering the minority perspective: 'on the other hand one man told me he was going home at Christmas and had no intention to come back to Spain' (O'Reilly 2000: 135–6). Finally, try to avoid using 'some people said this, and some said that' (which gets tedious and implies a number) by sharing contrasting views, focusing on more complex interactions between variables, and generally emphasising what you learned that is useful and insightful.

FOR YOUR TOOLKIT
Avoid the temptation to reduce findings to numerical summaries; this is disingenuous and loses sight of the significance of what you are trying to impart. Emphasise the research insights.

Acknowledge the agency of participants

I am often asked whether or not to write in the first person, and in active or passive voice. In my opinion, in light of the discussion in Chapter 3 about reflexive practice, and the entire tone of this book that argues for an interpretive approach to qualitative research that continually oscillates between data collection and its interpretation, then I cannot see how you could do other than acknowledge that you are part of the world you study. I have used my own voice and often the first or third person throughout. To avoid doing so denies your own self and positioning, and using the passive voice denies the agency of participants. Chapters do not analyse, papers do not argue – you do. Spaces weren't found to be babyish; children found the way some spaces were designed felt babyish to them (Birch et al 2007).

In a similar vein, Michael Billig (2013) makes an eloquent case for avoiding the overuse of noun phrases: imprecise jargon that reifies complexes of things while discounting people and actions. Phrases like 'translational mobilisation theory' (Allen 2018), 'integrated case management' (Hughes et al 2022), 'children's dental anxiety' (cited in Billig 2013), 'reflexivity' rather than 'being reflexive' (Chapter 3), sound clever but risk placing academic status above human lives and actions if they are overused. These are my own examples. Billig (2013: 98) entreats us to follow the earlier writings of Freud, who 'wrote about people and what they did, usually avoiding technical terminology as he did so. In Freud's passages of "action" language, his long dead patients live on as characters with their enduring problems.' Similarly, Sarah Pink and colleagues (2022: 19) often use the gerund version of concepts, such as evaluating, prototyping, transforming, 'to emphasise the ongoing and emerging nature of practice' as opposed to nouns that are bereft of action or agency.

In Chapter 3, I talked about how we should no longer be referring to our research participants as subjects or informants. Use pseudonyms where you can, and perhaps ask your participants to choose their own. Give more information that will help the reader understand the person and context. Also, use blended stories and free indirect speech where it is helpful and meaningful. As a reminder, free indirect speech involves quoting a style of phrase rather than exact words, and blended stories are accounts or narratives that are blended together to capture an essence or meaning rather than an identifiable person (Chapter 3).

FOR YOUR TOOLKIT

Writing in the first person, using active voice, avoiding the overuse of noun phrases, and using the gerund version of concepts all respect the iterative-inductive nature of qualitative research and the agency of participants.

Consider how your work looks and reads

Pay attention to what your text looks like to the eye. Look at headings and sub-headings: can readers easily understand the structure? Does the text make sense without examples and charts? Be sure long quotes are indented, but also consider what looks and flows better. Use charts and lists where it helps make things stand out and breaks up the flow. Expose the structure, invite readers in, put yourself (and participants) on the page, and don't forget the details (Portwood-Stacer 2021).

Box 9.3: An exciting and interactive way of communicating: the flip-flop trail

An exciting and interactive way of communicating has been employed by Caroline Knowles for her ethnographic study of the role of plastics (namely, the flip-flop) in the global interconnections that reproduce inequalities. It is a great example of how to share the richness of studies separately from the more analytical writing. To paraphrase: 'This website follows a footnote through the landscapes, lives and stories animating it. Following flip-flops teaches us about globalisation; about people and places we have yet to imagine … Caroline started this journey because she wondered what the ordinary everyday objects we take for granted can teach us about the world in which we live. There are several things we can learn from this journey about the precariousness of where and how we live today. To find out more about the fascinating global journey of a humble flip-flop follow the trail.' Each link on the trail (www.flipfloptrail.com) takes you to a place, and then to images and accounts related to the journey of the flip-flop. For example, in Kuwait we learn about oil production and distribution, about the workers in its production, their pay and conditions, and there are stories and quotes from the participants themselves. In China, we hear about Chinese socialism, its economic growth, and the role of Special Economic Zones, and we get to visit the 'plastic city' of Fuzhou, where profits from plastics have shaped architecture and design, and where flip-flop start-up businesses have flourished, and where migrant workers outnumber locals in multiples. The critical analysis is implicit, and is elaborated more in other publications (Knowles 2014, 2015). In the flip-flop trail, the details and insights are rich, descriptive, complex and comprehensive; photographs are colourful and bright; accounts are clear and succinct.

Pinker (2015: 67) warns us to watch out for the curse of knowledge: 'Imagine the reader over your shoulder,' he says, and check your use of jargon, abbreviations, acronyms, and technical vocabulary. Know your audience but also consider it could be broader than you thought. Imagine them as sophisticated and intelligent but not necessarily as knowledgeable as you in the same areas.

Final thoughts

Finally, be imaginative and creative (Box 9.3). Consider using some of the many available styles of communicating and interpreting that I mentioned at the start of the chapter, such as blogs and podcasts, dance and poetry (Mason 2018: 214). Have a look, for inspiration, at the online journal *Entanglements: Experiments in Multimodal Ethnography*, or the Sociological Review Foundation's magazine and 'artist in residence' features. The podcasts from our Brexit Brits Abroad project are now available through Spotify. Enjoy your writing and communications and then hopefully your audience or readers will enjoy your work too.

Speaking of writing

'I hate the thought of writing, but I love it when I get into it.'

'I thought I'd finished analysing my data until I realised all I'd done was summarise a few themes. That would be boring for anyone to read and wouldn't really help answer my research questions.'

'I'm so excited to present these findings: I've organised them around a timeline, comparing women and men of different ages; I've got some poignant stories to include, and a chart that summarises how the main themes fit together.'

'Who knew reading a novel would help me write well and give me a great concept to use as well: stories as life lived backwards. Thank you, Ruth Ozeki.'

Taking things further

Take things further by reading anything and everything with a critical eye. Portwood-Stacer (2021) has some surprising insights about writing **style**, layout and strength of argument. Pinker's (2015) book on **style** is enjoyable. The chapters by White and colleagues (2014) and Spencer and colleagues (2014) have some great **practical tips** and got me thinking in ways I hadn't thought before. Pat Thomson's (2017) research blog, Patter, has some fabulous imaginative and creative suggestions for **communicating differently**. There's a lovely special issue in *The Sociological Review* journal on **sociography** or writing differently (Kilby and Gilloch 2022). The report by Dutton and Sisya (2024) has a great layout accompanied by a short **animation**.

Listen to the related episode for this chapter on
Qualitative Research Methods for Everyone podcast:

Transformative and inspiring qualitative research

I conclude this book with a brief celebration of the transformative and inspiring work of a few qualitative researchers to emphasise the diverse potential for and impact of qualitative research.

- Davina Allen (2015, 2018), Cardiff University, sociologist and nurse academic, has developed TRACT, a web-based application for measuring, planning and managing the organisational components of nursing care, and translational mobilisation theory that facilitates an understanding of nursing practices.
- Keri Facer, University of Bristol, collaborates with engineers, artists, sociologists and philosophers to open up possibilities for personal and social change in the context of ecological crisis. She also works to connect schools, universities and the wider community (http://kerifacer.wordpress.com).
- Trisha Greenhalgh, primary healthcare academic and general practitioner, works prolifically at the interface of social science and medicine using narrative methods and structuration theory (for example, Greenhalgh et al 2014). She has an international profile and powerful social media influence, with over 181,000 followers on X (formerly Twitter), but at the time of writing has switched to Bluesky.
- Yvonne Jewkes (2013), University of Bath, has undertaken qualitative ethnographic research with prisoners and prison design that has led to progressive innovations in prison architecture in the UK, Ireland, Australia and New Zealand.
- Maggie O'Neill, University College Cork, uses biographical and participatory methods (including walking, filming, exhibitions) to examine the transformative effects of arts and science, and to produce knowledge that addresses and intervenes in public policy (see Chapter 7).
- Sarah Pink, anthropologist at Monash University, is an award-winning design and futures anthropologist and documentary filmmaker, whose work is influential internationally both inside and beyond academia (see Chapter 7).

Qualitative research has the potential to be transformative, to reveal possibilities, to generate meaningful insights, to be evocative, to emancipate, to yield significant insights, to inform policy, to evaluate processes and practices, to address the theory-practice gap, to give us hope. Enjoy your qualitative research journey.

References

Åberg, A.C., Sidenvall, B., O'Reilly, K., Hepworth, M. and Lithell, H. (2005) 'On Loss of Activity and Independence, Adaptation Improves Life Satisfaction in Old Age – A Qualitative Study of Patients' Perceptions', *Quality of Life Research*, 14: 1111–25.

Adler, P.A. and Adler, P. (2007) 'The Demedicalization of Self-Injury', *Journal of Contemporary Ethnography*, 36(5): 537–70.

Ahmed, S. (2006) *Queer Phenomenology: Orientations, Objects, Others*, Durham, NC: Duke University Press.

Aldridge, J. (2015) *Participatory Research. Working with Vulnerable Groups in Research and Practice*, Bristol: Policy Press.

Allen, D. (2015) *The Invisible Work of Nurses: Hospital, Organisation and Healthcare*, London: Routledge.

Allen, D. (2018) 'Translational Mobilisation Theory: A New Paradigm for Understanding the Organisational Elements of Nursing Work, *International Journal of Nursing Studies*, 79: 36–42.

Alzheimer's UK (2024) 'Dementia Experience Toolkit: Qualitative Data. Read About the Importance of Gathering Qualitative Data when Researching People Who Have Dementia', www.alzheimers.org.uk/dementia-professionals/dementia-experience-toolkit/working-with-data/qualitative-data

Anderson, R. (2011) 'Intuitive Inquiry: Exploring the Mirroring Discourse of Disease', In F.J. Wertz, K. Charmaz, L.M. McMullen, R, Josselson, A. Anderson and E. McSpadden, *Five Ways of Doing Qualitative Analysis*, New York: Guilford Press.

Archibald, M.M., Ambagtsheer, R.C., Casey, M.G. and Lawless, M. (2019) 'Using Zoom Videoconferencing for Qualitative Data Collection: Perceptions and Experiences of Researcher and Participants', *International Journal of Qualitative Methods*, 18. DOI: 10.1177/1609406919874596

Armitage, J.S. (2022) '"When I Least Expected It": An Autoethnography of Reporting Workplace Sexual Harassment and Compassionate Bystanders', *Journal of Contemporary Ethnography*, 51(1): 29–58.

Asad, T. (ed) (1973) *Anthropology and the Colonial Encounter*, London: Ithaca Press.

Atkinson, P., Coffey, A., Delamont, S., Lofland, J. and Lofland, L. (eds) (2001) *Handbook of Ethnography*. London: Sage.

Atkinson P., Delamont, S., Cernat, A., Sakshaug, J.W. and Williams R.A. (eds) (2019) *Sage Research Methods Foundations*, London: Sage.

Back, L. (2007) *The Art of Listening*. Oxford: Berg.

Back, L. (2012) 'Live Sociology: Social Research And Its Futures', *The Sociological Review*, 60(1): 18–39.

Back, L. (2021) 'Hope's Work', *Antipode*, 53: 3–20.

Back, L. and Puwar, N. (2012) 'A Manifesto for Live Methods: Provocations and Capacities', *The Sociological Review*, 60(S1): 6–17.

Baker, S.E. and Edwards, R. (2012) 'How Many Qualitative Interviews Is Enough?', National Centre for Research Methods, https://eprints.ncrm.ac.uk/id/eprint/2273/4/how_many_interviews.pdf

Barbour, R. and Kitzinger, J. (1998) *Developing Focus Group Research: Politics, Theory and Practice*, London: Sage.

Barbulescu, R. (nd) Feeding the Nation: Seasonal Migrant Workers and Food Security during COVID-19 Pandemic, UKRI Award ES/V015257/1, https://gtr.ukri.org/projects?ref=ES%2FV015257%2F1

Bartlett, R. (2015) 'Visualising Dementia Activism: Using the Arts to Communicate Research Findings', *Qualitative Research*, 15(6): 755–68.

Barton, B. (2007) 'Managing the Toll of Stripping: Boundary Setting among Exotic Dancers', *Journal of Contemporary Ethnography*, 36(5): 571–96.

Becker, H. (1998) *Tricks of the Trade: How To Think About Your Research While You're Doing It*, Chicago, IL: University of Chicago Press.

Bejarano, C.A., García, M.A.M., Juárez, L.L. and Goldstein, D.M. (2019) *Decolonizing Ethnography: Undocumented Immigrants and New Directions in Social Science*, Durham, NC: Duke University Press.

Benson, M. (2011) *The British in Rural France: Lifestyle Migration and the Ongoing Quest for a Better Way of Life*, Manchester: Manchester University Press.

Benson, M. (2020) 'Brexit and the Classed Politics of Bordering: The British in France and European Belongings', *Sociology*, 54(3): 501–17.

Benson, M. and Lewis, C. (2019) 'Brexit, British People of Colour in the EU-27 and Everyday Racism in Britain and Europe', *Ethnic and Racial Studies*, 42(13): 2211–28.

Benson, M. and O'Reilly, K. (2015) 'From Lifestyle Migration to Lifestyle in Migration: Categories, Concepts and Ways of Thinking', *Migration Studies*, 4(1): 20–37.

Benson, M. and O'Reilly, K. (2018) *Lifestyle Migration and Colonial Traces in Malaysia and Panama*, London: Palgrave Macmillan.

Benson, M. and O'Reilly, K. (2020a) 'British Citizens in Europe Left Navigating the (Brexit) Swamp', UK in a Changing Europe, https://ukandeu.ac.uk/british-citizens-in-europe-left-navigating-the-brexit-swamp

Benson, M. and O'Reilly, K. (2020b) 'Reflexive Practice in Live Sociology: Lessons from Researching Brexit in the Lives of British Citizens Living in the EU-27', *Qualitative Research*, 22(2): 177–193.

Benson, M., O'Reilly, K. and Collins, K. (2018) 'What Does Brexit Mean for UK Citizens Living in the EU27? Talking Citizens' Rights with UK Citizens across the EU27', Project Report. Goldsmiths, University of London. DOI: 10.25602/GOLD.00027351

Benton, M., Aliyyah, A., Benson, M., Collins, C., McCarthy, H. and O'Reilly, K. (2018) 'Next Steps: Implementing a Brexit Deal for UK Citizens Living in the EU-27', Migration Policy Institute.

References

Benton, T. and Craib I. (2023) *Philosophy of Social Science: The Philosophical Foundations of Social Thought*, 3rd edn, Bloomsbury Academic.

Berg, B. and Lune, H. (2012) *Qualitative Research for the Social Sciences*, 8th edn, Boston, MA: Pearson International Edition.

Bhana, A. (2006) 'Participatory Action Research: A Practical Guide for Realistic Radicals', In M. Terre Blanche, K. Durrheim and D. Painter (eds), *Research in Practice: Applied Methods for the Social Sciences*, Cape Town: University of Cape Town Press, pp 429–42.

Billig, M. (2013) *Learn to Write Badly: How to Succeed in the Social Sciences*, Cambridge UK: Cambridge University Press.

Bingham, A.J. (2023) 'From Data Management to Actionable Findings: A Five-Phase Process of Qualitative Data Analysis', *International Journal of Qualitative Methods*, 22. DOI: 10.1177/16094069231183620

Birch, J., Curtis, P. and James, A. (2007) 'Sense and Sensibilities: In Search of the Child-Friendly Hospital', *Built Environment*, 33(4): 405–16.

Bloom, S., Critten, S., Johnson, H. and Wood, C. (2020) 'A Critical Review of Methods for Eliciting Voice from Children with Speech, Language and Communication Needs', *Journal of Research in Special Educational Needs*, 20(4): 308–20.

Bluteau, J.M. (2021) 'Legitimising Digital Anthropology through Immersive Cohabitation: Becoming an Observing Participant in a Blended Digital Landscape', *Ethnography*, 22(2): 267–85.

Boellstorff, T. (2008) *Coming of Age in Second Life: An Anthropologist Explores the Virtually Human*, Princeton, NJ: Princeton University Press.

Boellstorff, T., Nardi, B., Pearce, C. and Taylor, T.L. (2012) *Ethnography and Virtual Worlds: A Handbook of Method*, Princeton, NJ: Princeton University Press.

Bourdieu, P. (1984) *Distinction: A Social Critique of the Judgement of Taste*, London: Routledge & Kegan Paul.

Bourdieu, P. (2003) 'Participant Objectivation', *Journal of the Royal Anthropological Institute*, 9: 281–94.

Bourdieu, P., Accardo, A., Balazs, G., Beaud S., Bonvin, F., Bourdieu, E. et al (1999) *The Weight of the World: Social Suffering in Contemporary Society*, translated by Priscilla Parkhurst Ferguson, Susan Emanuel, Joe Johnson and Shaggy T. Warren, Stanford, CA: Stanford University Press.

Bourgois, P. and Schonberg, J. (2009) *Righteous Dopefiend*, Berkeley, CA: University of California Press.

Braun, V. and Clarke, V. (2022) *Thematic Analysis. A Practical Guide*, London: Sage.

Brown, N. (2021) *Making the Most of Your Research Journal*, Bristol: Policy Press.

Burawoy, M. (2000) 'Introduction. Reaching for the Global', In M. Burawoy et al, *Global Ethnography*, Berkeley, CA: University of California Press, pp 1–26.

Burawoy, M., Blum, J.A., George, S., Gille, Z., Gowan, T. and Haney, L. et al (2000) *Global Ethnography*, Berkeley, CA: University of California Press.

Burawoy, M. (1998) 'The Extended Case Method', *Sociological Theory*, 16(1): 4–33.

Busetto, L., Wick, W. and Gumbinger, C. (2020) 'How to Use and Assess Qualitative Research Methods', *Neurological Research and Practice*, 2(14). DOI: 10.1186/s42466-020-00059-z

Calvey, D. (2021) 'Being on Both Sides: Covert Ethnography and Partisanship with Bouncers in the Night-Time Economy', *Journal of Organizational Ethnography*, 10(1): 50–64.

Campbell, S., Dowlen, R. and Fleetwood-Smith, R. (2023) 'Embracing Complexity within Creative Approaches to Dementia Research: Ethics, Reflexivity, and Research Practices', *International Journal of Qualitative Methods*, 22: 1–15.

Candea, M. (2018) *Comparison in Anthropology: The Impossible Method*, Cambridge University Press.

Candea, M. and Yarrow, T. (2023) 'Emergent Explanation', In P. Heywood and M. Candea (eds), *Beyond Description. Anthropologies of Explanation*, London/Ithaca, NY: Cornell University Press, pp 81–103.

Chandler, A. (2019) 'Boys Don't Cry? Critical Phenomenology, Self-Harm and Suicide', *The Sociological Review*, 67(6): 1350–66.

Charmaz, K. (2011) 'A Constructivist Grounded Theory Analysis of Losing and Regaining a Valued Self', In F.J. Wertz, K. Charmaz, L.M. McMullen, R, Josselson, A. Anderson and E. McSpadden, *Five Ways of Doing Qualitative Analysis*, New York: Guilford Press.

Charmaz, K. (2014) *Constructing Grounded Theory: A Practical Guide through Qualitative Analysis*, 2nd edn, London: Sage.

Choi, K.H. (2020) 'Reflective Journals in Qualitative Inquiry' [blog], QualPage, 3 December, https://qualpage.com/2020/12/03/reflective-journals-in-qualitative-inquiry

Clifford, J. (1988) *The Predicament of Culture*, Cambridge, MA: Harvard University Press.

Clifford, J. and Marcus, G.E. (eds) (1986) *Writing Culture. The Poetics and Politics of Ethnography*, Berkeley, CA: University of California Press.

Cole, A.L. and Knowles, J.G. (2001) *Lives in Context: The Art of Life History Research*, Walnut Creek, CA: Altamira Press.

Condon, L., Bedford, H., Ireland, L., Kerr, S., Mytton, J., Richardson, Z. et al (2019) 'Engaging Gypsy, Roma, and Traveller Communities in Research: Maximising Opportunities and Overcoming Challenges', *Qualitative Health Research*, 29(9): 1324–33.

Crang, M. and Cook, I. (2007) *Doing Ethnographies*, London: Sage.

Crow, G. (2020) *What are Community Studies?*, London: Bloomsbury Academic.

Crow, G. (2022) '"Amusing and Fun", "Arresting", or "the Wrong Pictures"? Methodological Lessons from Using Photo-Elicitation in a Study of Academic Retirement', *Sociological Research Online*, 15: 1–20. DOI: 10.1177/13607804221133117

Crowther, J., Horton, S., Wilson, K. and Lloyd-Williams, M. (2022) 'A UK Qualitative Study of Living and Dying with Dementia in the Last Year of Life', *Palliative Care and Social Practice*, 16: 1–11.

Cubellis, L.C., Schmid, C. and von Peter, S. (2021) 'Ethnography in Health Services Research: Oscillating between Theory and Practice', *Qualitative Health Research*, 31(11): 2029–40.

Curtis, P., James, A. and Birch, J. (2007) 'Space to Care: Children's Perceptions of Spatial Aspects of Hospitals', Full research report. ESRC End of Award Report, RES-000-23-0765. ESRC, Swindon, pp 1–25.

Danby, M. and O'Reilly, K. (2018) 'What Does Brexit Mean for UK Citizens Living in the EU27? Talking Brexit with 18–35 Year Old UK Citizens in Southern Spain', Project Report, Goldsmiths, University of London, London. DOI: 10.25602/GOLD.00027353

Davies, C.A. (2008) *Reflexive Ethnography. A Guide to Researching Selves and Others*, London: Routledge.

Dean, J. (2017) *Doing Reflexivity: An Introduction*, Bristol: Policy Press.

de Gialdino, I.V. (2009) 'Ontological and Epistemological Foundations of Qualitative Research', *Forum Qualitative Sozialforschung, Forum: Qualitative Social Research*, 10(2). DOI: 10.17169/fqs-10.2.1299

Denzin, N.K. (2013) *Interpretive Autoethnography*, 2nd edn, London: Sage.

Desmond, M. (2006) 'Becoming a Firefighter', *Ethnography*, 7(4): 387–421.

Dodworth, K. (2021) '"A Real African Woman!" Multipositionality and Its Effects in the Field', *Ethnography*, 22(2): 164–83.

Dowlen, R. (2019) The 'In the Moment' Musical Experiences of People with Dementia: A Multiple-Case Study Approach, PhD Thesis, University of Manchester.

Dowling, M. (2007) 'From Husserl to van Maanen: A Review of Different Phenomenological Approaches', *International Journal of Nursing Studies*, 44(1): 131–42.

Dutton, A. and Sisya, K. (2024) *Exploring what Young People in Together for Childhood Know, Think, and Do about Child Abuse*, London: NSPCC.

Ellis, C., Adams, T.E. and Bochner, A.P. (2011) 'Autoethnography: An Overview', *Forum Qualitative Sozialforschung Forum: Qualitative Social Research*, 12(1).

Emerson, R.M., Fretz, R.I. and Shaw, L.L. (2011) *Writing Ethnographic Fieldnotes*, 2nd edn, Chicago, IL: University of Chicago Press.

Falzon, M. (ed) (2009) *Multi-Sited Ethnography: Theory, Praxis and Locality in Contemporary Research*, Aldershot: Ashgate.

Fell, M.J., Roelich, K. and Middlemiss, L. (2022) 'Realist Approaches in Energy Research to Support Faster and Fairer Climate Action', *Nature Energy*, 7: 916–22.

Fetterman, D.M. (2010) *Ethnography Step by Step*, 3rd edn, London: Sage.

Finch, H., Lewis, J. and Turley, C. (2014) 'Focus Groups', In J. Ritchie, J. Lewis, C. McNaughton Nicholls and R. Ormston (eds), *Qualitative Research Practice*, 2nd edn, London: Sage, pp 211–366.

FitzGerald, S., O'Neill, M. and Wylie, G. (2020) 'Social Justice for Sex Workers as a 'Politics of Doing': Research, Policy and Practice', *Irish Journal of Sociology*, 28(3): 257–79.

Fleetwood-Smith, R. (2020) Exploring the Significance of Clothing to People with Dementia Using Sensory Ethnography, PhD Thesis, University of West London.

Fratsea, L.M. and Papadopoulos, A. (2021) 'The Social and Spatial Mobility Strategies of Migrants: Romanian Migrants in Rural Greece', In J.F. Rye and K. O'Reilly (eds), *International Labour Migration to Europe's Rural Regions*, London: Routledge, pp 37–51.

Geertz, C. (1973) *The Interpretation of Cultures*, New York: Fontana.

Giabiconi, J. (2013) 'Serendipity ... Mon Amour? On Discomfort as a Prerequisite for Anthropological Knowledge', *Social Anthropology*, 21(2): 199–212.

Giddens, A. (1984) *The Constitution of Society: Outline of the Theory of Structuration*, Cambridge: Polity.

Glaser, B.G. and Strauss, A. (1967) *The Discovery of Grounded Theory*, Chicago, IL: Aldine.

Gobo, G. (2008) *Doing Ethnography*, London: Sage.

Goffman, A. (2014) *On the Run: Fugitive Life in an American City*, Chicago, IL: University of Chicago Press.

Gomensoro, A. and Burgos Paredes, R. (2017) 'Combining In-Depth Biographical Interviews with the LIVES History Calendar in Studying the Life Course of Children of Immigrants', In C. Bolzman, L. Bernardi and J.M. Le Goff (eds), *Situating Children of Migrants across Borders and Origins. Life Course Research and Social Policies, Volume 7*, Dordrecht: Springer, pp 151–71.

Goode, J. (ed) (2019) *Clever Girls. Autoethnographies of Class, Gender and Ethnicity*, Cham: Springer.

Gram E.G., Brodersen, J.B., Hansen, C., Pickles, K., Smith, J. and Jønsson, A.R.B. (2023) 'Fictitious Cases as a Methodology to Discuss Sensitive Health Topics in Focus Groups', *International Journal of Qualitative Studies on Health and Well-Being*, 18(1). DOI: 10.1080/17482631.2023.2233253

Greenhalgh, T., Wherton, J., Sugarhood, P., Hinder, S., Procter, R. and Stones, R. (2013) 'What Matters to Older People with Assisted Living Needs? A Phenomenological Analysis of the Use and Non-Use of Telehealth and Telecare', *Social Science & Medicine*, 93: 86–94.

Greenhalgh, T.R., Stones, R. and Swinglehurst, D. (2014) 'Choose and Book: A Sociological Analysis of Resistance to an Expert System', *Social Science and Medicine*, 104: 210–19.

Gubrium, J.F. and Holstein, J.A. (2012) 'Narrative Practice and the Transformation of Interview Subjectivity', In J.F. Gubrium, J.A. Holstein, A.B. Marvasti and K.D. McKinney (eds), *The Sage Handbook of Interview Research: The Complexity of the Craft*, London: Sage, pp 27–44.

Gunaratnam, Y. (2003) *Researching 'Race' and Ethnicity: Methods, Knowledge and Power*, London: Sage.

Hallett, T. (2019) 'Book Review: *Bits and Pieces of Ethnographic Data on Trial*, by Steven Lubet', *Contemporary Sociology*, 48(3): 255–61.

Hammersley, M. (2009) 'Against the Ethicists: On the Evils of Ethical Regulation', *International Journal of Social Research Methodology*, 12(3): 211–25.

Hannerz, U. (2003) 'Being There ... and There ... and There! Reflections on Multi-Site Ethnography,' *Ethnography*, 4(2): 201–16.

Harding, S. (1986) *The Science Question in Feminism*, Milton Keynes: Open University Press.

Harrison, T.C., Taylor, J.L., Johnson, A.H., Ortega, L.C., Lowe, J. and Blozis, S. (2023) 'The Life-Course Perspectives of Mexican American Men with Mobility Limitation', *Qualitative Health Research*, 33(10): 897–910.

Hayes, L. (2017) *Stories of Care: A Labour of Law. Gender and Class at Work*, London: Palgrave.

Hayes, M. (2018) *Gringolandia. Lifestyle Migration under Late Capitalism*, Minneapolis, MN: University of Minnesota Press.

Heyl, B.S. (2001) 'Ethnographic Interviewing', In P. Atkinson, A. Coffey, S. Delamont, J. Lofland and L. Lofland (eds), *Handbook of Ethnography*, London: Sage, pp 369–83.

Hine, C. (2000) *Virtual Ethnography*, London: Sage.

Hippolyte-Blake, D., Dreschler, A., Rose, A., Rae, P., Archer, J., Garrod, T.J. (2022) 'A Qualitative Study of the Incentives and Barriers that Influence Preferences for Rural Placements during Surgical Training in Australia', *ANZ Journal of Surgery*, 92(3): 341–5.

Holmes, M. (2010) 'The Emotionalization of Reflexivity', *Sociology*, 44(1): 139–54.

Horst, H. and Miller, D. (eds) (2012) *Digital Anthropology*, Oxford: Berg.

Hughes, G., Shaw, S. and Greenhalgh, T. (2022) 'Why Doesn't Integrated Care Work? Using Strong Structuration Theory to Explain the Limitations of an English Case', *Sociology of Health & Illness*, 44: 113–29.

Ingold, T. and Vergunst, J.L. (2008) *Ways of Walking: Ethnography and Practice on Foot*, Aldershot: Ashgate.

Iphofen, R. and O'Mathúna, D. (eds) (2021) *Ethical Issues in Covert, Security and Surveillance Research. Advances in Research Ethics and Integrity, Volume 8*, Leeds: Emerald Publishing Limited.

Irani, E. (2018) 'The Use of Videoconferencing for Qualitative Interviewing: Opportunities, Challenges and Considerations', *Clinical Nursing Research*, 28(1): 3–8.

Jacobs, A., Dreessen, K. and Pierson, J. (2008) '"Thick" Personas – Using Ethnographic Methods for Persona Development as a Tool for Conveying the Social Science View in Technological Design', *Observatorio (OBS*)*, 2(2): 079–097.

Jakobsen, H. (2012) 'Focus Groups and Methodological Rigour outside the Minority World: Making the Method Work to Its Strengths', *Qualitative Research*, 12(2): 111–30.

Jessee, E. (2018) 'The Life History Interview', In P. Liamputtong (ed), *Handbook of Research Methods in Health Social Sciences*, Singapore: Springer.

Jewkes, Y. (2013) 'What Has Prison Ethnography to Offer in an Age of Mass Incarceration?', *Criminal Justice Matters*, 91(1): 14–15.

Jewkes, Y. and Laws, B. (2021) 'Liminality Revisited: Mapping the Emotional Adaptations of Women in Carceral Space', *Punishment and Society*, 23(3): 394–412.

Jones, R. (2004) 'Blended Voices: Crafting a Narrative from Oral History Interviews', *The Oral History Review*, 31(1): 23–42.

Josselson, R. (2011) in F.J. Wertz, K. Charmaz, L.M. McMullen, R, Josselson, A. Anderson and E. McSpadden, *Five Ways of Doing Qualitative Analysis*, New York: Guilford Press.

Kahneman, D. (2012) *Thinking, Fast and Slow*, London: Penguin.

Kara, H. (2020) *Creative Research Methods. A Practical Guide*, Bristol: Policy Press.

Keen, S., Lomeli-Rodriguez M. and Joffe, H. (2022) 'From Challenge to Opportunity: Virtual Qualitative Research during COVID-19 and Beyond', *International Journal of Qualitative Methods*, 21. DOI: 10.1177/16094069221105075

Kerr, J., Kinsella, R., Turley, C., Legard, R., McNaughton Nicholls, C. and Barnard, M. (2009) 'Qualitative Follow-Up of the British Gambling Prevalence Survey 2007', London: National Centre for Social Research.

Kilby, J. and Gilloch, G. (2022) 'Sociography: Writing Differently', *The Sociological Review*, 70(4): 635–55.

Kitzinger J. (1995) 'Introducing Focus Groups', *British Medical Journal*, 311: 299–302.

Knoblauch, H. (2005) 'Focused Ethnography', *Forum Qualitative Sozialforschung Forum: Qualitative Social Research*, 6(3).

Knowles, C. (2014) *Flip-Flop: A Journey through Globalisation's Backroads*, London: Pluto Press.

Knowles, C. (2015) 'The Flip-Flop Trail and Fragile Globalisation', *Theory, Culture and Society*, 32(7–8): 231–44.

Krueger, R.A. (1994) *Focus Groups: A Practical Guide for Applied Research*, 2nd edn, London: Sage.

Krueger, R.A. and Casey, M.A. (2015) *Focus Groups: A Practical Guide for Applied Research*, 5th edn, Thousand Oaks, CA: Sage.

Kusenbach, M. (2003) 'Street Phenomenology: The Go-Along as Ethnographic Research Tool', *Ethnography*, 4(3): 455–85.

Kvale S. and Brinkmann, S. (2015) *InterViews: Learning the Craft of Qualitative Research Interviewing*, 3rd edn, London: Sage.

Ladner, S. (2014) *Practical Ethnography*, London: Routledge.

Lave, J. and Wenger, E. (1991) *Situated Learning: Legitimate Peripheral Participation*, Cambridge: Cambridge University Press.

Legard, R., Keegan, J. and Ward, K. (2003) 'In-Depth Interviews', In J. Richie and J. Lewis (eds), *Qualitative Research Practice*, London: Sage, pp 139–68.

Legge, K., Hartfree, Y., Stafford, B., Magadi, M., Beckhelling, J., Nyhagen Predelli, L. et al (2006) *The Social Fund. Current Role and Future Direction*, York: Joseph Rowntree Foundation.

Leung, L. (2015) 'Validity, Reliability, and Generalizability in Qualitative Research', *Journal of Family Medicine and Primary Care*, 4(3): 324–27.

Lewis-Dagnell, S., Parsons, S. and Kovshoff, H. (2023) 'Creative Methods Developed to Facilitate the Voices of Children and Young People with Complex Needs about Their Education: A Systematic Review and Conceptual Analysis of Voice', *Educational Research Review*, 39. DOI: 10.1016/j.edurev.2023.100529.

Lewis-Kraus, G. (2016) 'The Trials of Alice Goffman', *The New York Times Magazine*, 12 January, www.nytimes.com/2016/01/17/magazine/the- trials-of-alice-goffman.html.

Linneberg, M.S. and Korsgaard, S. (2019) 'Coding Qualitative Data: A Synthesis Guiding the Novice', *Qualitative Research Journal*, 19(3): 259–70.

Lleisiau Bach Little Voices (2022) 'Methodology', www.lleisiaubach.org/about-us/methodology

Lobe, B., Morgan, D. and Hoffman, K.A. (2020) 'Qualitative Data Collection in an Era of Social Distancing', *International Journal of Qualitative Methods*, 19. DOI: 10.1177/1609406920937875

Lubet, S. (2015a) 'Ethics on the Run. Review of *On the Run: Fugitive Life in an American City* by Alice Goffman', *The New Rambler Review*, 26 May, http://newramblerreview.com/book-reviews/law/ethics-on-the-run

Lubet, S. (2015b) 'Did This Acclaimed Sociologist Drive the Getaway Car in a Murder Plot?', *New Republic*, 27 May, https://newrepublic.com/article/121909/did-sociologist-alice-goffman-drive-getaway-car-murder-plot

Lubet, S. (2017) *Interrogating Ethnography. Why Evidence Matters*, New York: Oxford University Press.

Lubit, A.J. and Gidley, D. (2021) 'Becoming Part of a Temporary Protest Organization through Embodied Walking Ethnography', *Journal of Organizational Ethnography*, 10(1): 79–94.

Lumsden, K. (2019) *Reflexivity: Theory, Method, and Practice*, London: Routledge.

Lundy, L. (2007) '"Voice" is Not Enough: Conceptualising Article 12 of the United Nations Convention on the Rights of the Child', *British Educational Research Journal*, 33(6): 927–42.

Madden, R. (2010) *Being Ethnographic: A Guide to the Theory and Practice of Ethnography*, London: Sage.

Madriz, M. (2000) 'Focus Groups in Feminist Research', In N. Denzin and Y.S. Lincoln (eds), *Handbook of Qualitative Research*, London: Sage, pp 361–76.

Malinowski, B. (1922) *Argonauts of the Western Pacific: An Account of Native Enterprise and Adventure in the Archipelagoes of Melanesian New Guinea*, New York: Dutton.

Malterud, K., Siersma, V.D., Guassora, A.D. (2016) 'Sample Size in Qualitative Interview Studies: Guided by Information Power', *Qualitative Health Research*, 26(13): 1753–60.

Mannay, D. (2010) 'Making the Familiar Strange: Can Visual Research Methods Render the Familiar Setting more Perceptible?', *Qualitative Research*, 10(1): 91–111.

Marcus, G. (2012) 'Foreword', In T. Boellstorff, B. Nardi, C. Pearce and T.L. Taylor, *Ethnography and Virtual Worlds. A Handbook of Method*, Princeton, NJ: Princeton University Press, pp xiii–xvii.

Markham, A. (2013) 'Remix Cultures, Remix Methods: Reframing Qualitative Inquiry for Social Media Contexts', In N. Denzin and M. Giardina (eds), *Global Dimensions of Qualitative Inquiry*, Walnut Creek, CA: Left Coast Press, pp 63–81.

Marzano, M. (2021) 'Covert Research Ethics', In R. Iphofen and D. O'Mathúna (eds), *Ethical Issues in Covert, Security and Surveillance Research. Advances in Research Ethics and Integrity, Volume 8*, Leeds: Emerald Publishing Limited, pp 41–53.

Mason, J. (1996) *Qualitative Researching*, London: Sage.

Mason, J. (2018) *Qualitative Researching*, 3rd edn, London: Sage.

May, T. and Perry, B. (2017) *Reflexivity: The Essential Guide*, London: Sage.

Mbohou, L.F.N. and Tomkinson, S. (2022) 'Rethinking Elite Interviews through Moments of Discomfort: The Role of Information and Power', *International Journal of Qualitative Methods*, 21. DOI: 10.1177/16094069221095312

McLeod, J. and Thomson, R. (2009) *Researching Social Change*, London: Sage.

McMullen, L.M. (2011) 'A Discursive Analysis of Teresa's Protocol: Enhancing Oneself, Diminishing Others', In F.J. Wertz, K. Charmaz, L.M. McMullen, R, Josselson, A. Anderson and E. McSpadden, *Five Ways of Doing Qualitative Analysis*, New York: Guilford Press.

Mies, M. (1983) 'Towards a Methodology for Feminist Research', In G. Bowles and R. Duelli Klein (eds), *Theories of Women's Studies*, London: Routledge & Kegan Paul, pp 117–40.

Miller, D. (2011) *Tales from Facebook*, Cambridge: Polity.

Moore, J.W. (1973) 'Social Constraints on Sociological Knowledge: Academics and Research Concerning Minorities', *Social Problems*, 21(1): 65–77.

Morawska, E.T. (1996) *Insecure Prosperity: Small-Town Jews in Industrial America, 1890–1940*, Princeton, NJ: Princeton University Press.

Morawska, E. (2009) *A Sociology of Immigration: (Re)Making Multifaceted America*, Basingstoke: Palgrave Macmillan.

Morgan, D. (1988) *Focus Groups as Qualitative Research*, London: Sage.

Morgan, D.L. (ed) (1993) *Successful Focus Groups: Advancing the State of the Art*, Newbury Park, CA: Sage.

Morosanu, R. (2016) *An Ethnography of Household Energy Demand in the UK. Everyday Temporalities of Digital Media Use*, London: Palgrave Macmillan.

Morrow, V. (2001) 'Using Qualitative Methods to Elicit Young People's Perspectives on their Environments: Some Ideas for Community Health Initiatives', *Health Education Research*, 16(3): 255–68.

Murthy, D. (2008) 'Digital Ethnography: An Examination of the Use of New Technologies for Social Research', *Sociology*, 42(5): 837–55.

Nair, D. (2021) '"Hanging Out" while Studying "Up": Doing Ethnographic Fieldwork in International Relations', *International Studies Review*, 23(4): 1300–27.

Nyumba, T.O., Wilson, K., Derrick, C.J. and Mukherjee, N. (2018) 'The Use of Focus Group Discussion Methodology: Insights from Two Decades of Application in Conservation', *Methods in Ecology and Evolution*, 9: 20–32.

Oakley, A. (1981) 'Interviewing Women: A Contradiction in Terms?', In H. Roberts (ed) *Doing Feminist Research*, London: Routledge & Kegan Paul, pp 30–61.

Oakley, A. (2016) 'Interviewing Women Again: Power, Time and the Gift', *Sociology*, 50(1): 195–213.

Oliver, C. (2008) *Retirement Migration*, London: Routledge.

O'Neill, M. (2011) 'Participatory Methods and Critical Models: Arts, Migration and Diaspora', *Crossings: Journal of Migration & Culture*, 2(1): 13–37.

O'Neill, M. (2018) 'Walking, Well-being and Community: Racialized Mothers Building Cultural Citizenship using Participatory Arts and Participatory Action Research', *Ethnic and Racial Studies*, 41(1): 73–97.

O'Reilly, K. (2000) *The British on the Costa del Sol*, London: Routledge.

O'Reilly, K. (2002) 'Britain in Europe/The British in Spain. Exploring Britain's Changing Relationship to the Other', *Nations and Nationalism*, 8(2): 179–94.

O'Reilly, K. (2009) *Key Concepts in Ethnography*, London: Sage.

O'Reilly, K. (2012a) *Ethnographic Methods*, 2nd edn, London: Routledge.

O'Reilly, K. (2012b) *International Migration and Social Theory*, Basingstoke: Palgrave.

O'Reilly, K. (2012c) 'Ethnographic Returning, Qualitative Longitudinal Research and the Reflexive Analysis of Social Practice', *Sociological Review*, 60(3): 518–36.

O'Reilly, K. (2015) 'Ethnography: Telling Practice Stories', In R.A. Scott and S.M. Kosslyn (eds), *Emerging Trends in the Social and Behavioral Sciences: An Interdisciplinary, Searchable, and Linkable Resource*. DOI: 10.1002/9781118900772. etrds0120

O'Reilly, K. (2017a) 'The British on the Costa Del Sol Twenty Years on: A Story of Liquids and Sediments', *Nordic Journal of Migration Research*, 7(3): 139–47.

O'Reilly, K. (2017b) 'What Does Brexit Mean for British Citizens Living in the EU27? Talking Brexit with the British in Spain', Project report, Goldsmiths, University of London. DOI: 10.25602/GOLD.00027354

O'Reilly, K. (2018a) 'What Does Brexit Mean for UK Citizens Living in the EU27? Talking Brexit with the British in Spain II', Project report, Goldsmiths, University of London. DOI: 10.25602/GOLD.00027355

O'Reilly, K. (2018b) 'Far More Britons Live in Europe than Government Statistics Suggest', *The Conversation*, 25 April, https://theconversation.com/profiles/karen-oreilly-466788

O'Reilly, K. (2020a) 'Brexit and the British in Spain', Project report, Goldsmiths, University of London. DOI: 10.25602/GOLD.00028223

O'Reilly, K. (2020b) '"Our Own Government Has Done Absolutely Nothing for Us": Brexit and the British in Spain' [blog], https://blogs.lse.ac.uk/brexit/2020/03/16/our-own-government-has-done-absolutely-nothing-for-us-brexit-and-the-british-in-spain

O'Reilly, K. and Rye, J.F. (2021) 'The (Re)Production of the Exploitative Nature of Rural Migrant Labour in Europe', In J.F. Rye and K. O'Reilly (eds), *International Labour Migration to Europe's Rural Regions*, London: Routledge, pp 228–45.

O'Reilly, K. and Scott, S. (2023a) 'Class, Migration and Bordering at Work: The Case of Precarious Harvest Labour in the UK', *Nordic Journal of Migration Research*, 13(2): 1–17. DOI: 10.33134/njmr.507

O'Reilly, K. and Scott, S. (2023b) 'Harvest Work, Migration, and the Structured Phenomenology of Time', *Journal of Ethnic and Migration Studies*, 49(15): 4033–51.

Owen, S. (2001) 'The Practical, Methodological and Ethical Dilemmas of Conducting Focus Groups with Vulnerable Clients', *Journal of Advanced Nursing*, 36(5): 652–8.

Palinkas, L.A., Horwitz, S.M., Green, C.A., Wisdom, J.P., Duan. N. and Hoagwood, K. (2015) 'Purposeful Sampling for Qualitative Data Collection and Analysis in Mixed Method Implementation Research', *Administration and Policy in Mental Health and Mental Health Services Research*, 42(5): 533–44.

Palmas L. Q. (2021) 'Frontera Sur: Behind and Beyond the Fences of Ceuta and Melilla', *Ethnography*, 22(4): 451–73.

Parsons, J., Atherton, H., Hillman, S., Beckett, D., Clarke, L. and Bick, D. (nd) Pregnant Women's Perceptions and Acceptance of Vaccinations during the COVID-19 Pandemic: A Qualitative Study, NIHR Award ID: NIHR203598, https://fundingawards.nihr.ac.uk/award/NIHR203598

Parsons, S., Ivil, K., Kovshoff, H. and Karakosta, E. (2021) '"Seeing Is Believing": Exploring the Perspectives of Young Autistic Children through Digital Stories', *Journal of Early Childhood Research*, 19(2): 161–78.

Patton, M.Q. (2002) *Qualitative Research and Evaluation Methods*, 3rd edn, Thousand Oaks, CA: Sage.

Pauwels, L. (2019) 'Visual Elicitation in Interviews', In P. Atkinson, S. Delamont, M.A. Hardy and Williams, M. (eds), *Sage Research Methods: Foundations*, London: Sage, pp 1–10.

Payne, G. and Williams, M. (2005) 'Generalization in Qualitative Research', *Sociology*, 39(2): 295–314.

Pedrini, L., Brown, D. and Navarini, G. (2021) 'The Antifascist Boxing Body: Political Somatics in Boxe Popolare', *Ethnography*, 22(3): 311–33.

Pelto, P.J. (2013) *Applied Ethnography. Guidelines for Field Research*, Walnut Creek, CA: Left Coast Press.

Pietkiewicz, I. and Smith, J.A. (2014) 'A Practical Guide to Using Interpretative Phenomenological Analysis in Qualitative Research Psychology', *Czasopismo Psychologiczne – Psychological Journal*, 20(1): 7–14.

Pink, S. (2007) *Doing Visual Ethnography: Images, Media and Representation in Research*, 2nd edn, London: Sage.

Pink, S. (2009) *Doing Sensory Ethnography*, London: Sage.

Pink, S. and Morgan, J. (2013) 'Short-Term Ethnography: Intense Routes to Knowing', *Symbolic Interaction*, 36(3): 351–61.

Pink, S., Fors, V., Lanzeni, D., Duque, M., Sumartojo, S. and Strengers, Y. (2022) *Design Ethnography. Research, Responsibilities, and Futures*, London: Routledge.

Pinker, S. (2015) *The Sense of Style*, London: Penguin.

Plummer, K. (2001) *Documents of Life 2*, 2nd edn, London: Sage.

Pope, C. and Mays, N. (2020) *Qualitative Research in Health Care*, 4th edn, Oxford: Wiley Blackwell.

Portwood-Stacer, L. (2021) *The Book Proposal Book. A Guide for Scholarly Authors*, Bristol: Policy Press.

Postill, J. (2010) 'Introduction: Theorising Media and Practice', In B. Brauchler and J. Postill (eds), *Theorising Media and Practice*, Oxford: Berghahn Books, pp 1–34.

Prince, J., Austin, J., Shewring, L., Birdsey, N., McInnes, K. and Roderique-Davis, G. (2014) *Attitudes to Parenting Practices and Child Discipline*, No. 13/2014, Cardiff: Welsh Government Social Research, https://gov.wales/attitudes-parenting-practices-and-child-discipline-0

Priya, A. (2021) 'Case Study Methodology of Qualitative Research: Key Attributes and Navigating the Conundrums in Its Application', *Sociological Bulletin*, 70(1): 94–110.

Puddephatt, A. J., Shaffir, W., Kleinknecht, S.W. (eds) (2009) *Ethnographies Revisited. Constructing Theory in the Field*, London/New York: Routledge.

Rashid, M., Hodgson, C.S. and Luig, T. (2019) 'Ten Tips for Conducting Focused Ethnography in Medical Education Research', *Medical Education Online*, 24(1). DOI: 10.1080/10872981.2019.1624133

Ravitch, S.M. and Carl, M.N. (2020) *Qualitative Research: Bridging the Conceptual, Theoretical, and Methodological*, 2nd edn, Thousand Oaks, CA: Sage Publishing.

Reay, D. (2004) '"Mostly Roughs and Toughs": Social Class, Race and Representation in Inner City Schooling', *Sociology*, 38(5): 1005–23.

Renold, E., Milne, B., Bragg, S., Ringrose, J., Timperley, V., Young, H. et al (2023) *'We Have to Educate Ourselves': How Young People Are Learning about Relationships, Sex and Sexuality*, London: NSPCC.

Reyes, V. (2020) 'Ethnographic Toolkit: Strategic Positionality and Researchers' Visible and Invisible Tools in Field Research', *Ethnography*, 21(2): 220–40.

Ringrose, J., Regehr, K. and Milne, B. (2021) *Understanding and Combatting Youth Experiences of Image-Based Sexual Harassment and Abuse*, London: UCL Collaborative Social Science Domain.

Ringrose, J., Regehr, K. and Whitehead, S. (2021) 'Teen Girls' Experiences Negotiating the Ubiquitous Dick Pic: Sexual Double Standards and the Normalization of Image Based Sexual Harassment', *Sex Roles*, 85(9): 558–76.

Ritchie, J. and Ormston, R. (2014) 'The Applications of Qualitative Methods to Social Research', In J. Ritchie, J. Lewis, C.M. Nicholls and R. Ormston (eds), *Qualitative Research Practice*, 2nd edn, National Centre for Social Research, London: Sage, pp 28–46.

Ritchie, J., Lewis, J. Nicholls, C.M. and Ormston, R. (eds) (2014) *Qualitative Research Practice*, 2nd edn, National Centre for Social Research, London: Sage.

Rivas, C. (2018) 'Writing a Research Report', In C. Seale (ed), *Researching Society and Culture*, 4th edn, London: Sage, pp 535–54.

Rivoal, I. and Salazar, N. (2013) 'Contemporary Ethnographic Practice and the Value of Serendipity', *Social Anthropology*, 21(2): 178–85.

Rock, P. (2001) 'Symbolic Interactionism and Ethnography', In P. Atkinson, A. Coffey, S. Delamont, J. Lofland and L. Lofland (eds), *Handbook of Ethnography*, London: Sage, pp 26–38.

Rosa, H. (2015) *Social Acceleration. A New Theory of Modernity*, New York: Columbia University Press.

Rubin, H.J. and Rubin, I.S. (2011) *Qualitative Interviewing. The Art of Hearing Data*, 3rd edn, London: Sage.

Russell, L. and Barley, R. (2020) 'Ethnography, Ethics and Ownership of Data', *Ethnography*, 21(1): 5–25.

Rye, J.F. and O'Reilly, K. (eds) (2021) *International Labour Migration to Europe's Rural Regions*, London: Routledge.

Said, E.W. (2021 [1978]) *Orientalism* (reissued version), London: Penguin Modern Classics.

Saldaña, J. (2015) *The Coding Manual for Qualitative Researchers*, London: Sage.

Samardzic, T., Wildman, C., Barata, P.C. and Morton, M. (2023) 'Considerations for Conducting Online Focus Groups on Sensitive Topics', *International Journal of Social Research Methodology*, 1–6. DOI: 10.1080/13645579.2023.2185985

Schatzki, T. (2005) *The Practice Turn in Contemporary Theory*, London: Routledge.

Scheper-Hughes, N. (2004) 'Parts Unknown: Undercover Ethnography of the Organs-Trafficking Underworld', *Ethnography*, 5(1): 29–73.

Scott, R.A. and Kosslyn, S.M. (eds) (2015) *Emerging Trends in the Social and Behavioral Sciences: An Interdisciplinary, Searchable, and Linkable Resource*, Hoboken, NJ: John Wiley & Sons.

Seale, C. (2018) 'Sampling', In C. Seale, *Researching Society and Culture*, London: Sage.

Shah, A. (2017) 'Ethnography? Participant Observation, a Potentially Revolutionary Praxis', *HAU: Journal of Ethnographic Theory*, 7(1): 45–59.

Shah, S. and Jones, N. (2023) 'RIghts and CHoices for Women with Cerebral Palsy (RICH Study): A Qualitative Study to Understand What Works in the Provision of Their Maternity Care', National Institute of Health Research, https://fundingawards.nihr.ac.uk/award/NIHR203677

Shaw, C. (1966 [1930]) *The Jack Roller. A Delinquent Boy's Own Story*, Chicago, IL: University of Chicago Press.

Shove E., Pantzer, M. and Watson, M. (2012) *The Dynamics of Social Practice: Everyday Life and How It Changes*, London: Sage.

Silverman, D. (2009) *Doing Qualitative Research*, 3rd edn, Newbury Park, London: Sage.

Skeggs, B. (2001) 'Feminist Ethnography', In P. Atkinson, A. Coffey, S. Delamont, J. Lofland and L. Lofland (eds), *Handbook of Ethnography*, London: Sage, pp 426–42.

Small, M.L. (2009) '"How Many Cases Do I Need?" On Science and the Logic of Case Selection in Field-Based Research', *Ethnography*, 10(1): 5–38.

Smith, B. (2010) 'Narrative Inquiry: Ongoing Conversations and Questions for Sport and Exercise Psychology Research', *International Review of Sport and Exercise Psychology*, 3(1): 87–107.

Smith, D.W. (2018) 'Phenomenology', In E.N. Zalta (ed), *The Stanford Encyclopedia of Philosophy* (Summer edn), https://plato.stanford.edu/entries/phenomenology

Spencer, D. (2014) 'Sensing Violence: An Ethnography of Mixed Martial Arts', *Ethnography* 15(2): 232–54.

Spencer, L. and Pahl, R. (2006) *Rethinking Friendship. Hidden Solidarities Today*, Princeton, NJ: Princeton University Press.

Spencer, L., Ritchie, J., O'Connor, W., Morrell, G. and Ormston, R. (2014) 'Analysis in Practice', In J. Ritchie, J. Lewis, C.M. Nicholls and R. Ormston (eds), *Qualitative Research Practice*, 2nd edn, National Centre for Social Research, London: Sage, pp 295–347.

Squire, C. (2008) 'Approaches to Narrative Research', NCRM Review Papers, http://eprints.ncrm.ac.uk/419/1/MethodsReviewPaperNCRM-009.pdf

Squire, C. and Andrews, M. (2014) *What Is Narrative Research?* (What Is? Research Methods series), London: Bloomsbury.

Stake, R.E. (2003) 'Case Studies', In N.K. Denzin and Y.S. Lincoln (eds), *Strategies of Qualitative Inquiry*, London/Thousand Oaks, CA: Sage, pp 134–64.

Statham, P. (2019) 'Living the Long-Term Consequences of Thai-Western Marriage Migration: The Radical Life-Course Transformations of Women Who Partner Older Westerners', *Journal of Ethnic and Migration Studies*, 46(8): 1562–87.

Stones, R. (2005) *Structuration Theory*, Basingstoke: Palgrave Macmillan.

Stones, R., Botterill, K., Lee, M. and O'Reilly, K. (2019) 'One World Is Not Enough: The Structured Phenomenology of Lifestyle Migrants in East Asia', *British Journal of Sociology*, 70(1): 44–69.

Strauss, A.L. and Corbin, J. (1998) *Basics of Qualitative Research: Techniques and Procedures for Developing Grounded Theory*, 2nd edn, Thousand Oaks, CA: Sage Publications.

Stuesse, A. (2016) *Scratching Out a Living. Latinos, Race, and Work in the Deep South*, Oakland, CA: University of California Press.

Sundler, A.J., Lindberg, E., Nilsson, C. and Palmér, L. (2019) 'Qualitative Thematic Analysis Based on Descriptive Phenomenology', *Nursing Open*, 6(3): 733–9.

Taghipour, A. (2014) 'Adopting Constructivist versus Objectivist Grounded Theory in Health Care Research: A Review of the Evidence', *Journal of Midwifery and Reproductive Health*, 2(2): 100–4.

Terkel, S. (1970) *Hard Times. An Oral History of the Great Depression*, Pantheon Books.

Teskereci, G. and Boz, I. (2019) '"I Try to Act Like a Nurse": A Phenomenological Qualitative Study', *Nurse Education in Practice*, 37: 39–44.

Tevington, P., Davis, W.J., Urban, J. B. and Linver, M.R. (2023) '"Been There, Done That But Also Not Quite": Discoveries and Limitations in an Evaluative, Short-Term, and Multi-Sited Ethnography of the Boy Scouts of America', *Ethnography*, 0(0). DOI: 10.1177/14661381231181625

Thomas, W.I. and Thomas, D.S. (1928) *The Child in America: Behavior Problems and Programs*, New York: Knopf.

Thompson, P. (1988) *The Voice of the Past*, 2nd edn, Oxford: Oxford University Press.

Thompson, C. and Reynolds, J. (2019) 'Reflections on the Go-Along: How "Disruptions" Can Illuminate the Relationships of Health, Place and Practice', *The Geographical Journal*, 185 (2): 156–67.

Thomson, P. (2017) 'Play with Your Data' [blog], https://patthomson. net/2017/08/17/play-with-your-data

Tonkiss, F. (2012) 'Focus Groups', In C. Seale (ed), *Researching Society and Culture*, London: Sage, pp: 237–56.

Törnqvist, M. and Holmberg, T. (2021) 'The Sensing Eye: Intimate Vision in Couple Dancing', *Ethnography*, 0(0). DOI: 10.1177/14661381211038430

Tsing, A.L. (2005) *Friction. An Ethnography of Global Connection*, Princeton, NJ: Princeton University Press.

Tuckman, B. and Jenson, M. (1977) 'Stages of Small-Group Development Revisited', *Group and Organisational Studies*, 2(4): 419–27.

Ulibarri, N., Cravens, A.E., Nabergoj, A.S., Kernbach, S. and Royalty, A. (2019) *Creativity in Research. Cultivate Clarity, Be Innovative, Make Progress in Your Research Journey*, Cambridge: Cambridge University Press.

Wall, S. (2015) 'Focused Ethnography: A Methodological Adaptation for Social Research in Emerging Contexts', *Forum Qualitative Sozialforschung Forum: Qualitative Social Research*, 16:1. DOI: 10.17169/fqs-16.1.2182

Wertz, F. J. (2011) 'A Phenomenological Psychological Approach to Trauma and Resilience', In F.J. Wertz, K. Charmaz, L.M. McMullen, R, Josselson, A. Anderson and E. McSpadden, *Five Ways of Doing Qualitative Analysis*, New York: Guilford Press.

Wertz, F.J., Charmaz, K., McMullen, L.M., Josselson, R., Anderson, A. and McSpadden, E. (2011) *Five Ways of Doing Qualitative Analysis*, New York: Guilford Press.

Westmarland, N. (2001) 'The Quantitative/Qualitative Debate and Feminist Research: A Subjective View of Objectivity', *Forum Qualitative Sozialforschung Forum: Qualitative Social Research*, 2(1).

White, C. and Sisya, K. (2023) *The Power of Young Voices in Plymouth Together for Childhood*, London: NSPCC.

White, C., Woodfield, K., Ritchie, J. and Ormston, R. (2014) 'Writing Up Qualitative Research', In J. Ritchie, J. Lewis, C.M. Nicholls and R. Ormston (eds), *Qualitative Research Practice*, 2nd edn, National Centre for Social Research, London: Sage, pp 367–400.

Whyte, W.F. (1993) *Street Corner Society: The Social Structure of an Italian Slum*, 4th edn, Chicago, IL: University of Chicago Press.

Wilkerson, J.M., Iantaffi, A., Grey, J.A., Bockting, W.O. and Rosser, B.S. (2014) 'Recommendations for Internet-Based Qualitative Health Research with Hard-to-Reach Populations', *Qualitative Health Research*, 24(4): 561–74.

Wilkinson, S. (1998) 'Focus Groups in Feminist Research', *Women's Studies International Forum*, 21(1): 111–25.

Wilkinson, S. (1999) 'Focus Groups: A Feminist Method', *Psychology of Women Quarterly*, 23(2): 221–44.

Williams, H. (2021) 'The Meaning of "Phenomenology": Qualitative and Philosophical Phenomenological Research Methods', *The Qualitative Report*, 26(2): 366–85.

Williksen, S. (2009) 'Moods Behind the Silences', *Ethnography*, 10(1): 115–27.

Willis, P. and Trondman, M. (2000) 'Manifesto for Ethnography', *Ethnography* 1(1): 5–16.

Willis P. and Trondman M. (2021) 'More Bread Less Circus', *Ethnography*, 22(2): 154–63.

Yeo, A., Legard, R., Keegan, J., Ward, K., McNaughton Nicholls, C. and Lewis, J. (2014) 'In-Depth Interviews', In J. Ritchie, J. Lewis, C. McNaughton Nicholls, R. Ormston (eds), *Qualitative Research Practice*, 2nd edn, National Centre for Social Research, London: Sage, pp 177–210.

Index

References to information in boxes are shown in **bold**

www.ingramcontent.com/pod-product-compliance
Lightning Source LLC
Chambersburg PA
CBHW081144020426
42333CB00021B/2664